Modifying a Table

CHAPTERS FOUR AND FIVE

You can change the contents of a Paradox table in DataEntry, Edit, or CoEdit mode. DataEntry lets you enter new records, which are added to the table when you are done. Edit lets you enter new records or modify existing records. CoEdit is similar to Edit but is meant for use with networks.

```
Editing Employee table: Record 23 of 23                          Edit  ──▼

EMPLOYEE═══════First name═════      ═════Last name═════      ════════════Address═══════
     2  │  Alice            Walter              326 B. 31 St.
     3  │  Joseph           Miller              2036 Park Ave.
     4  │  Samuel           Smithson            203 West St.
     5  │  Sally            Bean                1465 Oak St.
     6  │  Albert           Cruz                1237 Flatbush Ave.
     7  │  Evelyn           Adams               3345 Church Ave.
     8  │  Rosalyn          Rogers              2242 Pensylvania Ave.
     9  │  Robert           Lin                 457 First St.
    10  │  George           Silk                237 Edison st.
    11  │  Harriet          Noble               34 Shady Lane
    12  │  Samuel           Schmaltz            590 Ocean Ave.
    13  │  Dianne           Lee                 1634 Bancroft Way
    14  │  Francine         Bowen               2113 University Ave.
    15  │  Henry            Ware                1742 Dutch Elm St.
    16  │  William          Channing            22 The Circle
    17  │  Josephine        Buckminster         3322 Bridgeway
    18  │  Jean             Abbott              4445-2312 Technology Blvd.
    19  │  Edward           Channing            180 Poplar St.
    20  │  Andrea           Norton              2311 First St.
    21  │  Joseph           Tuckerman           45 Arcroft Circle
    22  │  Jane             Walker              848 Broadway
    23  │  Edward           Channing            505 Haight St.
```

The Paradox Edit screen

In Table View, the cursor is always at the end of the field. Field View lets you move the cursor within a field to make it easier to edit its contents.

Use of the keys in Field View:

Key	Action	Key	Action
Home	Moves cursor to the first character	Up and Down arrow	Move cursor up or down one line (in wrapped fields only)
End	Moves cursor to the last character	Ctrl-Left arrow and Ctrl-Right arrow	Move cursor one word left or right
Del	Deletes a character		
Ins	Toggles from insert mode to type-over mode	Backspace	Deletes the letter left of the cursor
Left and Right arrow	Move cursor left or right one character	Ctrl-Backspace	Deletes the contents of the field

THE
ABC'S
OF
Paradox

THE

ABC'S

OF

Paradox ®

Charles Siegel

SYBEX ®

San Francisco · Paris · Düsseldorf · Soest

Acquisitions Editor: Dianne King
Developmental Editor: Lyn Cordell
Copy Editor: Linda Ackerman
Technical Editor: Linwood P. Beacom
Word Processors: Chris Mockel and Scott Campbell
Series Designer: Jeffrey James Giese
Chapter Art and Book Layout: Ingrid Owen
Technical Art: Jeffrey James Giese
Screen Graphics: Delia Brown
Typesetter: Bob Myren
Proofreader: Vanessa Miller
Indexer: Paul Geisert
Cover Designer: Thomas Ingalls + Associates
Cover Photographer: Mark Johann
Screen reproductions produced by XenoFont

dBASE II and dBASE III are trademarks of Ashton-Tate.
Lotus 1-2-3 and Lotus Symphony are trademarks of Lotus Development Corporation.
Paradox is a trademark of Borland Software.
pfs:FILE is a trademark of Software Publishing Corp.
Quattro and Reflex are trademarks of Borland International.
VisiCalc is a trademark of VisiCorp.
XenoFont is a trademark of XenoSoft.

SYBEX is a registered trademark of SYBEX, Inc.

SYBEX is not affiliated with any manufacturer.

Every effort has been made to supply complete and accurate information. However, SYBEX assumes no responsibility for its use, nor for any infringements of patents or other rights of third parties which would result.

Library of Congress Card Number: 89-63175
ISBN 0-89588-573-5
Manufactured in the United States of America
10 9 8 7 6 5

To the Siegel children—
David, Etta, Rose, Milton, and Leon—
and to all the good times.

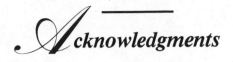

Acknowledgments

Thanks to the people at SYBEX who contributed to this book—particularly Lyn Cordell, my developmental editor, and Dianne King, who made it all possible.

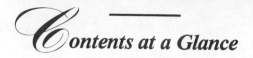

Contents at a Glance

*T*able of Contents

Part II   *Multitable Databases*

13

BREAKING DOWN YOUR DATA

14

SETTING UP A MULTITABLE DATABASE

15

ADDING DATA TO A MULTITABLE DATABASE

16

CREATING REPORTS FOR MULTITABLE DATABASES

17

USING QUERIES WITH MULTITABLE DATABASES

Part III Shortcuts and Special Techniques

18

TOOLS FOR MANAGING FILES

19

VALIDATING DATA

Introduction

This book is for people who are not computer experts, but who simply want to learn, as quickly as possible, to use Paradox for practical tasks—such as keeping track of mailing lists, customer records, or other data.

Paradox is the ideal program for this sort of person, because it makes managing data easy. As promised, Paradox gives you "immediate database power." Its easy-to-understand menu system lets you manage data in sophisticated ways without memorizing commands. Techniques that used to require complex programming are at your fingertips with Paradox.

In addition to the easy-to-use features you need to manage your own data, Paradox also includes an entire programming language and programming aids for computer professionals who set up systems for other people. Having a programmer set up this sort of system saves you some learning time, but makes you dependent on outside advice whenever you want to do something new. This book will free you from dependence on programmers and let you use Paradox to create your own practical applications, but it will not take up your time with obscure features that are only useful to programmers.

So many manuals come with your copy of Paradox that it can be intimidating just to look at them. But the manuals are so lengthy only because they are filled with technical information that is necessary for programmers but not for most users. You do not need to know most of what is in the manuals to use the full power of Paradox to manage your own data.

This book uses an easy-to-follow tutorial approach. It takes you through the Paradox features you need to know step-by-step, so you can learn the program as quickly as possible—and then get down to your real business.

*H*ow to Use This Book

If you bought your copy of Paradox, opened the box, saw how many manuals there were, and ran straight to the bookstore to find a simpler introduction to the program, then begin with Appendix A, which tells you how to install Paradox on your computer. If you are working in an office or school where Paradox is already installed, you can begin with Chapter 1. In any case, you should have Paradox running and available when you read this book. Its step-by-step approach assumes you are at the computer keyboard, using the program as you learn.

You do not have to memorize the things this book has you do. Paradox is so easy to use that you just need to familiarize yourself with the program's basic organization; then, you will be able to do most things intuitively when you are working on your own. If you make an error, Paradox usually tells you what you've done wrong, and how to correct it.

Part I of this book, "Single-Table Databases," contains the simplest and most important things you need to learn. It shows you how to create a database, enter and edit data, and produce reports—the basic skills you need to manage any simple database. In this first section you'll learn enough to let you manage many common business applications, such as mailing lists and lists of product specifications.

Part II, "Multitable Databases," shows you how to manage more complicated data. What you learn in this section can save you a great deal of work if, for example, you need to keep several different kinds of records about individual employees.

Paradox makes it easy to use multitable databases, but you may not need them right now. When you get to Part II, you should read Chapter 13 to learn when multitable databases are useful. If you do not need them immediately, you might want to get to work on single-table databases, and skip Part II until you need it.

Part III, "Shortcuts and Special Techniques," introduces some Paradox features that let you do things either more easily or more effectively. If you do choose to apply what you learned in Part I immediately, consider reading Chapters 18 and 20 in Part III either before or soon after you begin your practical work. What you learn in these chapters will definitely save you effort.

If you find that you are making typographical errors and you would like Paradox to help catch them, you can also read Chapter 19, "Validating Data."

On the other hand, you might want to read the entire book, from beginning to end, so that you feel completely confident with Paradox before using it in a practical application. How quickly you move from this tutorial to your own use of the program is a matter of personal style. Whichever way you apply it, this book produces an easy and direct introduction to Paradox.

Conventions Used in This Book

This book is designed to help you learn Paradox quickly and easily. To make instructions clear, numbered steps walk you through tasks that you can perform on your own computer. Words to be typed into your computer are printed in boldface, as follows: "After making that menu choice, type the name **Smith**." Frequent illustrations show you what your screen should look like at critical points.

These conventions will make it easy for you to follow the instructions in this book as you work on your own computer. Now you are ready to begin.

Part I

SINGLE-TABLE DATABASES

WHAT IS A DATABASE?

DATABASE STRUCTURE

MULTITABLE DATABASE

INTRODUCTION TO PARADOX

COMPUTER BASICS

A simple database might be a list of names, addresses, and telephone numbers, or it could be a list of all the classes given at a school, including their teachers and the times they meet. Any collection of repetitive data can be a database.

Before computers came along, this sort of list was usually kept in a file folder, a Rolodex, or on index cards. Usually, each sheet of paper or card had a form printed on it, with blank spaces where you were supposed to fill in the data. Each Rolodex card, for example, might be printed with a form to show where you should fill in the name, address, city, state, zip code, and phone number.

Understanding Database Structure

When you work with a computer database, such as Paradox, you must create a similar form—one designed to fit whatever type of data you want to record—before you actually enter any data. This determines the *structure* of the database, and using Paradox, it is very easy to create or change this structure to suit your particular needs.

As you can see, the people who first designed computer databases occasionally applied everyday terms, such as *structure*, in new ways, to describe the same sorts of techniques that were always used for data kept in files or on index cards. There are a couple of other terms that are so common you'll probably be familiar with them:

- A *record* is the computerized version of the information that used to go on one index card or on one sheet of paper in a file. A single record includes the name, address, and telephone number of one person, or all the information about one class, or any other relevant data about one entity. A simple database is a list of records.

- A *field* is the computerized version of a single blank space on an index card or form, where one piece of data would be written. For example, in an address book, the first name might be one field, the last name might be another field, and the zip code might be a third field.

As you will see, you can actually define database fields in any way you want, just as you can design a paper form in any way you want. You could, for example, have a single field for the entire name rather than one for the first and another for the last name. However, it is generally best to break down the name, as you'll soon see.

Rather than storing individual records on separate cards, computers store records in *tables*. Figure 1.1 shows a typical Paradox database table. Each horizontal row represents a single record—one person's name and address—which would go on a single index card if you were working with paper. The vertical columns represent the fields in the database; the name at the top of each column is the name of a field. Notice that the records in the sample table are numbered. Counting is one thing computers are very good at, and virtually all computer databases number their records in this way.

```
Editing Record table: Record 22 of 28                         Edit

RECORD First name      Last name       Address          City      State
   1    Samuel         Schmaltz        590 Ocean Ave.      Brooklyn      NY
   2    Harriet        Noble           34 Shady Lane       Greenwich     CT
   3    Evelyn         Adams           3345 Church Ave.    Brooklyn      NY
   4    Henry          Ware            1742 Dutch Elm St   San Raphael   CA
   5    Josephin       Buckminister    3322 Bridgeway      Sausalito     CA
   6    Edward         Channing        180 Poplar St.      Mill Valley   CA
   7    Alice          Walter          326 B. 31 St.       Far Rockaway  NY
   8    William        Channing        22 The Circle       Ross          CA
   9    Joseph         Miller          2036 Park Ave.      New York      NY
  10    Joseph         Tuckerman       45 Arcroft Circle   San Mateo     CA
  11    Samuel         Smithson        203 West St.        Rye           NY
  12    Albert         Cruz            1237 Flatbush Ave   Brooklyn      NY
  13    George         Silk            237 Edison St.      New Brunswick NJ
  14    Andrea         Norton          2311 First St.      Mill Valley   CA
  15    Joan           Garfield        4437 Elm St.        Hoboken       NJ
  16    Dianne         Lee             1634 Bancroft Way   Berkeley      CA
  17    Robert         Lin             457 First St.       Paramus       NJ
  18    Jane           Walker          848 Broadway        San Raphael   CA
  19    Edward         Channing        505 Haight St.      San Francisco CA
  20    Sally          Bean            1465 Oak St.        Yonkers       NY
  21
  22                   ◄
```

Figure 1.1: A sample database in tabular form

*W*hy Have Multitable Databases?

There are some obvious advantages to using a computer to maintain a database, even one as simple as a list of names, addresses, and phone numbers.

You can print out the list, with very little effort, in any form you choose. If you want to telephone everyone on the list, you can print names and telephone numbers. If you want to do a mailing, you can print the names and addresses on mailing labels—obviously much easier than manually typing them onto envelopes.

You can also sort the data in any order. For example, you might want to print your labels in zip code order for a bulk mailing; and, after you are done, you might want to print a list of names and addresses in alphabetical order, so you can find names easily. Using a computer, you can rearrange the order of your records effortlessly.

Finally, a computer allows you quick access to records that meet certain criteria. For example, if you want to produce mailing labels only for people who live in a certain state or zip code, the computer will find them for you instantly. You can also use more complex criteria. Rather than finding just the people who live in California, you might want the people who live either in California or in Nevada or in Utah. You might want the people who live in California or in Nevada or in Utah whose last names begin with the letter *A* or *B*. A computer can search for complex criteria just as easily as it can search for simple criteria.

Apart from these clear advantages of using a computer, which are valuable even if you only work with simple applications, there is a less obvious reason for computerizing complex data.

When large businesses first began to use computers, people wrote programs that stored data in the same way it had always been stored in paper files. For example, there might be one program for the Benefits Department that contained each employee's name, address, social security number, phone number, and the benefits that he or she had used and was eligible for; another program for the Payroll Department with each employee's name, address, social security number, phone number, hourly wage, and number of hours worked each week; and a third program for the Human Resources Development Department with each employee's name, address, social security number, phone number, educational history, and special training courses.

You do not need more examples to see that in a big company, the basic data on each employee, such as name, address, social security number, and phone number, could be recorded in a dozen places. Of course, if an employee moved, the address would have to be changed a dozen times.

This was not only extra work; it also made it more likely that there would be an error or an oversight somewhere, so that the company might have several different addresses on record for the same employee.

This is the way it had to be when records were kept on paper, but programmers soon began to invent better ways to do things with computers. New programs made it possible to type each employee's name, address, social security number, and phone number only once. Then the benefits program could combine this data with the person's benefits records, while the payroll department combined the same information with the employee's wage and hours records, and so on. In paper files, all the relevant data for each person had to be repeated on the form used by each department. Because computers can access data much more quickly than people can, they are able to look in several places and find the relevant data without any delay.

After trying several complex ways to do this, computer scientists came up with a fairly simple model they called the *relational* database. Data is kept in two or more tables, which are "related" to each other by a *key field*. For example, a company might assign each employee an employee number to serve as the key field. There could be one table with employee number, name, address, social security number, and phone number; a second table with employee number, hourly wage, and number of hours worked each week; and a third table with employee number, educational history, and special training courses taken. The tables must have some common field, such as employee number, so that they can be related to each other.

This, of course, is a *multitable database*. A database management program can use the employee number to pull elements from separate tables and combine them in the form that each department needs. People in the Human Resources Department can print or display reports that look just like the forms they used to have in their paper files; they need never know that the name and address they are looking at came from one table in the database, while the educational history came from another table.

If someone moves, the address has to be changed only once. A relational database management system will use the new address in a dozen different reports that it produces for various departments.

What Is Paradox?

Paradox is a highly sophisticated database management system that is remarkably easy to use. The "paradox" of the program is this unusual combination of power and simplicity.

Before Paradox, there were easy-to-use programs that let you maintain simple, single-table databases. But these were inadequate for many applications. Programs that let you manage multitable databases required you to program—or at least use obscure, complex commands—to relate one table to another.

Paradox was the first program that made it easy to manage multitable databases. With Paradox everything is laid out on the screen for you. All you need to do is make selections from menus and fill out forms that appear on the screen as a result of your choices.

Even if you are only using a single-table database, Paradox is valuable because it is so easy to use. Once you've familiarized yourself with the program's organization, you will be able to do most things intuitively.

Paradox becomes even more valuable, though, when your data becomes a bit more complex and you want to move from a single-table to a multitable database. With Paradox, anyone who can use basic software applications, such as a word processing or spreadsheet package, can also manage multitable databases in ways that used to be the province of professional programmers.

A Few Computer Basics

Before beginning with Paradox, you should know a few basics about your computer. If you have used other applications, you can skip this section or just skim it. Read this section carefully if you are just starting to use your computer.

How to Save Your Work on Disk

With most programs, the data you enter is only held in your computer's Random Access Memory (RAM), which remains active only while the computer is turned on. RAM is very fast, but it is not permanent; if there is a power failure, or if you turn off your computer, any data in RAM is lost.

To save your data permanently, you can record it on a magnetic disk—either on a portable floppy disk or on a hard disk inside your computer. Because it uses mechanical motion, a disk works much more slowly than RAM, and saving data requires you to wait for a moment.

To minimize the amount of data that would be lost in case of accidental loss of power, Paradox automatically saves your data at certain intervals.

Paradox also saves your work when you exit from the program. When you are done entering data in Paradox, do not simply turn your computer off; choose the menu option that exits from Paradox first, or you may lose data. In the next chapter you will learn how to use the menu Exit option.

Remember also that hard disks sometimes fail, and floppy disks can be damaged. You should back up all your work regularly on an extra set of floppy disks, and store them in a safe place.

How to Use Your Keyboard

If you are new to the IBM XT, AT, or PS/2 keyboard, look at Figure 1.2 to see how these keyboards are laid out.

The main section of your computer keyboard is similar to a standard typewriter; it includes all the letters, numbers, and special characters, such as the asterisk and ampersand, and has the spacebar at the bottom. It also includes, at the right, a numeric keypad that is similar to an adding machine, with the ten digits near each other to allow quick number entry; these keys also have arrows and words on them, whose purpose you will learn in a moment.

The computer keyboard also has two Shift keys, on the right and left; as with a typewriter, you hold one of these keys down while you press another character to type that character in uppercase (or to type the special symbols above the number keys).

The Caps Lock key is like the typewriter key that locks the shift so all characters are in uppercase. There is one important exception, however; Caps Lock makes only letters uppercase; it does not affect numbers or

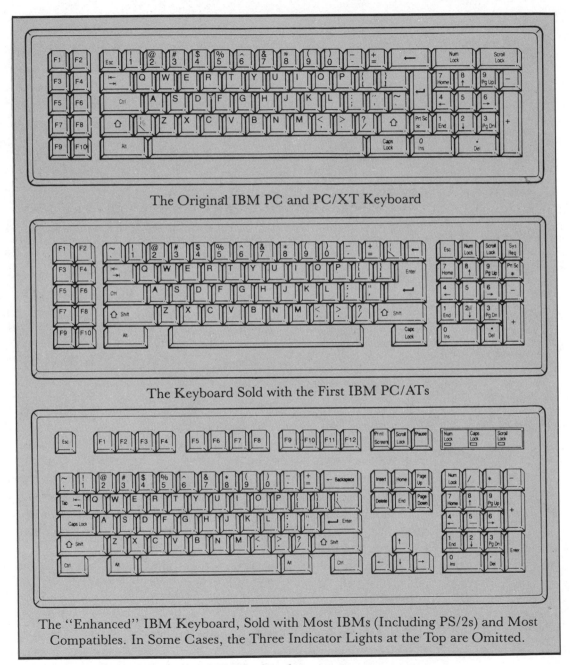

The Original IBM PC and PC/XT Keyboard

The Keyboard Sold with the First IBM PC/ATs

The "Enhanced" IBM Keyboard, Sold with Most IBMs (Including PS/2s) and Most Compatibles. In Some Cases, the Three Indicator Lights at the Top are Omitted.

Figure 1.2: The IBM-PC/XT, AT, and PS/2 keyboards

special characters. You must use the Shift key to affect these characters.

Apart from the usual typewriter keys, you should become familiar with several special keys on your computer.

The Enter Key

The Enter key, located at the center-right of the typewriter portion of your keyboard, is a bit like the carriage return key of a typewriter. (If you have an old keyboard, this key might actually be labeled ↵ or Carriage Return.) Like a typewriter's carriage return, one of its uses is to move you to the next line. In many applications, Enter also moves you to the next entry, even if it is not on a new line. Finally, this key is often used to complete an entry; what you type appears on the screen, but is not actually sent to the computer's memory until you press Enter.

The Ctrl and Alt Keys

The Ctrl (Control) and Alt (Alternate) keys are above and below the Shift key on the left side of the keyboard. Like the Shift key, they do nothing by themselves, but are used to obtain an alternative response from some other key that you press with them—something different from that key's usual use.

The Tab Key

The key above the Ctrl key, labeled with arrows pointing in opposite directions, is the Tab key. This key is similar to the tab on a typewriter, except it works in both directions. Used alone, Tab moves you one tab to the right. Used with the Shift key, it moves you one tab to the left; that is why it has a left arrow above and a right arrow below.

The Esc Key

The Esc (Escape) key is located near the upper-right of the XT keyboard, above the numeric keypad, but at the upper-left of the AT and PS/2 keyboards. As its name indicates, it lets you escape from something you are doing. One of its main uses in Paradox is to back out of menu choices. As you will see in the next chapter, if you mistakenly make the wrong selection on a menu and are presented with a submenu you do not want, you can usually press Esc to escape from a submenu back to the previous menu.

The Ctrl-Break Key

On XT keyboards, the Scroll Lock key is above the numeric keypad, to the right. On most keyboards—though not all—the word *Break* is written on the front of the Scroll Lock key, to indicate that this key functions as the Break key when it is used in conjunction with the Ctrl key.

On the AT and PS/2 keyboards, the key to the far right of the top row of keys says Pause. The word Break should be written on the front of this key to indicate that it is the Break key when used in conjunction with the Ctrl key.

Pause and Scroll Lock are not used by Paradox, but the Ctrl-Break combination is used to cancel an operation that you are working on; it abandons the operation without saving what you have already done. Ctrl-Break is like Esc, but stronger; you can often use it to get out of operations that you cannot get out of with Esc.

The Cursor Keys and the Num Lock Key

The keys on the numeric keypad have arrows and words as well as numbers on them. The arrows are used to move the *cursor*—the highlight on your screen that shows you where you are working at the moment.

The four arrow keys move the cursor left, right, up, and down. In Paradox, how far they move it depends on what you are doing. Sometimes, the ← and → keys move the cursor just one character to the left or right, but more often, they move it one field to the left or right.

How can the same keys both enter numbers and move the cursor? The gray key labeled Num Lock immediately above them changes these keys from one function to the other. If you have been using them to move the cursor and then want to enter numbers, just press Num Lock. When you are done entering numbers, press Num Lock again, and you will be able to move the cursor again.

If you have an XT keyboard, you only have the arrows on the numeric keypad to move the cursor. If you have an AT or a PS/2, your keyboard has an additional set of arrow keys between the type-writer keyboard and the numeric keypad that can also be used to move the cursor. These extra keys are handy when you want to use the keypad for entering numbers and move the cursor at the same time. With Paradox, it is usually equally convenient to use either set of arrow keys; you'll soon discover which is more comfortable for you.

Remember, if the arrow keys on your keypad fail to move the cursor, you can probably correct the problem by pressing Num Lock.

The Home and End Keys

On the numeric keypad (and, if you have an AT or PS/2, also on separate keys above the arrow keys), you will find two keys marked Home and End. These are a bit like the arrow keys, except that they move the cursor farther. Pressing Home takes you to the top of a table, and pressing End moves you to the bottom. Ctrl-Home and Ctrl-End take you to the table's far left and far right, respectively. When you're in a menu, rather than a table, Home and End move you directly to the leftmost and rightmost choices.

The PgUp and PgDn Keys

Also on the numeric keypad (and on separate keys above the arrow keys on the AT and PS/2), you will find keys marked PgUp (Page Up) and PgDn (Page Down). Most of your Paradox tables will have far more records than your computer screen can display; pressing these keys will move you up and down through your data one full screen at a time.

The Ins and Del Keys

Right below the numeric key pad (and, on the AT and PS/2, also above the arrow keys) are the Ins (Insert) and Del (Delete) keys. These do what their names imply; they insert or delete either a character, a field, or an entire record, depending on what you are doing in Paradox at the time.

The Backspace Key

The Backspace key on an XT keyboard is in the upper-right corner of the typewriter portion of the keyboard. It is labeled with a left-pointing arrow. On the AT and PS/2 keyboards, Backspace is in the same location, but it has the word *Backspace* as well as a left-pointing arrow on it.

Do not confuse the Backspace key with the ← key, which merely moves the cursor to the left. Backspace moves the cursor one space to the left, but it also erases the character in that position.

The Function Keys

The function keys, numbered from F1 to F10, are arranged vertically on the far left of the XT keyboard. On the AT and PS/2, they are arranged across the top of the keyboard and numbered from F1 to F12.

These keys were added to the keyboard so programmers could make it easy for users to perform common tasks by pressing a single key. As you will see in the next chapter, Paradox includes a template you can place on the function keys to remind you what they do.

GETTING STARTED

Before you can start Paradox, it must be installed on your computer. If you do not have the program installed, see Appendix A for directions. Appendix A also includes a brief discussion of subdirectories.

Once you have Paradox installed, all you have to do to start the program is

1. Get into the subdirectory that you want to work in. If you are working in the subdirectory that contains the program, type the command **CD \PARADOX3** and press Enter. If you are working in a separate subdirectory, use the same command with the name of that directory. If you are using the name LEARNPAR for the directory you want to use with this book, for example, type the command **CD \LEARNPAR** and press Enter.

2. Type the command **PARADOX3** and press Enter.

After a moment, you should see a title screen that says "Borland International" and "Paradox Relational Database." In the lower-right corner of the screen, you will see the word "Loading" followed by three blinking dots. Notice that the light indicating your computer is accessing its hard disk is on. The program is being read from the disk into RAM. After a few seconds, you should see the main menu screen.

The Paradox Main Menu

When Paradox has started properly, you will see the screen shown in Figure 2.1.

The words along the top of the screen are the Paradox main menu selections. Notice that View is highlighted. The first choice on any Paradox menu is the *default* choice. Because this first option is already highlighted when the menu appears, you can select it by simply pressing Enter.

The phrase "View a table" under the menu line is a *help line* that tells you what you can do by choosing the currently highlighted option.

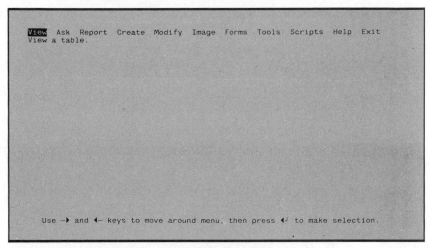

```
View  Ask  Report  Create  Modify  Image  Forms  Tools  Scripts  Help  Exit
View a table.




















Use → and ← keys to move around menu, then press ↵ to make selection.
```

Figure 2.1: *The Paradox main menu and work area*

The blank space that takes up most of the screen is called the *work area*. This is where tables you are working on will appear.

At the bottom of the screen is a line of instructions telling you to use the ← and → keys to move around the menu and then press Enter to choose an option. You can see how easy Paradox is to use; most of the time it tells you what to do.

How to Use the Paradox Menu System

Try using → to move the cursor through the main menu options. By the time you are done with this book, you will be familiar with all of the menu options. For now, look at the help line as you move the cursor to get a basic idea of the things Paradox can do.

- *View* lets you view a Paradox table.

- *Ask* lets you ask the program to find specific information— for example, the names of people who live in a certain zip code.

- *Report* lets you design and produce reports. You specify the information and choose the format.

- *Create* lets you create a new table. As you saw in Chapter 1, this involves defining the table's structure—that is, deciding what blanks will have to be filled in.

- *Modify* lets you change an existing table. You can add new records, edit existing records, sort the records in a different order, or actually change the structure of a table.

- *Image* lets you change the way data appears on your screen. It also lets you search through the database and create graphs of your data.

- *Forms* lets you create custom forms for data entry. This option is mainly used to design simple forms that make data entry easy for novices.

- *Tools* lets you use special utilities that are designed to perform specific tasks. For example, it lets you rename or delete tables.

- *Scripts* lets you automate repetitive tasks. You can record a long series of keystrokes and play them back automatically whenever you need them again.

- *Help* gives you information about using Paradox.

- *Exit* is the option you choose when you are done using Paradox. As its help line mentions, Exit automatically saves changes for you.

This gives you an overview of the things Paradox does; as you can see, the menu structure is not hard to grasp.

There are also a couple of shortcuts that let you move the cursor around the menu more quickly. Try the following steps to see how they work:

1. Press → with the cursor on Exit. It moves back to View. Press ← when the cursor is on View. It moves back to Exit.

2. Press Home and End a few times. The cursor moves back and forth between Exit and View.

These shortcuts work on all Paradox menus. The cursor wraps around from the far left to the far right, saving you keystrokes when you move among menu options. Home and End take you directly to the choices on the far left and far right of the menu.

*H*ow to Back Out of Submenus

Some choices from the main menu will give you forms to fill in or ask you questions, but most of them will present you with submenus that offer more choices. If you make a mistaken choice and do not want to use the submenu that appears, you can press the Esc key to back out of that submenu and return to the previous menu. To see how these submenus work, follow these steps:

1. Use the arrow keys to move the cursor to Image and then press Enter.

2. A submenu replaces the main menu, offering new choices that give you different ways of modifying the image (see Figure 2.2); below the submenu a help line appears for each highlighted option, as on the main menu.

3. Use the arrow keys to move through the Image submenu.

4. Whenever you are ready, press Esc. The submenu will disappear and the main menu will reappear on the screen, with the cursor still on Image, the last choice made from the main menu.

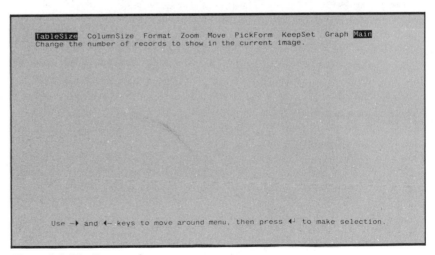

Figure 2.2: The Image submenu

*M*aking Faster Menu Choices

While you are a still a beginner, you will find it useful to move the cursor through the menus and read the help line, as you decide what selection to make.

Once you are used to the Paradox menu system, there is a faster way to make choices from the menus. No matter where the cursor is, all you need to do is press the first letter of the menu choice you want to make that choice instantly. Try these steps to see how this faster method works:

1. Make sure that the main menu is on the screen. If it is not, press Esc until it appears.

2. Press M. Paradox will display the Modify submenu, just as if you had moved the cursor to Modify and pressed Enter.

3. Press Esc to return to the main menu. Notice that the cursor is on Modify.

After you have used Paradox for a while, you will become so familiar with the menu system that you will make menu and submenu choices instantly, just by pressing a few letters.

*B*eware of the Beep

Try using the ↑ or ↓ key (instead of the ← or → key) to move the cursor around the main menu; or try pressing a character on the keyboard that is not the first letter of one of the menu choices. In either case, Paradox beeps to tell you that you have made an error.

Paradox has two different beeps to indicate errors. If you try to cross a boundary that can't be crossed, it emits a low-pitched beep. If you try to enter invalid data in a table, it emits a high-pitched beep.

*H*ow to Use the Paradox Function Keys

As you have seen, you use the Paradox menu to do all the basic tasks involved in managing a database, such as creating tables, adding data, and creating reports. But some of these tasks can be done more quickly using the function keys. In addition, there are some special functions that you can accomplish only by using these keys.

To make it easy for you to remember what the function keys do, Paradox includes templates for you to place next to them. You should have received two plastic templates with your copy of Paradox.

One template is a rectangle with the center removed. It is for the XT keyboard, which has two rows of function keys at the left. If you have this kind of keyboard, simply place the template around the function keys.

The other template is a long strip designed to be used with the AT or PS/2 keyboard, which has a single row of function keys at the top. Notice that this template has the numbers of the function keys, from F1 to F12, listed across it. Use these numbers to align the template with the function keys on your keyboard. The template has adhesive backing to hold it in place.

Either template puts the name Paradox uses for each function key next to that key. Notice that some keys have only one name, written in black. Other keys have two, three, or four names, written in black, red, green, and purple.

Like some of the other keys on your keyboard, the function keys can be used in combination with the Alt, Ctrl, or Shift key. When the name on the template is black, it describes the function key used by itself. When the name is red, you must hold down Alt while you press the function key to perform the function. Green means you must hold down Ctrl, and purple means you must hold down Shift while pressing the function key. Your template has a legend that explains this color coding; it is on the far-left if you have an AT or PS/2 keyboard, and on the lower-right if you have an XT keyboard.

*H*ow to Get Help

You can get help while using Paradox from either the menu or the function keys. To get help from the main menu, just select the Help option, as you would any other menu choice. Follow these steps to get a feel for the Paradox help system:

1. Either use the arrow keys to move the cursor to Help and press Enter, or simply press H, and the screen shown in Figure 2.3 will appear. Note the submenu at the top of the screen.

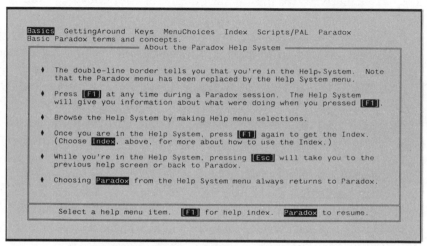

Figure 2.3: *The first screen of the Paradox help system*

2. Select Keys from the submenu. Either use your arrow keys to move the cursor to the word Keys and press Enter, or just press the letter K. A guide to your computer keyboard will appear on the screen with a new submenu above it (see Figure 2.4).

3. To return to the Paradox main menu immediately, you may select Paradox from this submenu, either by using the arrow keys and Enter or by pressing P. To return to the previous menu, the main help menu, just press Esc. Then you can press Esc again to back out of the main help menu to the Paradox main menu.

Notice that the help screens are always surrounded by double lines; this is your clue that you are in the help system. You can always get out of the help system either by selecting Paradox from any submenu or by pressing Esc repeatedly until you have backed through all of the submenus.

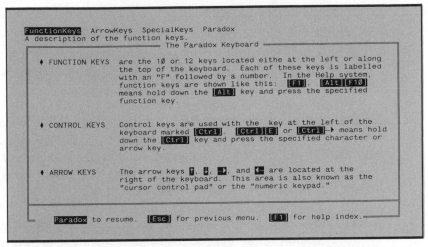

Figure 2.4: The help screen for Paradox keys

You can also get help by using the function keys. You will see on your template that F1 is labeled Help in black, meaning that you press the key by itself to get help.

1. Press F1. You'll see the same screen that appeared when you selected Help from the main menu.

2. Press Esc to return to the main menu.

Wherever you are in the program and whatever you are doing, you can always press F1 to get help. And because the Paradox help system is context sensitive, it always provides help with whatever task you are doing at the time you press F1.

*H*ow to Exit from Paradox

It is important that you exit from Paradox when you are finished working, to make sure that your data is saved. When you choose Exit from the main menu, Paradox displays a simple submenu from which you must choose Yes, to confirm that you are ready to exit the program, or No, to cancel the request.

1. Be sure the main menu is on your screen. If it isn't, press Esc until it appears.

2. Press End to move the cursor to the rightmost menu choice, Exit, or use the arrow keys to move the cursor to Exit.

3. Press Enter, and the Exit submenu appears. Notice that the cursor is on No, the default choice. Press Enter to choose No, so that you return to the main menu.

Since you will be choosing Exit and then choosing Yes whenever you finish using Paradox, this will probably be one of the first combinations of menu choices that you will learn to use the fast way, by pressing the initial letters of your choices without pressing Enter. Use this quick method now to actually leave Paradox.

1. Move the cursor so it is no longer on Exit. This puts you in a typical position that you might be in when you are done with a Paradox session and want to quit the program.

2. Press E to choose Exit from the menu.

3. Press Y to choose Yes, and your system prompt will appear.

From this exercise, you can see how quickly you will be able to go through the menus once you have memorized the initial letters of the menu choices that you use most frequently.

Now that you are oriented, and can move around in Paradox easily, you are ready to create a database.

3

CREATING A
PARADOX TABLE

Featuring

**STRUCTURING
A TABLE**

**DEFINING
THE FIELDS**

**CORRECTING
ERRORS**

**SAVING
YOUR WORK**

**THE
MENU KEY**

In this chapter, you will create a table to hold a list of employees, which you will use as a sample database for the rest of this book. In addition to names and addresses, this table will include the date each employee was hired, his or her hourly wage and score on an aptitude test, as well as a field for comments. These extra fields will be useful in illustrating Paradox's capabilities.

How to Plan a Table's Structure

Before creating a table, you must think carefully about how much you need to break down the data for the application you have in mind. As a general rule, it is good to break the data into as many fields as possible, because it is easy to access data in a separate field.

If you created a single name field, for example, and then entered the names of one or two hundred employees, you couldn't print a report arranged in alphabetical order by last name. If you had a separate field for last names, Paradox could easily sort the table with the entries in that field arranged in alphabetical order; but with no separate field, you would be out of luck.

Likewise, if you enter city, state, and zip code as three separate fields, it will be easy for you to sort in zip code order when you produce mailing labels, and also to find the employees who live in a certain city or state.

On the other hand, you are unlikely to use the middle name or initial by itself, so you can generally keep this in the same field as the first name.

It is a bit less convenient to work with extra fields, so you should avoid creating fields that you will not need. On the other hand, people using Paradox or other databases have had to reenter hundreds of names and addresses by hand, in order to place last names or zip codes in a separate field. When you are in doubt about how to break down your data, it is best to err on the side of caution by creating more fields than you'll actually need. As you'll see, it's easy to delete a field that you aren't using.

How to Create a Table

It is very easy to create a table using Paradox. In fact, you are probably already familiar enough with the menu system to realize that you must begin by selecting Create from the main menu. Start the program, if necessary, and follow these steps:

1. Make sure you are in the Paradox main menu. If you are in a submenu, press Esc until you return to the main menu.

2. Either use the arrow keys to move the cursor to Create and then press Enter or do it the quick way by just pressing C.

3. Paradox will prompt you to enter the name of the table you want to create. Type **Employee** and press Enter.

There are a few rules to remember when you name a table:

- The name can have no more than eight characters.
- The name cannot include spaces. If the name has two words, use a hyphen or an underscore to separate them.
- Two tables cannot have the same name.

Of course, you should also choose a name that describes what is in the table. You will find this pays off when you have to keep track of a number of tables.

Understanding the Paradox Screen

After you enter the table name, you will see the Create screen, shown in Figure 3.1. There are some features of this screen that you will notice in most Paradox screens:

- *The mode indicator* The word Create highlighted at the upper-right of the screen tells you where you are in the program. At times, you will see Main, Edit, and other words as mode indicators, telling you the general part of the program you are currently using.

- *The status message*   The help line on the upper-left, which now reads "Creating new Employee table," tells you more about the task you are currently performing.

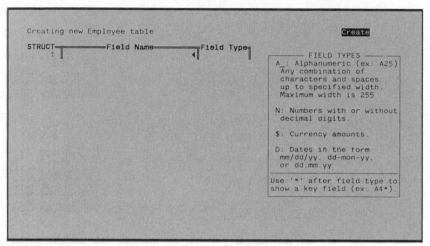

Figure 3.1: The screen for creating a new table

In addition, the Create screen provides help in the box on the right. Like many Paradox screens, it almost tells you what you need to do.

There is one other feature you will often see on Paradox screens that does not appear on this one. To the right of the status message on many Paradox screens, small arrows indicate whether there are more records above or below the current record. If there are more records above the record the cursor is on, a small arrow points upward; a small arrow pointing downward indicates more records below the cursor.

How to Enter Field Names and Types

The way the Create screen is laid out makes it clear how to create a new table. All you have to do is enter the names and types of fields in the columns provided. The box on the right of the screen reminds you of the abbreviations for the four types of data you can enter in the column headed Field Type. Let's look at the differences between these types:

- A_: Alphanumeric fields can hold any type of characters, including letters, numbers, blank spaces, and special characters such as $ or &. The underscore after the A reminds you that you must enter a number in that space to indicate the maximum number of characters the field will be able to hold.

- N: Number fields hold numbers with or without decimals. You should remember that Paradox will automatically round off numbers with more than 15 digits (including decimals).

- $: Currency fields are just like number fields, except that they automatically display numbers with two decimal places and with commas separating thousands, millions, and so on. In addition, negative numbers are enclosed in parentheses in currency format. As you will see in a later chapter, you can make Paradox display numbers in almost any format. Choosing Currency as a field type is just a convenience that saves you the work of setting up the display to show amounts of money.

- D: Dates can be entered in one of three forms: *mm/dd/yy, dd-mon-yy,* or *dd.mm.yy.* For example, December 22, 1990, can be entered as 12/22/90, as 22-Dec-90, or as 22.12.90. You can also use one digit numbers (1/2/90, 2-Jan-90, or 2.1.90) and enter extra digits in the year (12/31/2001). Paradox's special Date field type also allows you to sort in order of date, select dates that come before or after another date, or even to subtract one date from another to see how much time is between them.

There is one other field type called the Short Number, symbolized by S, but this is meant to be used only by programmers and developers. Its only advantage is that it takes up less memory than the ordinary Number field type.

There is one simple rule to remember about data types: any entry that is not actually a number used in a calculation, an amount of money, or a date, is alphanumeric.

Under the box with the list of field types, there is a note that says

Use '*' after the field type to show a key field

Key fields are used mainly when you are working with multitable databases, which you will learn about in Part II of this book.

To create your sample table, just type in the names and types of its fields. If you make a typographical error, see the next section, "How to Correct Errors."

If you have followed the instructions in the previous section, your computer is now displaying the screen for creating a new table. Notice that there is an arrow at the top-right of the Field Name column, to show where your next entry will go. The cursor is a small blinking line at the left of the same column. Follow these steps to create your first Paradox table.

1. Type **First name** and press Enter. Note that the first letter of the field name is capitalized whether you type it in upper- or lowercase; other letters will be either upper- or lowercase, depending on how you type them. After you press Enter, notice that the arrow and the cursor move to the right, to the Field type column.

2. Type **A15** and press Enter to indicate that the First name column is an alphanumeric field with no more than 15 characters. Notice that the A appears in uppercase, regardless of how you type it.

3. The arrow and cursor move to a position directly below the first field name you entered, and you may now enter a second field name. Notice that this is field number 2 according to the numbers in the STRUCT column at the left of the Field Name column. Type **Last name** and press Enter.

4. The cursor moves to the position to get the field type of field 2. Type **A20** and press Enter. This lets you have last names up to 20 characters long.

5. The cursor is now ready for you to enter the name of field 3. Type **Address** and press Enter.

6. Type **A30** for the type of field 3, and press Enter.

7. For the name of field 4, type **City** and press Enter. For its type, type **A15** and press Enter.

8. For the name of field 5, type **State** and press Enter. For its type, type **A2** and press Enter. Only two characters are needed, because you will use the usual postal abbreviations for state names.

9. For the name of field 6, type **Zip** and press Enter. For its type, type **N** and press Enter. For now, you will make the field type for zip codes numeric; in a moment, though, you will change its type.

10. For the name of field 7, type **Date hired** and press Enter. For its type, type **D** and press Enter.

11. For the name of field 8, type **Hourly wage** and press Enter. For its type, type **$** and press Enter.

12. For the name of field 9, type **Test score** and press Enter. For its type, type **N** and press Enter.

13. For the name of field 10, type **Comments** and press Enter. For its type, type **A100** and press Enter.

That completes the structure of your first database table. As you can see, Paradox is very flexibile about field names. For example, unlike table names, they can contain blank spaces. The few rules that do apply to field names are listed here for reference:

- Field names cannot exceed 25 characters in length.

- Field names cannot begin with a blank space, though they can contain blank spaces.

- Field names cannot contain double quotes ", square brackets [], curly brackets {}, parentheses ( ), or a hyphen followed immediately by a greater-than sign to form an arrow ->. Nor can they contain a number sign # by itself.

- Two fields in the same table cannot have the same name.

Notice that numbers *can* be used in field names. If you wanted separate fields for people's home and business addresses, for example, you could name them Address 1 and Address 2.

*C*orrecting Errors

Paradox will not accept an invalid field type. To see how the program traps this error, try adding an extra field to your table.

1. For the name of field 11, type **Dummy field** and press Enter.

2. For the type of field 11, type **x** and press Enter. Paradox will make a low-pitched beep to tell you this is an error, and the message "Not a Paradox field type" will appear in the lower-right corner of the screen, as shown in Figure 3.2.

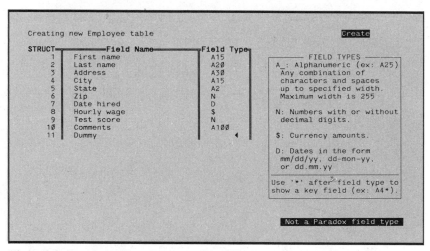

Figure 3.2: *Paradox will not accept an invalid field type*

3. The cursor will still be in position for you to enter the type of field 11. Type **N** and press Enter.

Of course, you might make some other typographical error that Paradox won't catch. Before you save any table, look at it carefully. It's easy to correct or completely change a field name or type. Just use the arrow keys to move the cursor through the list. The cursor will be at the end of each field name or type. Press Backspace to erase one character at a time, or use Ctrl-Backspace to erase the entire entry; then type in the correction.

If you tried to use this table structure, you would find that it is better to make the Zip field alphanumeric than numeric, because Paradox does not display the initial zero of numbers. In the following exercise, you'll make this change, and you'll also change the name of this field and then change it back, just for practice.

1. The cursor should be ready for you to type in the name of field 12. Press ↑ six times to move the cursor to field 6.

2. Type a blank space and then type the word **code** to change the field name from Zip to Zip code.

3. Press either → or Enter to move the cursor to the field type of field 6.

4. Press the Backspace key to erase what is there, and type **A5** to change the type to alphanumeric.

5. Press ← to move the cursor back to the name of field 6, then press the Backspace key five times to erase the word "code" and the blank space that you just added, changing the field name back to Zip.

6. Try making an error. Press ← to move the cursor to the column that contains the number of field 6, and try typing **8** to change the number of this field. The message "Cannot edit this field..." will appear on the lower-right.

This method may seem unwieldy because you can only make changes by erasing everything back to the error, or by deleting the entire entry. Another method called *Field Editing* lets you use the arrow keys to move within a field without erasing characters, but you generally do not need anything this sophisticated to change field names and types. Here, you will just use the simpler method of editing. You will learn about Field Editing in Chapter 5.

Deleting a field is also extremely easy.

1. Use ↓ to move the cursor to field 11.

2. Press Del, and the dummy field you created disappears.

It's that simple, and you can insert new fields just as easily.

1. Press ↑ nine times to move the cursor up to field 2.

2. Press Ins. A space opens up for a new field 2, and all the other fields move down one, as shown in Figure 3.3.

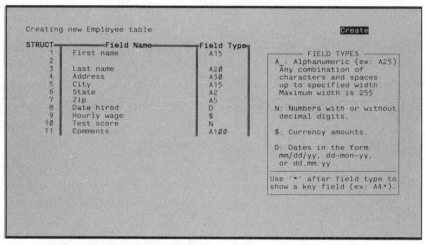

Figure 3.3: Inserting a new field

3. Press → to move the cursor to the name of field 2, type **Middle name**, and press Enter.

4. For the type of field 2, type **A9**.

5. Since you do not actually need a middle name field, press Del to delete it.

Saving Your Work: the DO-IT! Key

You will use the DO-IT! (F2) key frequently; whenever you have completed your work and are ready to save it you press DO-IT!

1. Double check the Employee table structure for typographical errors.

2. Make any necessary corrections, using the editing skills that you just learned.

3. Press F2, the DO-IT! key, to save your work.

Paradox will display the message "Creating Employee," and there will be a brief pause while it writes the structure you have just created on the disk. Then the main menu will reappear.

*H*ow to Use the Menu Key

In Chapter 2, you learned to move through the menu and submenu systems. While you were working on the Employee table in this chapter, though, the main menu disappeared, and you did not return to it until you pressed DO-IT! to finish creating the table.

In addition to the main menu system, you can call up special menus by pressing the Menu key. Look at the template on your function keys, and you will see that F10 is labeled Menu.

*C*alling Up the Create Menu

You can use F10, the Menu key, to call up either Paradox's main menu or its special menus, which appear when you press F10 in certain Paradox modes. For example, when you are using the screen to create the structure of a database, and the mode indicator on the upper-right of your screen says Create, pressing the Menu key calls up the special Create menu. The Create menu is straightforward, and provides a good introduction to the use of the Menu key.

One use of the Create menu is to cancel your work. For example, if you decide not to define a new table, or to rearrange the fields so extensively that you might as well start over, you can choose Cancel from the menu. Let's try it now.

1. Make sure you are in the main menu.

2. Use the arrow keys to move the cursor to Create and press Enter (or just press C to select Create).

3. When Paradox asks you to enter a new table name, type **Dummy** and press Enter. A screen for creating the new Dummy table, much like the screen you used to create the Employee table, appears.

4. Try pressing Esc. Paradox displays an error message telling you to use the menu to cancel the structure definition.

5. Notice that the cursor is still in place to receive the name of field 1. Ignore the error message, type **First name** and press Enter. The error message disappears as soon as you start typing.

6. Press F10, the Menu key. The special Create menu appears at the top of the screen, offering these choices:

   Borrow Help DO-IT! Cancel

   A help line like the help line of the main menu appears below these options.

7. Press the → key three times to move the cursor to Cancel. Notice the different help lines that appear as the cursor moves.

8. Press Enter to select Cancel. The Create screen disappears and the main menu returns.

Paradox does not let you use the Esc key to cancel your work, because too much would be lost if you pressed it by mistake. You can cancel your work, though, by pressing Ctrl-Break. Since this requires pressing two keys, you are not likely to do it by mistake. Pressing Ctrl-Break is equivalent to selecting Cancel from the Create menu.

As you've probably realized, two of the four choices on the Create menu simply offer another way to do something you can do more easily with the function keys. Selecting Help from the Create menu is the same as pressing F1, the Help key; and selecting DO-IT! is the same as pressing F2, the DO-IT! key. You will look at Borrow, the most powerful option on this menu, in the next section.

You can back out of the Create menu—or out of any other special menu—just as you back out of submenus, by pressing Esc.

1. Make sure you are in the main menu, move the cursor to Create, and press Enter (or just press C to select Create).

2. Paradox will ask you to enter a new table name. Type **Dummy** and press Enter to call up the screen for creating the Dummy table.

3. Press the Menu key, F10, to display the Create menu at the top of the screen.

4. Press Esc to back out of the Create menu. The menu disappears, and Paradox returns you to the Create screen.

This illustrates how to use Esc to back out of the special Create menu. Since you do not want to use the Create screen again at this time, cancel it by pressing Ctrl-Break.

*B*orrowing a Table Structure

The Borrow option on the Create menu lets you incorporate the structure of another table into a new table you are defining. Let's say you want to create a new table that includes names and addresses like those in the Employee table. Rather than typing all the field names and types over again, you can just borrow them.

1. From the main menu, select Create.

2. Enter **Dummy** as the name of the new table, and Paradox displays the Create screen.

3. For the name of field 1, type **Company** and press Enter. For its type, type **A15** and press Enter.

4. For the name of field 2, type **Region** and press Enter. For its type, type **A10** and press Enter.

5. To insert the structure of the Employee table between fields 1 and 2, press F10, the Menu key. Borrow is highlighted when the menu appears, so just press Enter to select Borrow.

6. Paradox asks you for the name of the table whose structure you want to borrow. Type **Employee** and press Enter.

The entire structure of the Employee table is inserted between fields 1 and 2 in the STRUCT table. Note that Borrow always inserts the structure you are borrowing above the field where the cursor is positioned.

You could now edit the structure of the new table and then save it. You could use the arrow and Del keys to delete unnecessary fields, for example. Often it is more efficient to borrow and modify an existing structure in this way than it is to type in a new structure.

You do not actually want to save this structure, so you can cancel it. Then you might want to exit from Paradox and take a break:

1. Press F10, the Menu key, to call up the Create menu.

2. Press C to select Cancel. Paradox will take a moment to cancel this structure and return you to the main menu.

3. If you want to exit from Paradox, press E, and then Y.

ENTERING DATA IN PARADOX TABLES

Now that you have created the Employee table, you can enter some sample data in it. As you'll see in this chapter, the basic methods of entering and changing data are the same as those you used to create the structure of the table.

*H*ow to Move Around a Table

Before you actually begin entering data, let's call up the screen Paradox provides for data entry, so you can get a little practice moving the cursor around it.

1. Be sure you are in the Paradox main menu. If necessary, start Paradox, as you did in Chapter 2, or press Esc until you return to the main menu.

2. Select Modify. Either use the arrow keys to move the cursor to Modify and press Enter, or just press M.

3. Select DataEntry, either by using the arrow keys and pressing Enter or by pressing D.

4. When Paradox prompts you to enter the name of a table to add records to, type **employee** and press Enter. Paradox will display the DataEntry screen, shown in Figure 4.1.

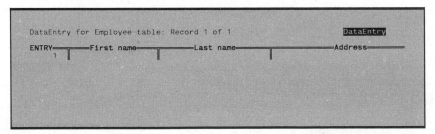

```
DataEntry for Employee table: Record 1 of 1                    DataEntry
ENTRY══════╤═══First name═══════╤═══════Last name═══════╤════════Address═══════
     1     │                    │                       │
```

Figure 4.1: *DataEntry in a table*

Notice that your computer screen is not wide enough to display the entire Employee table, with all its fields. It displays only First name, Last name, and Address. The rest of the fields are beyond the right edge of the screen. You can view the remaining fields by using the arrow keys, as follows:

1. Notice that the cursor is now in the First name field, and that there is an arrow at the right of that field like the one that appeared in the current field when you were creating the structure. Press the → key to move to the Last name field, and then press it again to move to the Address field. Notice that the table moves to the left so that the entire Address field appears on the screen.

2. Another way to move to the next field is by pressing Enter. The table moves to the left, and the First name field disappears beyond the left edge of your screen as the City field appears on the right edge.

3. Press → six more times to move through all of the fields; the Comments field now takes up the entire screen. Notice that, all this time, the status message has been "DataEntry for Employee table: Record 1 of 1."

4. Press → once more. The cursor moves back to the First name field, and Paradox automatically creates a second record. The number 2 appears in the leftmost column, and the status message changes accordingly.

5. Press Del to delete record 2, and the cursor returns to record 1.

6. Press ↓. Paradox again automatically creates record 2 when you move the cursor. Press Del to delete record 2 again.

7. If you hold Ctrl down while you press the arrow keys, you will move through the table a screen at a time instead of a field at a time. With the cursor in First name, press Ctrl →. All the fields that were completely displayed before disappear beyond the left edge of the screen. Address, because it was only partly displayed before is now the leftmost field, as shown in Figure 4.2.

8. Press Ctrl → two more times to move to the Comments field, then press Ctrl ← three times to move back to the left edge of the table. (You could also use Ctrl-Home and Ctrl-End to move to the extreme left and right edges of the table.)

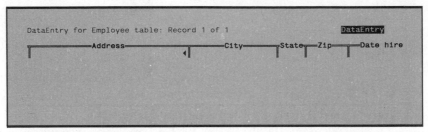

Figure 4.2: Pressing Ctrl with an arrow key moves the cursor one full screen

9.   The cursor is now in the leftmost field, which holds the record numbers. Try pressing **2** to change the record number. Paradox displays an error message in the lower-right corner of your screen, "Cannot Edit this field . . .".

10.   Press → (or Enter) to move the cursor to the First name field, and the error message disappears.

You can also use the Tab key to move around a table. Tab moves you one field to the right, like →, and Shift-Tab moves you one field to the left, like ←.

When you have a table with many records, you will also find it convenient to use the Home key, which moves you to the first record, and the End key, which moves you to the last record.

*H*ow to Enter Data

The methods used to enter data and correct errors are similar to those used to define the structure of a database. You just type the appropriate data in each field, and press Enter to move to the next one. To make corrections, use the arrow keys to move to the field you want to change and the Backspace key to erase mistakes. Follow these steps to enter a sample employee record:

1.   Make sure the cursor is in the First name field of record 1, where you left it when you finished moving around the table.

2.   Type **John** and press Enter. The cursor moves to Last Name.

3. Type **Fairfield** and press Enter. The cursor moves to Address.

4. Type **4437 Elm St.** and press Enter. The cursor moves to City.

5. Type **Hoboken** and press Enter. The cursor moves to State.

6. Type **NJ** and press Enter. The cursor moves to Zip.

7. Type **07031** and press Enter. The cursor moves to Date hired.

8. You will enter dates in the American format, *mm/dd/yy.* Type **02/04/86** and press Enter. The cursor moves to Hourly wage, and Paradox displays the date as 2/04/86, without the leading zero for the month.

9. Notice that the cursor is now at the right of the Hourly wage field, though it has always been at the left of the fields until now. This shows you that Hourly wage is a numeric field. Paradox usually right-justifies numbers, so the ones column lines up; text is usually left-justified, so the first letters line up. Let's say John's wage is $11.00 per hour. Type **11** and press Enter. Because this is a currency field, the number is automatically displayed with two decimal places.

10. When the cursor moves to the Test score field, type **600** and press Enter. The cursor moves to Comments.

11. Type **Was very impressive at personal interview. Possible advancement** and press Enter. The cursor moves to record 2, at the left edge of the table.

12. Let's say you now notice that you've made an error in the name. It is actually not John Fairfield, but Joan Garfield. To correct this error, press ↑ to move to the First name field of record 1.

13. Notice that the cursor is at the end of the name. Press Backspace twice to erase the *hn* in John. Type **an** to change the name to Joan and press Enter.

14. The cursor is now at the end of Fairfield. Press Ctrl-Backspace (hold down Ctrl and then press Backspace) to erase the entire name, and then type **Garfield**.

15. Press ↓ and then ← to return to the First name field of record 2.

By now, you should be fairly comfortable entering data, moving around the table, and making corrections, because these techniques are the same ones you used to create the table's structure in the last chapter.

To get more practice with data entry and to prepare the Employee table for exercises in later chapters, you need to enter some additional records. In the following list, commas separate the fields, but these should not be entered. If there is no comment, just press Enter to leave the Comments field blank and move to the next record. You might also try entering some invalid data. Type a nonexistent or an incomplete date, or press a letter when the cursor is in a numeric field to confirm that Paradox does not accept invalid entries. Here is the list of new employee records for you to enter:

- Alice, Walter, 326 B. 31 St., Far Rockaway, NY, 11601, 12/3/79, 8.65, 488

- Joseph, Miller, 2036 Park Ave., New York, NY, 10033, 3/22/81, 10.25, 503, May be promoted again soon

- Samuel, Smithson, 203 West St., Rye, NY, 10580, 12/1/83, 15.60, 599

- Sally, Bean, 1465 Oak St., Yonkers, NY, 10715, 11/13/89, 11.15, 715, Excellent test score

- Albert, Cruz, 1237 Flatbush Ave., Brooklyn, NY, 11226, 1/15/84, 10.50, 540

- Evelyn, Adams, 3345 Church Ave., Brooklyn, NY, 11235, 4/17/76, 10.33, 466, Long-term employee

- Rosalyn, Rogers, 2242 Pennsylvania Ave., Mt. Vernon, NY, 10507, 7/17/82, 14.56, 723, Occasional customer complaints about service

- Robert, Lin, 457 First St., Paramus, NJ, 07652, 11/25/86, 11.23, 588

- George, Silk, 237 Edison St., New Brunswick, NJ, 08901, 3/1/85, 8.65, 322

- Harriet, Noble, 34 Shady Lane, Greenwich, CT, 06830, 7/12/74, 14.05, 622

- Samuel, Schmaltz, 590 Ocean Ave., Brooklyn, NY, 11226, 2/3/69, 8.32, 321, No potential for advancement

Do not press DO-IT! when you are done entering these records, because there might be errors in them that you want to correct first.

Paradox actually stores newly entered data in a special temporary table named Entry. It only adds data to a permanent table when you press DO-IT! Then, when you select DataEntry again, the program creates a new temporary Entry table to receive the next batch of new data. This temporary Entry table prevents accidental changes to existing data in permanent tables as you move around and make corrections during DataEntry.

You make changes to the temporary Entry table just as you do when you are defining a table's structure: Use the arrow keys to move from field to field. The cursor appears at the end of each field, and you can then use the Backspace key to erase letters one by one, or press Ctrl-Backspace to erase an entire field, and type the correct entry. You can also insert or delete a record by pressing Ins or Del, as you did when you were defining the table's structure.

When you start looking for errors in your new records, you will find it is a nuisance not to be able to see an entire record on the screen. You have to keep using the arrow key to compare each record with the original data. Fortunately, there is another way to look at your data, which allows you to see an entire record at once.

How to Use Form View

In Form View, Paradox automatically creates a form to hold each record in your table. As you can see in Figure 4.3, the form resembles an electronic index card. Notice that the top of the screen says you are using form F. Paradox always gives this name to forms it creates automatically. It is also possible to create custom forms for data entry, which Paradox names F1, F2, and so on. This advanced option is mainly for programmers who are setting up systems. For simple Paradox applications, the automatic form is all you'll need.

```
 DataEntry for Employee table with form F: Record 12 of 12          DataEntry

                                                        Employee    #     12

     First name:  Samuel
     Last name:   Schmaltz
     Address:     590 Ocean Ave.
     City:        Brooklyn
     State:       NY
     Zip:         11226
     Date hired:  2/03/69
     Hourly wage:               8.32
     Test score:                321
     Comments: No potential for advancement                              ◄
```

Figure 4.3: *A record in Form View*

Correcting Errors in Form View

To enter Form View, press the Form Toggle key, F7, which switches you in and out of Form View. If you press this key when your data is displayed as a table, it takes you into Form View; if you press it again, it takes you back to Table View.

In Form View, you can move around and change data as you did in Table View. However, because a form takes up the whole screen, and the ↑ and ↓ keys move only one line at a time, you must press PgUp or PgDn to move from record to record in Form View. Follow these steps to try it out:

1. Make sure the cursor is on one of the fields of record 12; if not, use the arrow keys to move it.

2. Press F7, Form Toggle. Paradox displays a message to tell you it is creating a form. After a moment, record 12 appears in Form View.

3. Try using all four arrow keys to move the cursor. Notice that the cursor appears at the end of any field you move it to. If there are errors in any field, use the Backspace key to erase them, and then type the correct data.

4. Press PgUp to move to record 11. Correct any errors.

5. Press Ins and a new, blank record 11 is inserted.

6. Press PgDn, and notice that the record that was number 11 is now number 12. When a new record is inserted, the record following it moves down one, just as it would if you pressed Ins in Table View.

7. Press PgUp to return to the blank record 11, and press Del to delete it. Notice that the record that became number 12 when you inserted the blank record becomes record 11 again when you delete the blank.

8. Press PgUp and correct any errors in record 10. Continue to press PgUp and correct any errors until you've checked record 1.

9. Press F7 to return to Table View. Notice that the cursor now occupies the same field of record 1 that it did in Form View.

Now that you're satisfied your new records are accurate, you are ready to add them to the permanent Employee table. Follow these steps to do so:

1. Press DO-IT! (F2). Paradox displays a message saying that it is adding the data from the Entry table to the Employee table. When it is done, it again displays the table. The records are the same, but the table name on the upper-left has change from ENTRY to EMPLOYEE.

2. Press Menu (F10) to call up the main menu.

3. Press M to select Modify.

4. Press D to select DataEntry.

5. Paradox asks you for the name of the table to add records to. Type **Employee** and press Enter.

The message at the top of the screen says

DataEntry for Employee table: Record 1 of 1

That doesn't mean that the 12 records you already entered in the Employee table have disappeared. You are in the first and only record of the new temporary Entry table, which will again be added to the Employee table when you press DO-IT!.

*E*ntering Data in Form View

You can also enter data in Form View, so that all the fields of a record are visible at once. Try entering a record in Form View to see how this is done.

1. Make sure you are still in the First name field of record 1 of the Entry table.

2. Press F7 to toggle to Form View. The cursor remains in the First name field.

3. Type **Dianne** and press Enter.

4. Type **Lee** in the Last Name field, and press Enter.

5. Type **1634 Bancroft Way** in the Address field and press Enter.

6. Type **Berkeley** in the City field and press Enter.

7. Type **CA** in the State field and press Enter.

8. Type **94703** in the Zip field and press Enter.

9. Type **4/15/86** in the Date hired field and press Enter.

10. Type **9.5** in the Hourly wage field and press Enter. The wage will automatically be displayed as 9.50.

11. Type **602** in the Test score field and press Enter.

12. Type **Retesting may be necessary** in the Comments field and press Enter.

After you have pressed Enter in the last field of record 1, the cursor moves to the first field of record 2. There is no need to enter more records at this time, so just press DO-IT! (F2) to end this data entry session.

Paradox adds the new record to the Employee table, and then displays the entire table. The status message at the top of the screen now says, "Viewing Employee Table." This means that you can only view the table at present; you cannot make changes. Try pressing Backspace to erase a letter, and Paradox will display the error message shown in Figure 4.4, which tells you that you must choose Edit or Coedit to make changes.

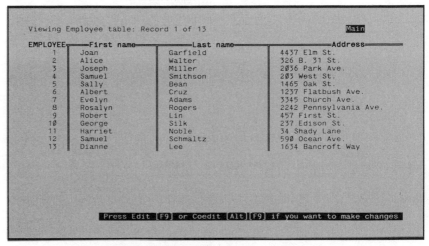

Viewing Employee table: Record 1 of 13   Main

EMPLOYEE	First name	Last name	Address
1	Joan	Garfield	4437 Elm St.
2	Alice	Walter	326 B. 31 St.
3	Joseph	Miller	2036 Park Ave.
4	Samuel	Smithson	203 West St.
5	Sally	Bean	1465 Oak St.
6	Albert	Cruz	1237 Flatbush Ave.
7	Evelyn	Adams	3345 Church Ave.
8	Rosalyn	Rogers	2242 Pennsylvania Ave.
9	Robert	Lin	457 First St.
10	George	Silk	237 Edison St.
11	Harriet	Noble	34 Shady Lane
12	Samuel	Schmaltz	590 Ocean Ave.
13	Dianne	Lee	1634 Bancroft Way

Press Edit [F9] or Coedit [Alt][F9] if you want to make changes

Figure 4.4: *The updated Employee table, with error message*

You will choose Edit in Chapter 5. As you will see, you can enter data directly into a permanent table by selecting Edit instead of DataEntry from the Modify menu. For now, you might want to take a break. To exit from Paradox, press Menu (F10) to call up the main menu. Then press E and Y.

5

EDITING DATA IN PARADOX

**USING
EDIT MODE**

**THE
EDIT KEY**

**FIELD
EDITING**

**PARADOX
POWER KEYS**

In the last chapter, you used the DataEntry option, which lets you add records to a table and make changes to these new records, but does not let you change records that were added in an earlier session. The Edit option is virtually identical to DataEntry, except that it also gives you access to earlier records.

Unlike DataEntry, which creates a temporary Entry table that is added to the actual table later, Edit gives you direct access to the table you are working on. You can move to the bottom of the table and add new records, in much the same way you did in DataEntry. But in Edit mode you can also change any existing record in the table in the same way, whereas DataEntry mode only lets you correct records that you've added during the current session.

Other Edit mode basics are the same as in DataEntry: you can move around the table, toggle from Table View to Form View, and make data changes, all in the same way.

This chapter focuses on shortcuts and more powerful ways of editing. Most of these techniques can be used in DataEntry as well as Edit mode, although it is more common to use them in Edit.

How to Edit a Paradox Table

To get started, take a little time to practice using Edit in the same ways that you have already used DataEntry. By following these steps, you'll get a feel for the similarities and minor differences between these two modes:

1. Make sure you are in the Paradox main menu. If necessary, start the program, press the Menu key (F10) to call up the menu, or press Esc until you get back to the main menu.

2. Press M to select Modify.

3. Press E to select Edit.

4. When Paradox prompts you for the name of the table to edit, press Enter to get a list of tables.

5. Make sure the cursor is on Employee and press Enter again. The Employee table will appear, with all the entries you have already made. The cursor will be on the record number of record 1, as shown in Figure 5.1. Notice the message at the top of the screen, which verifies that you are editing the Employee table.

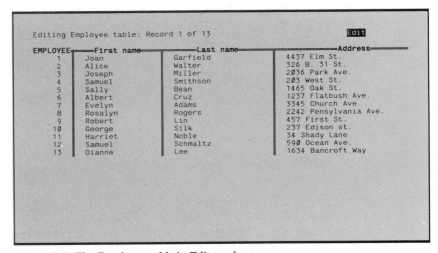

```
Editing Employee table: Record 1 of 13                           Edit
EMPLOYEE      First name             Last name             Address
     1        Joan                   Garfield              4437 Elm St.
     2        Alice                  Walter                326 B. 31 St.
     3        Joseph                 Miller                2036 Park Ave.
     4        Samuel                 Smithson              203 West St.
     5        Sally                  Bean                  1465 Oak St.
     6        Albert                 Cruz                  1237 Flatbush Ave.
     7        Evelyn                 Adams                 3345 Church Ave.
     8        Rosalyn                Rogers                2242 Pensylvania Ave.
     9        Robert                 Lin                   457 First St.
    10        George                 Silk                  237 Edison st.
    11        Harriet                Noble                 34 Shady Lane
    12        Samuel                 Schmaltz              590 Ocean Ave.
    13        Dianne                 Lee                   1634 Bancroft Way
```

Figure 5.1: The Employee table in Edit mode

Let's say you discovered that you were right the first time about the name of the employee in record 1. You can change it just as you did in DataEntry.

6. Press → to move the cursor to the First name field of record 1. Press Backspace twice to erase the *an*. Then type **hn** to make the first name John and press Enter.

7. Press Ctrl-Backspace to erase the last name. Then type **Fairfield** as the last name. Now that you have made that correction, you can add new records.

8. Press ← to move back to the First name field. Then press ↓ 13 times to move through all the existing records to the first name of a new record. Paradox will add a blank record 14.

9. Type the following entries in the specified columns, pressing Enter after each entry:

Column	Entry
First name	**Francine**
Last name	**Bowen**
Address	**2113 University Ave.**
City	**Palo Alto**
State	**CA**
Zip	**94301**
Date hired	**7/23/84**
Hourly wage	**12**
Test score	**432**

10. Press Enter to skip the Comment field and move to the next record. Then press Form Toggle (F7) to enter the next record in Form View. Paradox presents the same data entry form you used before. The message

appears at the top, and the cursor is still in the First name field.

11. As you did in step 9, type the following entries, pressing Enter after each one:

Column	Entry
First name	**Henry**
Last name	**Ware**
Address	**1742 Dutch Elm St.**
City	**San Raphael**
State	**CA**
Zip	**94904**

Column	Entry
Date hired	**12/22/77**
Hourly wage	**12.5**
Test score	**664**
Comments	**Very loyal employee**

Your screen should look like Figure 5.2. Press Enter to move to record 16.

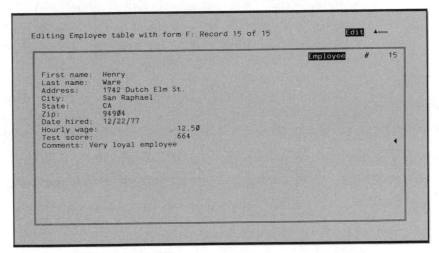

```
Editing Employee table with form F: Record 15 of 15                    Edit  ▲───

                                                         Employee    #    15

   First name:   Henry
   Last name:    Ware
   Address:      1742 Dutch Elm St.
   City:         San Raphael
   State:        CA
   Zip:          94904
   Date hired:   12/22/77
   Hourly wage:                    12.50
   Test score:              664
   Comments: Very loyal employee                                            ◄
```

Figure 5.2: Editing in Form View

That takes you through the basics of the Edit mode, and you are almost ready to move on to more powerful features. First, though, take time to enter a few more records—both to accustom yourself to entering data in Form View and to add data you will need for examples in later chapters.

Remain in Form View and add the following records (do not enter the commas):

- William, Channing, 22 The Circle, Ross, CA, 94957, 2/22/81, 15.55, 641

- Josephine, Buckminster, 3322 Bridgeway, Sausalito, CA, 94965, 4/1/79, 14.25, 533, In special training program

- Jean, Abbott, 4445-2312 Technology Blvd., Menlo Park, CA, 94025, 4/15/88, 9.45, 601, On executive track

- Edward, Channing, 180 Poplar St., Mill Valley, CA, 94943, 10/17/79, 12.50, 403

- Andrea, Norton, 2311 First St., Mill Valley, CA, 94945, 6/16/85, 15.05, 722

- Joseph, Tuckerman, 45 Arcroft Circle, San Mateo, CA, 94406, 7/6/82, 12.75, 421

- Jane, Walker, 848 Broadway, San Raphael, CA, 94901, 2/12/87, 14.15, 560, Steady progress in training program

- Edward, Channing, 505 Haight St., San Francisco, CA, 94122, 6/15/88, 4.45, 325, Frequent absenteeism

You should now have more data than your screen can display. Edward Channing should be record 23. After you enter his name, press Form Toggle (F7) and you will see that record 1 has disappeared from the top of the table, as shown in Figure 5.3.

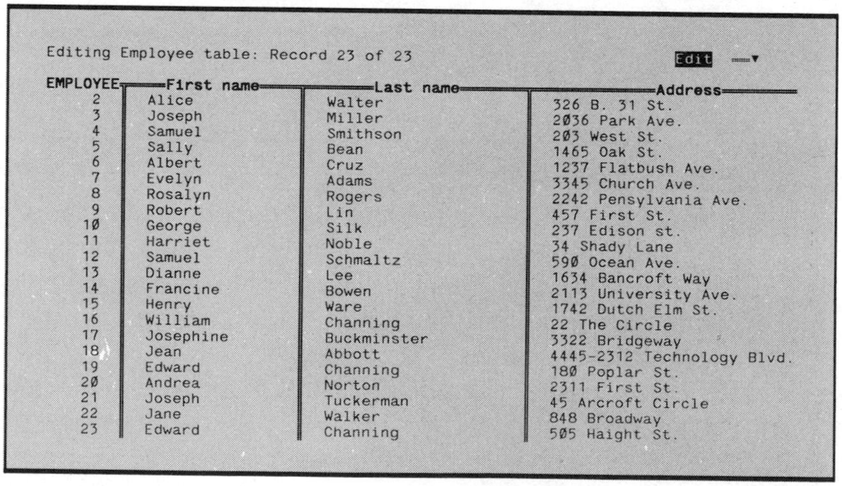

```
Editing Employee table: Record 23 of 23                        Edit   ▬▼
EMPLOYEE╤══════First name══════╤══════Last name══════╤═══════════Address═══════
     2  │ Alice               │ Walter              │ 326 B. 31 St.
     3  │ Joseph              │ Miller              │ 2036 Park Ave.
     4  │ Samuel              │ Smithson            │ 203 West St.
     5  │ Sally               │ Bean                │ 1465 Oak St.
     6  │ Albert              │ Cruz                │ 1237 Flatbush Ave.
     7  │ Evelyn              │ Adams               │ 3345 Church Ave.
     8  │ Rosalyn             │ Rogers              │ 2242 Pensylvania Ave.
     9  │ Robert              │ Lin                 │ 457 First St.
    10  │ George              │ Silk                │ 237 Edison st.
    11  │ Harriet             │ Noble               │ 34 Shady Lane
    12  │ Samuel              │ Schmaltz            │ 590 Ocean Ave.
    13  │ Dianne              │ Lee                 │ 1634 Bancroft Way
    14  │ Francine            │ Bowen               │ 2113 University Ave.
    15  │ Henry               │ Ware                │ 1742 Dutch Elm St.
    16  │ William             │ Channing            │ 22 The Circle
    17  │ Josephine           │ Buckminster         │ 3322 Bridgeway
    18  │ Jean                │ Abbott              │ 4445-2312 Technology Blvd.
    19  │ Edward              │ Channing            │ 180 Poplar St.
    20  │ Andrea              │ Norton              │ 2311 First St.
    21  │ Joseph              │ Tuckerman           │ 45 Arcroft Circle
    22  │ Jane                │ Walker              │ 848 Broadway
    23  │ Edward              │ Channing            │ 505 Haight St.
```

Figure 5.3: Record 1 has scrolled off the top of the screen

Some Editing Shortcuts

By now, you should be accustomed to the basic methods of entering and changing records. You are ready to learn faster and more versatile ways to do the same things. These methods can save you a great deal of time when you are actually working with practical Paradox applications.

Using the Edit Key

After you have finished entering a batch of names, you can press DO-IT! to save your work. If you want to return to editing again, you can do so without going through the menu structure simply by pressing the Edit key (F9).

After you press DO-IT! to end your editing, the table remains on the screen, but you can only view it and cannot make any changes. Because people often want to edit a table they are already viewing, Paradox lets you do this by pressing a single key, rather than pressing DO-IT! to end data entry, and then choosing DataEntry again as you did in the last chapter.

1. Press DO-IT! (F2). The highlighted message, Ending Edit, appears. After the table is saved, your screen should look the same as it did when you were editing, except that the status message at the top says Viewing Employee table. Now that you are viewing rather than editing, you can no longer make changes.

2. Press Backspace to try to make a change. An error message appears on the bottom of the screen saying

   Press Edit [F9] or Coedit [Alt][F9] if you want to make changes

3. Press Edit (F9). The screen should look the same except that the status message on the top says Edit again. Now, you can make changes in the data.

Coedit is similar to Edit, but it is designed for people who work on *networks,* groups of computers that share the same data. Coedit also offers certain advantages when you are using multitable databases, as you will see in Part II of this book.

How to Move around a Table Quickly

With the additional data you have entered, you can now take advantage of keys that let you move up and down the table more quickly. The Home key moves you to the first record of the table, and the End key moves you to the last. PgUp moves you up one screen, and PgDn moves you down one screen. Follow these steps to try them out:

1. Press Home. The table moves down a bit and the last record disappears as the cursor moves to the first record.

2. Press End. The cursor moves to the last record, and the first record disappears from the screen again.

3. Press PgUp. The table is not large enough to scroll up an entire screen, but goes as far up as it can, and the cursor again moves to the first record.

4. Press PgDn. The table scrolls down an entire screen. All the records that were visible before, except the last one, disappear. Only the final two records and the blank space following them are visible, as shown in Figure 5.4. The cursor is on the record at the top of the screen.

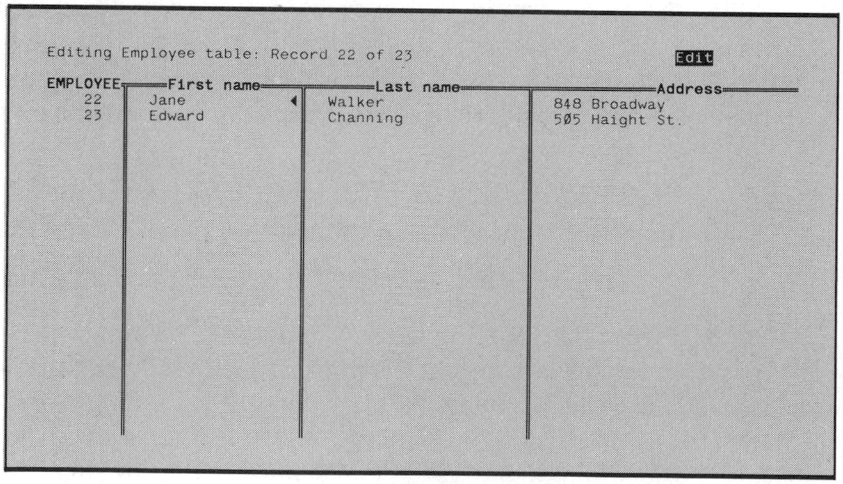

```
Editing Employee table: Record 22 of 23                    Edit
EMPLOYEE     First name              Last name                Address
   22     Jane              ◄    Walker              848 Broadway
   23     Edward                 Channing            5Ø5 Haight St.
```

Figure 5.4: PgDn has scrolled beyond the last record

5. Press End. The cursor moves to the last record, and the table is displayed with the last record at the bottom of the screen.

In general, when you are working with long tables, Home and End are used to move all the way through the table and PgUp and PgDn to move through the table one screen at a time, so you can look at all the records. You can see, though, that End also has the advantage of displaying as many records as possible with the cursor on the last record of the table.

How to Use Field Editing

You have learned to make changes in your data by using the Backspace key to erase everything from the end of a field back to the error (or by using Ctrl-Backspace to erase the entire field) and then typing in the correct data. Of course, this can be inconvenient if you have a very long field where only the first letter is incorrect. There is a way to move the cursor within a field without erasing what is already there, so that you can change just one or two letters in the field rather than retyping it all. Paradox calls this method Field Editing, or Field View.

You begin Field Editing by pressing the Field View key combination (Alt-F5). (You can also begin Field Editing by pressing Ctrl-F, but it is easier for beginners to use the function keys and take advantage of the template.)

Once you have begun Field Editing, the keys that used to move you around the entire table will move you just within the field. In general, they do the same things, but on a much smaller scale. Table 5.1 summarizes the differences. Eventually, you will become used to them. For now, you should glance at the table and concentrate on these important points:

- Usually, the ← and → keys move you a field to the left or right. In Field View, they move you just one character to the left or right.

- Usually, the Del key deletes an entire record. In Field Editing, it deletes a single character.

- Usually, the Enter key moves you to the next field. In Field View, it ends Field Editing and takes you back to the usual editing mode.

Table 5.1: Keys That Function Differently in Field View and Table View

Key	Field View	Table View
←	Moves left one character	Moves left one field
→	Moves right one character	Moves right one field
Ctrl ←	Moves left one word	Moves left one screen
Ctrl →	Moves right one word	Moves right one screen
↑	Moves up one line (works only in fields that have more than one line)	Moves up one record
↓	Moves down one line (works only in fields that have more than one line)	Moves down one record
Home	Moves to the first character of the field	Moves to the first record of the table
End	Moves to the Last character of the field	Moves to the last record of the table
Del	Deletes a character	Deletes a record
Ins	Toggles between Insert and Typeover modes	Inserts a record
Enter	Ends field editing	Moves to the next field

There is another important feature of Field Editing that is a bit more subtle. Usually, pressing the Ins key inserts a new record. When you are doing Field Editing, though, the Ins key toggles between Insert and Typeover modes.

When you first begin, you will be in Insert mode. If you move the cursor to the left and then type new characters, they will be inserted before the character the cursor is on, and all the characters that follow will be pushed to the right. If you press the Ins key and toggle into Typeover mode, however, the characters that you type will replace the characters that are already there. If you press Ins again, you will toggle back to Insert mode.

Finally, Backspace and Ctrl-Backspace erase the character to the left of the cursor and the entire word, respectively, as they usually do.

The only difference is that in Field View, the cursor can be anywhere within a word when you press Backspace to erase the letter to its left.

These differences will be clear when you look at an example. Let's say that you find out, once again, that you've entered the wrong name in the first record, that it actually is Joan Garfield after all. Now you can make the change a little more easily.

1. Press Home to move to the first record of the table. You should already be in the First name field. If not, use ← or → to move the cursor to that field.

2. Press the Field View key combination (Alt-F5) to begin Field Editing. Notice that the cursor turns into a small box, indicating that you are in Field View.

3. Press ← once to move the cursor. Then press Backspace to erase the *h* in John and type **a** to change the name to Joan.

4. Press Enter to leave Field Editing, and Enter again to move to the Last name field. Now press Alt-F5 to begin Field Editing.

5. Press Home to move the cursor to the first letter of the field, as shown in Figure 5.5. You want to type a G over the F that is there now.

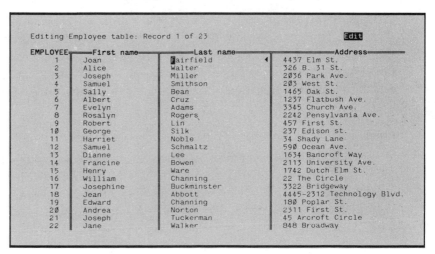

Editing Employee table: Record 1 of 23			Edit

EMPLOYEE	First name	Last name	Address
1	Joan	Fairfield ◄	4437 Elm St.
2	Alice	Walter	326 B. 31 St.
3	Joseph	Miller	2036 Park Ave.
4	Samuel	Smithson	203 West St.
5	Sally	Bean	1465 Oak St.
6	Albert	Cruz	1237 Flatbush Ave.
7	Evelyn	Adams	3345 Church Ave.
8	Rosalyn	Rogers	2242 Pensylvania Ave.
9	Robert	Lin	457 First St.
10	George	Silk	237 Edison st.
11	Harriet	Noble	34 Shady Lane
12	Samuel	Schmaltz	590 Ocean Ave.
13	Dianne	Lee	1634 Bancroft Way
14	Francine	Bowen	2113 University Ave.
15	Henry	Ware	1742 Dutch Elm St.
16	William	Channing	22 The Circle
17	Josephine	Buckminster	3322 Bridgeway
18	Jean	Abbott	4445-2312 Technology Blvd.
19	Edward	Channing	180 Poplar St.
20	Andrea	Norton	2311 First St.
21	Joseph	Tuckerman	45 Arcroft Circle
22	Jane	Walker	848 Broadway

Figure 5.5: Using Field Editing to move the cursor within a word

6. Press Ins to toggle to Typeover mode. Notice that the cursor changes slightly when you do this. In Insert mode, it was a box with a blinking line in it; in Typeover mode, the blinking line disappears. Toggle back and forth a few times to see the difference in the cursor.

7. Type a capital **G** to correct the first letter of the name. Notice that the cursor moves to the right, just as in ordinary typing. You could type over an entire word if you wanted to.

8. Press → to move the cursor to the *i* and press Del to delete it. Then press Enter to leave Field Editing mode.

That's all there is to Field Editing, and once you get used to it, you will find it very convenient.

Remember that Field Editing is a general feature of Paradox. You can use it when you have chosen DataEntry from the menu, or when you have chosen Edit. You can even use it when you are defining the structure of a table. It is discussed in this chapter only because it is used most commonly to edit data.

*U*sing the Paradox Power Keys

There are a few special power keys in Paradox. By pressing one of these keys you can make an entry in an entire field, correct an error, or find a certain name, city, or other value in your database. These are not function keys indicated on your template, but are usually a letter, which stands for a specific task, combined with the Ctrl or Alt key.

*T*he Ditto Key

When you are entering repetitive data, the Ditto key, Ctrl-D, is very useful. Just press Ctrl-D, and the field your cursor is in will automatically be filled by the data in the field above. Imagine, for example, that the company has decided to hire Edward Channing's wife, Alice.

1. With the cursor in the First name field of record 23, Edward Channing, press ↓ to add a blank record 24 and to move the cursor to its First name field.

2. Type **Alice** and press Enter to move to the Last name field.

3. Press Ctrl-D (hold down Ctrl and press D). The name Channing appears in the Last name field. Press Enter.

4. Use Ctrl-D to enter the address, city, state, and zip code from the previous record.

5. Type **7/14/90** in the Date hired field and press Enter.

6. Press Ctrl-D for Hourly wage and press Enter.

7. Type **348** for Test score and press Enter. Then press Enter again to skip the Comments field.

The Ditto key is most often used with a list that requires you to enter the same city name repeatedly.

The Undo Key

The Undo key, Ctrl-U, lets you change your mind and undo your previous edits, one at a time, by repeatedly pressing Ctrl-U. Or, you can undo changes by selecting Undo from the Edit menu.

1. Press Home to move to the First name field of the first record; then press Ctrl-Backspace to erase the first name.

2. Press ↓ to move to the second record, and type **xxx** to change the name from Alice to Alicexxx.

3. Press ↓ to move to the third record, and Del to delete it. Then press Ctrl-U to undo the deletion. The third record reappears, and Paradox displays the message, "Record 3 reinserted."

4. Press Ctrl-U to undo the previous change. The xxx following Alice disappears, and Paradox displays the message, "Changes for record 2 undone."

5. Press the Menu key (F10) to call up the Edit menu. Then press → to move the cursor to Undo, and press Enter. Now press Y to confirm the change, and the first name of record 1 reappears.

If you have ever done data entry, you will realize how useful this feature can be.

The Zoom and Zoom Next Keys

The Zoom key (Ctrl-Z) and the Zoom Next key (Alt-Z) let you go directly to specific data that you are looking for. For example, they let you find a record with a certain last name or all the records with a certain state.

The Zoom key takes you to the first occurrence in the table of the value you are looking for. First move the cursor to the field that the value will be in and press the Zoom key. Paradox prompts you to enter a value. After you have found the first occurrence of that value using Zoom, the Zoom Next key takes you to its subsequent occurrences.

In the following example you'll deliberately make a few errors to show what to avoid and how to correct mistakes.

1. Make sure the cursor is still in the First name field of record 1 and press Ctrl-Z. When Paradox asks you to enter the value or pattern to search for, type **Channing** and press Enter. The message "Searching..." appears for a moment on the lower-right, followed by the message "Match not found." This is because you were looking for a last name but had the cursor in the First name field.

2. Press → to move the cursor to the Last name field. Then press Ctrl-Z, and when Paradox prompts you, type **Channing** and press Enter. The cursor moves to the first occurrence of that name, which is highlighted for a moment. Now press Alt-Z, for Zoom Next. The cursor moves to the next occurrence of the same name.

3. Press Ctrl-Z instead of Zoom Next. Paradox asks you for a name to search for, and suggests Channing. This prompt tells you that you've mistakenly chosen Zoom instead of Zoom Next. You could back out of this choice by pressing Esc, but instead press Enter. Notice that the cursor goes back to the first occurrence of Channing, not on to the next one.

4. Press Ctrl-Z. Paradox asks you for the value or pattern to search for and suggests Channing. Press Ctrl-Backspace to erase that suggestion; then type **Norto** and press Enter. Paradox tells you "Match not found."

5. Press Ctrl-Z. Paradox asks you what to search for and suggests Norto. Type **n** to change Norto to Norton and press Enter. Paradox takes you to the last name Norton.

6. Press Alt-Z. Paradox says "Match not found" since there is no other Norton in the table.

7. Press Ctrl-Z. Paradox suggests Norton as the value to search for. Press Ctrl-Backspace to erase Norton.

8. Type **garfield** (with a small *g*) and press Enter. Paradox says "Match not found." Press Ctrl-Z and Paradox suggests garfield as the value to search for.

9. Press the Field View key combination (Alt-F5). When the cursor turns into a box, as it always does in Field View, press Home to move the cursor to the *g*.

10. Press Ins to toggle into Typeover mode. Notice that the blinking line in the cursor box disappears. Now type **G** (be sure to use a capital *G*) and press Enter to leave Field View.

11. The suggested value is now Garfield. Press Enter to select it. The cursor moves to the last name Garfield and highlights it for a moment.

When you are editing, you will probably use the Zoom key most often to find a record you want to change. If one of your employees moves, for example, it is easiest to use Zoom to find that employee's record and then to change the address.

You can also use the Zoom key with *wildcards*—symbols that can stand for any letter or combination of letters. This feature is useful if you are not sure how a name is spelled, or are looking for several names with similar spellings.

Paradox has two wildcard operators:

- The at sign (@) stands for any character. For example, if you cannot remember whether a last name is spelled Smith or Smyth, you can search for Sm@th to find either spelling.

- Two periods (..) stand for any series of characters. For example, if you still cannot remember whether the employee's name was Fairfield or Garfield, you can search for ..rfield, which would find either one.

A Few Conveniences

Paradox provides a number of additional shortcuts that save time in editing or data entry. Although you can use the program perfectly well without knowing these tricks, you might find it helpful to keep them in mind.

- If you do not include the year in a date field, Paradox automatically uses the current year.

- If you press the spacebar while entering a date, Paradox fills in the current month, day, or year, depending on where you are in the date, followed by a separator (except after the year). Pressing the spacebar three times enters the current date.

- If you are entering a date in the *dd-Mon-yy* format, the first letter of the month is automatically capitalized and pressing the spacebar fills in the letters that follow. Thus, if you type **f** and press the spacebar twice, Paradox displays Feb.

- While typing number fields, you can press the spacebar to enter a decimal point.

- If a negative number is preceded by a left parenthesis (instead of a minus sign) you can press the spacebar twice to enter the decimal point and the right parenthesis.

Using the Edit Menu

Before concluding this chapter, let's look briefly at the Edit menu, shown in Figure 5.6.

1. Press The Menu key (F10).

2. Use the arrow keys to move the cursor and read the help lines for each choice, while you read the descriptions of the choices below.

3. When you are done, press Esc to back out of the menu.

You do not have to spend much time studying this menu, but you should be aware of it. You already used the Undo option when

```
Image  Undo  ValCheck  Help  DO-IT!  Cancel                     Edit
Resize or reformat an image; move to a field, record, or value; pick a form.
EMPLOYEE      First name            Last name              Address
        1     Joan                  Garfield               4437 Elm St.
        2     Alice                 Walter                 326 B. 31 St.
        3     Joseph                Miller                 2036 Park Ave.
        4     Samuel                Smithson               203 West St.
        5     Sally                 Bean                   1465 Oak St.
        6     Albert                Cruz                   1237 Flatbush Ave.
        7     Evelyn                Adams                  3345 Church Ave.
        8     Rosalyn               Rogers                 2242 Pensylvania Ave.
        9     Robert                Lin                    457 First St.
       10     George                Silk                   237 Edison st.
       11     Harriet               Noble                  34 Shady Lane
       12     Samuel                Schmaltz               590 Ocean Ave.
       13     Dianne                Lee                    1634 Bancroft Way
       14     Francine              Bowen                  2113 University Ave.
       15     Henry                 Ware                   1742 Dutch Elm St.
       16     William               Channing               22 The Circle
       17     Josephine             Buckminster            3322 Bridgeway
       18     Jean                  Abbott                 4445-2312 Technology Blvd.
       19     Edward                Channing               180 Poplar St.
       20     Andrea                Norton                 2311 First St.
       21     Joseph                Tuckerman              45 Arcroft Circle
       22     Jane                  Walker                 848 Broadway
```

Figure 5.6: The Edit menu

you learned about the Undo key (Ctrl-U). Help, DO-IT!, and Cancel are the same choices you learned about in the DataEntry menu.

You will learn about the other two menu choices in later chapters. Image changes the way data appears on the screen. It is the same as the Image option on the main menu, which is discussed in Chapter 8. ValCheck lets you screen out invalid data. It is among the special techniques that are discussed in Chapter 19.

You are probably ready to take a break by now. If so,

1. Press DO-IT! (F2)—or select DO-IT! from the Edit menu.

2. Press Menu (F10).

3. Press E for Exit and Y for Yes.

RESTRUCTURING
A TABLE

ADDING AND
RENAMING
FIELDS

MOVING AND
DELETING
FIELDS

CHANGING
FIELD LENGTHS

There will be times when you need to change the structure of a table you have already worked on—for example, to add new fields or to change the length of existing fields.

Restructuring a table is essentially no different from creating one. You can change the field names or field types of an existing table in the same way that you adjusted them while you were creating it.

The difference is that the table now contains data, so the changes you make could cause problems. For example, if you shorten a field, the data already in it might be too long to fit into its new, condensed length. You will learn in this chapter how Paradox handles this problem.

In general, this chapter presents slight variations of techniques you have already learned. It is simple and short, and should complete your knowledge of how to create and add data to tables. Then, you'll be ready to learn how Paradox can put data to work for you.

How to Change the Structure of a Table

Now that you have some experience with tables, you can see that the table structure itself is stored in a table named STRUCT. To change the structure, you simply edit this table. You can use the same editing methods that you would use with any other table.

Changes without Problems

First, let's look at forms of restructuring that rarely cause problems. The concepts are so easy that a few examples should suffice to get the point across.

How to Add a New Field

Let's say that you want to generate form letters that begin with a personal salutation. You need to add a field that holds the word Mr., Ms., Mrs., Miss, Dr., or whatever goes before a person's last name.

1. From the Paradox main menu, press M to select Modify and R to select Restructure.

2. When Paradox prompts you for a table name, type **employee** and press Enter. You should see the screen illustrated in Figure 6.1, which is just like the screen you used to create the table structure, except for the restructuring message at the top. Your cursor should be in the first record of the table, so just press Ins to insert a new record 1. All the other records move down one, as shown in Figure 6.2.

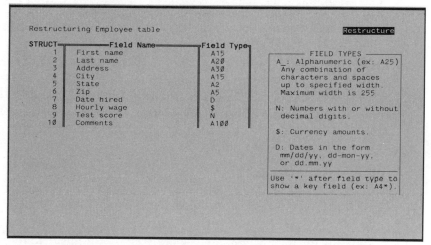

Figure 6.1: Modifying a table's structure

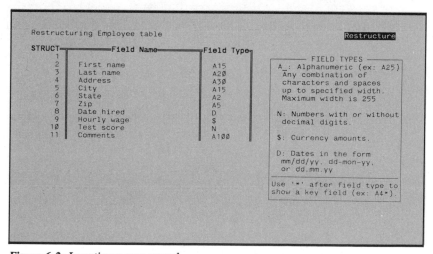

Figure 6.2: Inserting a new record

3. Press → to move the cursor to the Field Name column. Type **Honorific** (the technical term for Mr., Mrs., and so on) and press Enter. Type **A5** as the field type and press Enter. Now press DO-IT! to save the change. Paradox displays a message to tell you it is making the change. Then it displays the table with the Honorific field added.

4. Press F7 to toggle into Form View and see what an entire record looks like. Then press F7 again to toggle back to Table View.

5. Press the Edit key (F9) to edit the table. Then press → to move to the Honorific field of record 1. Type **Dr.** and press ↓ to move to record 2. Press DO-IT! (F2) to save the change.

Under ordinary circumstances, you would probably want to fill in all of the honorifics immediately, pressing ↓ after each one to go to the next record. Since this example will be discarded later, you do not need to fill in the fields in the other records.

How to Rename a Field

If you discover that nobody else where you work knows what the word honorific means, you can change the name of this field to something more common without any trouble. At the same time, you might want to change the name of the Test score field to show that the Standard Employee Aptitude Test is being used. Change the name to SEAT score.

1. Press the Menu key (F10) to call up the main menu. Then press M to select Modify and R to select Restructure.

2. When Paradox asks for the table name, type **employee** and press Enter. Paradox displays the screen for restructuring a table, with the cursor on field 1.

3. Press → to move the cursor to Field Name, and Ctrl-Backspace to erase the current name.

4. Type **Mr/Mrs/etc,** and press End to move the cursor to the last record. Press ↑ once to move to the field name of the Test score field.

5. Press Field View (Alt-F5) to toggle to Field Editing (the cursor changes to a box with a blinking line), and press Home to move to the first letter of the field. Press Ins to toggle to Typeover mode. The blinking line in the cursor disappears.

6. Press Caps Lock and type **SEAT**. Half way through, your screen will look like Figure 6.3. When you're finished, press Caps Lock again, and then press Enter to end Field Editing. Now press DO-IT! (F2) to save the changes. Paradox displays the table, and the name of the first field is now Mr/Mrs/etc.

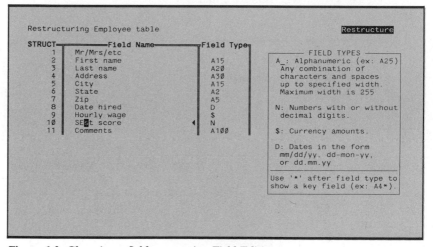

Figure 6.3: Changing a field name using Field Editing

7. Press the Form Toggle key (F7) to see the table in Form View. Notice that the name of the Test score field has also been changed to SEAT score. Press Form Toggle again to return to Table View.

*H*ow to Move a Field

Initially, it seems sensible to make Mr/Mrs/etc the first field of this table, since it comes before the name when you actually use it. Later, you might find that you would rather have it elsewhere. Let's see how to move a field in Paradox.

1. Press Menu (F10) to call up the main menu. Then press M to select Modify and R to select Restructure.

2. Type **employee** and press Enter. Now press ↓ seven times to move the cursor to record 8 and press Ins to insert a new record 8.

3. Press → to move the cursor to the Field Name of record 8, and type **Mr/Mrs/etc** exactly as it is typed in record 1 (see Figure 6.4).

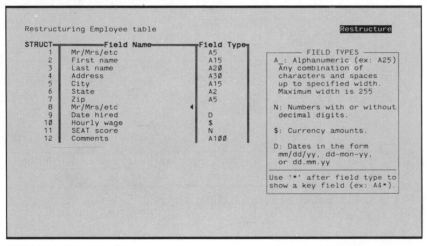

```
Restructuring Employee table                            Restructure

STRUCT      Field Name         Field Type
     1    Mr/Mrs/etc            A5                  FIELD TYPES
     2    First name           A15           A_: Alphanumeric (ex: A25)
     3    Last name            A20            Any combination of
     4    Address              A30            characters and spaces
     5    City                 A15            up to specified width.
     6    State                A2             Maximum width is 255
     7    Zip                  A5
     8    Mr/Mrs/etc                 ◀        N: Numbers with or without
     9    Date hired           D              decimal digits.
    10    Hourly wage          $
    11    SEAT score           N             $: Currency amounts.
    12    Comments             A100
                                             D: Dates in the form
                                              mm/dd/yy, dd-mon-yy,
                                              or dd.mm.yy

                                             Use '*' after field type to
                                             show a key field (ex: A4*).
```

Figure 6.4: Moving a field

4. Press any key that moves the cursor to another field: Enter, an arrow key, Home, or End. Paradox displays a message saying it is moving the field. Field 1 (where Mr/Mrs/etc used to be) disappears, and all the fields below it move up one. The data type is automatically entered in the new Mr/Mrs/etc field, which is now record 7. Press DO-IT! (F2) to make the change final.

In Chapter 8, you will learn that you can change the order in which fields appear on the screen without changing a table's actual structure. In practice, you'll rarely need to change the order of fields in the table itself.

How to Delete a Field

After all that trouble, you may decide that you do not need a Mr/Mrs/etc field at all. When you delete a field Paradox asks you to confirm that you did not press Del by mistake, because you lose all the data in a field when you delete it.

1. Press Menu (F10) to call up the main menu. Then press M to select Modify and R to select Restructure. Now type **employee** and press Enter. The screen for restructuring the Employee table appears.

2. Press ↓ six times to move the cursor to record 7, the Mr/Mrs/etc field, and press Del to delete that record. All the records below it move up one.

3. Press DO-IT! (F2). The message "Please confirm deletion of Mr/Mrs/etc field" appears on the lower-right, and a menu appears on the upper-left with two choices, Delete and Oops (see Figure 6.5). The cursor is already on Delete. Press Enter to confirm that you want to delete the field. After a moment, Paradox displays the table.

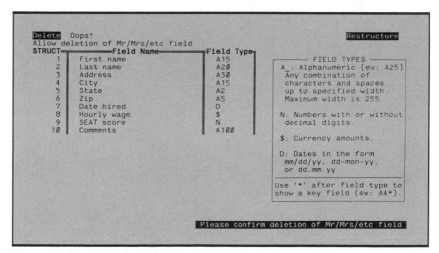

Figure 6.5: Confirming the deletion of a field

4. Press the Form Toggle key (F7). Paradox takes a moment to create a new form for the restructured table. When the table appears in Form View, you will see that the Mr/Mrs/etc field is gone. Press DO-IT! (F2) to finalize the change.

If you did not want to delete the field, you could have chosen Oops from the menu to indicate that you pressed Del by mistake. Then you would have to type the name of the deleted field back into the structure (though not necessarily in the same place it was before) to undo the deletion.

Changes with Possible Problems

As you saw when you deleted a field, restructuring a table is a bit trickier when you are doing something that could cause you to lose data. The choices are straightforward when you are deleting a field: either do it and lose all the data in the field, or don't do it and preserve the data. In other cases where data may be lost, Paradox gives you more choices.

How to Change Field Length

Increasing the length of a field does not create any problem with loss of data. After working with a table, you may find that one of the fields you created initially is not long enough to hold some of the data you now need to enter. In that case, you can just make the field as long as you need it to be.

1. Press Menu (F10) to call up the main menu. Then press M to select Modify and R to select Restructure. Type **employee** and press Enter.

2. Press → twice and ↓ once to move the cursor to the field type of field 2 (the Last name field). Press Backspace to erase the 0 of A20, and type **5** to change the field type to A25. Press DO-IT! (F2) to finalize the change.

3. After a brief delay, Paradox displays the table—with a longer Last name field. Press Edit (F9) to edit the table, and End to move to the last record.

4. Press ↓ to add a blank record and move to it. Type **Sam** as the first name and press Enter. Then type **Smithson-Robinson-Barnett** as the last name and press Enter.

5. Since you will be discarding this record later, just fill the rest of it with the same data you entered in the previous record. Press Ditto (Ctrl-D) followed by Enter to fill all the fields except the Comment field. Press DO-IT! (F2) to finalize the change.

The longer Last name field takes up more space on the screen, but it doesn't affect your existing data. On the other hand, you can run into problems when you shorten a field: data that is too long to fit into the new, shorter field may be lost. In this case, Paradox warns you that data may be lost, and gives you a menu with three choices for handling the problem:

- *Oops* means that you made the field too short by mistake. This choice returns you to restructuring your table, so you can make the field at least as long as it was.

- *Trimming* cuts off the end of any data that is too long, to make it fit into the new field. If any trimming is actually necessary, Paradox also keeps the original form of the trimmed records in a temporary table named Problems.

- *No-Trimming* removes records that are too long from the table you are changing, and places them in the temporary table called Problems. Then, if you wish, you can fix them and then add them to the restructured table.

If you have ever received a mailing with part of your address cut off, it is because the computer operator used something like the Trimming option.

No-Trimming is a better choice in most cases—if, for some reason, you can't just choose Oops to avoid the problem completely. If data is actually lost, edit each record in the temporary Problems table individually, so it fits in the new structure. Then add the corrected records to the original table. Later in the book, when you learn about tools for managing files, you will actually do this.

For now, choose Trimming, just to see how the option works, and then delete the record with the damaged data.

1. Press Menu (F10) to call up the main menu. Then press M to select Modify and R to select Restructure. Type **employee** and press Enter.

2. When the restructuring screen appears, press → twice and ↓ once to move to the field type of the Last name field. Press Backspace to erase the final 5 and type **0** to change the length to 20.

3. Press DO-IT! (F2). Paradox flashes the warning "Possible data loss for the Last name field," and offers the three menu choices mentioned previously (see Figure 6.6).

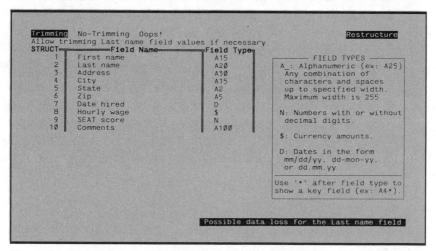

Figure 6.6: Shortening an alphanumeric field

4. Press Enter to select Trimming. Notice that the program displays the Problems table for an instant, to show you that the data loss did actually occur. You can work with this temporary

table just as you can with any other table, but it will be lost when you exit from Paradox or when Paradox creates another Problems table. After a moment, Paradox displays the restructured table. You can see that the last name has been cut off in the new record.

5. Press End to move to the last record. Then press Edit (F9) to enter Edit mode and Del to erase the damaged record. Now press DO-IT! to finalize the changes.

How to Change Data Type

You can also change the data type of any field, by selecting Modify and then Restructure (as above), using the Backspace key to delete the current data type of the field, and then typing a new one. Changing data types generally creates problems, and you will rarely—if ever— have a reason to do it.

Since alphanumeric fields can hold numbers as well as characters, for example, you can change a number field to an alphanumeric field. However, the field might not have enough characters to hold the largest numbers in your table. If you choose Trimming, any number too large to fit into the field will simply be truncated, as the long last name was above. It can make a big difference in the meaning of your data if you put a number in the millions in an alphanumeric field that is only big enough to hold numbers in the thousands.

You can also change an alphanumeric field to a date or number field. Any records that have inappropriate data will go into the Problems table. If you insist on changing a date field into a number field, all the records will go into the Problems table.

You can change a currency field into a number field (or vice versa) without any difficulty.

You will probably never have occasion to change data types on a table you have been using for a while. However, if you use the wrong data type when you first define a table's structure and discover your error when you begin to enter data, you will be glad this option exists.

Using the Restructure Menu

The Restructure menu will look very familiar to you.

1. Press Menu (F10) to call up the main menu. Then press M to select Modify and R to select Restructure.

2. Type **employee** and press Enter; then press Menu (F10), and the Restructure menu, shown in Figure 6.7, appears.

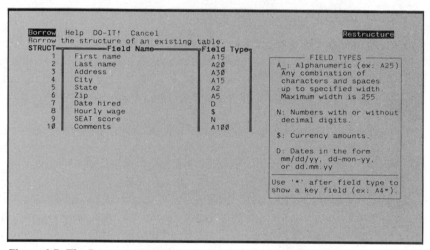

Figure 6.7: The Restructure menu

Notice that the menu has the same choices as the Create menu: Borrow, Help, DO-IT!, and Cancel.

Cancel is the most important. There will probably be occasions when you make too many changes in a table's structure, and become so confused that you just want to start over. At such times, the ability to call up the Restructure menu and choose Cancel is invaluable. Alternately, you can just press Ctrl-Break to cancel your work.

Borrow works just as it did in the Create menu: you can insert the structure of another table within the structure of the table you are modifying. Choosing Help or DO-IT! from the menu is the same as pressing F1 or F2.

Since you are already in the Restructure menu, you might as well use it to choose DO-IT!. You are probably ready to take a break; if so, you should also exit from the program.

You have now learned how to create and modify a table's structure and how to add and edit data. In the next chapters, you will begin to manipulate the table in more sophisticated ways.

SORTING A PARADOX TABLE

SORTING ON MULTIPLE FIELDS

DESCENDING SORTS

COMPLEX SORTS

SORT ORDER

Now that you can set up the table you want and put data in it, you are ready to learn how you can manipulate data that is already in a table, arranging it in different forms for different purposes. One of the easiest of these is sorting—rearranging the order of the records in the table. You simply select Sort from the Modify menu, and Paradox displays a screen that lets you choose which fields to sort on.

Paradox gives you two choices about where to put the results of the sort. You can either place the sorted records in a new table, or leave them in the same table. Using a new table preserves one set of records in their original order. Sorting in the same table changes the order permanently.

As a general rule, it is bad practice to keep two tables with the same data for any period of time. It means that you have to do twice as much updating work, and you will probably end up with discrepancies between the two tables. It only makes sense to place the results of a sort into a new table temporarily: you can use them in that table, then delete it before doing any new data entry or editing. If, for some reason, you must have your data in more than one order, it is much better to sort when you need to than to maintain the same data in two separate tables.

1. From the Paradox main menu, press M to select Modify and S to select Sort.

2. When Paradox asks for the name of the table to sort, type **employee** and press Enter. Press Enter again to keep the results in the same table.

Paradox displays the Sort screen shown in Figure 7.1, with the names of all the fields listed. For now, you can ignore the instructions at the top of the screen, although they will be helpful as a reminder when you are using the program.

If you want to sort on a single field, just type the number 1 next to that field. Let's say that you want to sort in zip code order to do a bulk mailing.

1. Press ↓ five times to move the cursor to Zip and type **1**.

2. Press DO-IT! (F2). Paradox displays a message to tell you it is sorting, and after a moment, displays the table in its new, sorted order.

3. Press Ctrl →, so that you can see the Zip field.

Your screen should look like Figure 7.2. Notice that the zip codes are in order.

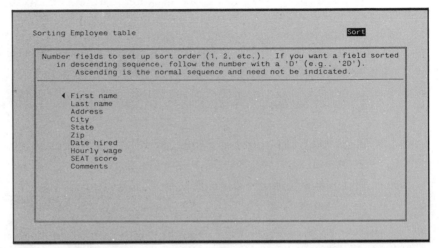

```
Sorting Employee table                                              Sort

   Number fields to set up sort order (1, 2, etc.).  If you want a field sorted
      in descending sequence, follow the number with a 'D' (e.g., '2D').
              Ascending is the normal sequence and need not be indicated.

          ◄ First name
            Last name
            Address
            City
            State
            Zip
            Date hired
            Hourly wage
            SEAT score
            Comments
```

Figure 7.1: The Sort screen

```
Viewing Employee table: Record 1 of 24                    Main  ▲──
┌───────Address═══════════════╤═════City══════╤═State╤═Zip═╤══Date hire═
│   34 Shady Lane             │ Greenwich     │ CT  │ 06830 │ 7/12/74
│ 4437 Elm St.                │ Hoboken       │ NJ  │ 07031 │ 2/04/86
│  457 First St.              │ Paramus       │ NJ  │ 07652 │ 11/25/86
│  237 Edison st.             │ New Brusnwick │ NJ  │ 08901 │ 3/01/85
│ 2036 Park Ave.              │ New York      │ NY  │ 10033 │ 3/22/81
│ 2242 Pensylvania Ave.       │ Mt. Vernon    │ NY  │ 10507 │ 7/17/82
│  203 West St.               │ Rye           │ NY  │ 10580 │ 12/01/83
│ 1465 Oak St.                │ Yonkers       │ NY  │ 10715 │ 11/13/89
│ 1237 Flatbush Ave.          │ Brooklyn      │ NY  │ 11226 │ 1/15/84
│  590 Ocean Ave.             │ Brooklyn      │ NY  │ 11226 │ 2/03/69
│ 3345 Church Ave.            │ Brooklyn      │ NY  │ 11235 │ 4/17/76
│  326 B. 31 St.              │ Far Rockaway  │ NY  │ 11601 │ 12/03/79
│ 4445-2312 Technology Blvd.  │ Menlo Park    │ CA  │ 94025 │ 4/15/88
│  505 Haight St.             │ San Francisco │ CA  │ 94122 │ 7/14/90
│  505 Haight St.             │ San Francisco │ CA  │ 94122 │ 6/15/88
│ 2113 University Ave.        │ Palo Alto     │ CA  │ 94301 │ 7/23/84
│   45 Arcroft Circle         │ San Mateo     │ CA  │ 94406 │ 7/06/82
│ 1634 Bancroft Way           │ Berkeley      │ CA  │ 94703 │ 4/15/86
│  848 Broadway               │ San Raphael   │ CA  │ 94901 │ 2/12/87
│ 1742 Dutch Elm St.          │ San Raphael   │ CA  │ 94904 │ 12/22/77
│  180 Poplar St.             │ Mill Valley   │ CA  │ 94943 │ 10/17/79
│ 2311 First St.              │ Mill Valley   │ CA  │ 94945 │ 6/16/85
```

Figure 7.2: A table sorted by zip code

*S*orting on Multiple Fields

If you wanted to sort alphabetically by name instead of zip code, a single field would not be enough, because several people might have the same last name. You would want records with the same last name to be alphabetized by first name also. To do this, you simply type **1** next to the Last name field and **2** next to the First name field.

1. Press Menu (F10). Then press M to select Modify and S to select Sort. Type **employee** and press Enter.

2. Press Enter to select Same. When the Sort screen appears, with the cursor next to First name, type **2**.

3. Press ↓ to move the cursor to Last name and type **1**. Your screen should look like Figure 7.3. Now press DO-IT! (F2).

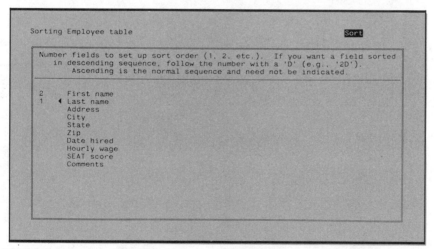

Figure 7.3: Sorting alphabetically by last and first names

Notice that the names are arranged in alphabetical order by last name, with the three Channings also alphabetized by first name.

The field that you put 1 next to is the primary sort field: all the records are arranged in that order. The field that you put 2 next to is only used as a tie-breaker if the primary sort field is the same in two records.

If you had a Middle name field, you would have typed a 3 next to it, to place the two Edward Channings in order by middle name.

How to Sort in Descending Order

Normally, sorted tables are arranged in what is called ascending order—from the lowest value to the highest. Thus, letters are arranged from A to Z, numbers from smallest to largest, and dates from earliest to latest.

There will be times when you want a table sorted in descending order, with the highest values first. To do this you put a D after the number you enter in the sort screen.

For example, you might want the employees listed in the order they were hired, with the most recent hires at the top of the list. To do this, you would sort on the date hired in descending order.

1. Press Menu (F10). Then press M to select Modify and S to select Sort.

2. Press Enter three times: once to get a list of tables, once to select the Employee table, and again to select Same.

3. Press ↓ six times to place the cursor next to Date hired and type **1d**. Note that the D is automatically capitalized.

4. Press DO-IT! When Paradox displays the sorted table, press Ctrl → twice so you can see the entire Date hired field.

Your screen should look like Figure 7.4. Notice that the most recently hired employees are at the top of the list.

How to Perform Complex Sorts

You can also combine ascending and descending sorts to arrange data in more complex ways. Let's say that you want an alphabetical list of the employees in each state, with the states listed in reverse alphabetical order. In this example, you will save the sorted list in a separate table, which you will use in the next chapter. You can call the

```
Viewing Employee table: Record 1 of 24                    Main  ▲—

 ┌─Date hired──┬──Hourly wage──┬──SEAT score─┐
        7/14/90              4.45            348
       11/13/89             11.15            715      Excellent test score
        6/15/88              4.45            325      Frequent absenteeism
        4/15/88              9.45            601      On executive track
        2/12/87             14.15            560      Steady progress in training
       11/25/86             11.23            588
        4/15/86              9.50            602      Retesting may be necessary
        2/04/86             11.00            600      Was very impressive at pers
        6/16/85             15.05            722
        3/01/85              8.65            322
        7/23/84             12.00            432
        1/15/84             10.50            540
       12/01/83             15.60            599
        7/17/82             14.56            723      Occasional customer complai
        7/06/82             12.75            421
        3/22/81             10.25            503      May be promoted again soon
        2/22/81             15.55            641
       12/03/79              8.65            488
       10/17/79             12.50            403
        4/01/79             14.25            533      In special training program
       12/22/77             12.50            664      Very loyal employee
        4/17/76             10.33            466      Long-term employee
```

Figure 7.4: In a descending sort the most recent date comes first

table Emp-stat to remind you that it lists the employees by state. (As you learned above, it is generally not a good practice to store the same data in two different tables. You are doing it here purely for instructional purposes.)

1. Press Menu (F10). Then press M to select Modify and S to select Sort. Now press Enter once to get a list of tables, and again to select Employee. Press N to select New.

2. When Paradox asks for the name of the new file, type **emp-stat** and press Enter. The sorting screen appears, with the message "Sorting Employee table into new EMP-STAT table." The cursor will be next to the First name field.

3. Type **3** next to First name and press ↓ to move the cursor to the Last name field.

4. Type **2** next to Last name and press ↓ three times to move the cursor to the State field.

5. Type **1D** next to State. (Be sure to include the *D*, so the states are arranged in descending order. Your screen should look like Figure 7.5.

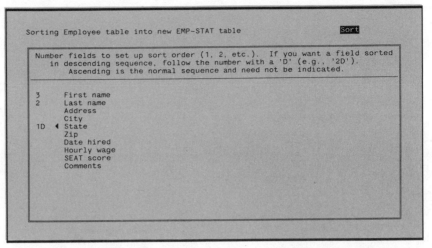

Figure 7.5: A complex sort

6. Press DO-IT! (F2). After a moment, Paradox displays the new Emp-stat table. You can see that there are a few groups of names arranged in alphabetical order: for example, records 1 to 8 are alphabetical.

7. Press Ctrl →, so you can see the State field. Notice that the states are in descending alphabetical order. The first eight records are NY, followed by NJ, CT, and CA.

This table would be easier to use if you could see the states and names at the same time. In the next chapter, you will learn how to view the table in this way.

Using the Sort Menu

Press the Menu key (F10) to see the Sort menu, shown in Figure 7.6. It presents only three options, which you already know how to use: Help, DO-IT!, and Cancel. All of these operations can also be done directly from the keyboard, by pressing the Help key (F1), the DO-IT! key (F2), or by pressing Ctrl-Break to cancel.

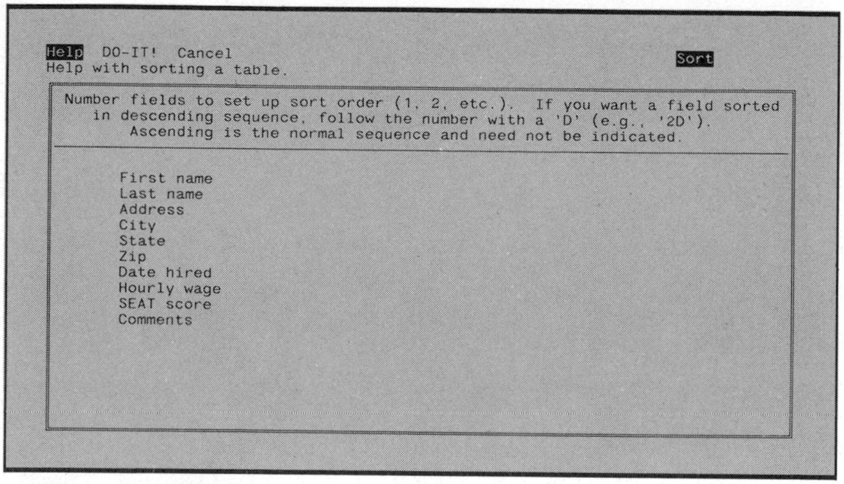

```
Help  DO-IT!  Cancel                                              Sort
Help with sorting a table.

    Number fields to set up sort order (1, 2, etc.).  If you want a field sorted
      in descending sequence, follow the number with a 'D' (e.g., '2D').
              Ascending is the normal sequence and need not be indicated.


        First name
        Last name
        Address
        City
        State
        Zip
        Date hired
        Hourly wage
        SEAT score
        Comments
```

Figure 7.6: The Sort menu

Sort Order: A Few Tricks

There are a couple of tricky points about sort order that may never cause you any problems, but that you should have in the back of your mind—just in case.

Alphanumeric fields can contain numbers as well as letters, and numbers in an alphanumeric field are treated as if they were characters. For example, if you are sorting an alphanumeric field, 99 would come after 100, just as XX would come after BAA.

An alphanumeric sort begins by comparing the first characters of the two words. If they are different, it arranges them in order, and if they are the same, it goes on to compare the second letter. If it is sorting 99 and 100, it will just compare the initial 9 with the initial 1, and decide that 100 comes first alphabetically. The way to make sure numbers in alphanumeric fields are sorted properly is to make them all the same length by adding leading zeros to smaller numbers: 099 would come before 100, since 0 comes before 1. (Of course, this trick isn't necessary for numeric or currency fields.)

Another point you should know about sort order is that, if you set up Paradox with the standard American format, uppercase letters all come before lowercase letters. Thus, if you have one last name that begins with a small letter, such as deBonnis, it will be at the end of the list after you sort (see Figure 7.7). This happens because Paradox normally sorts in ASCII order: numbers come first, followed by capital letters, small letters, letters with accent marks, and then Greek letters. (ASCII stands for American Standard Code for Information Interchange.)

```
Viewing Employee table: Record 25 of 25                    Main  ▲—

EMPLOYEE   First name        Last name              Address
    4      Francine          Bowen          2113 University Ave.
    5      Josephine         Buckminster    3322 Bridgeway
    6      Alice             Channing       505 Haight St.
    7      Edward            Channing       180 Poplar St.
    8      Edward            Channing       505 Haight St.
    9      William           Channing       22 The Circle
   10      Albert            Cruz           1237 Flatbush Ave.
   11      Joan              Garfield       4437 Elm St.
   12      Dianne            Lee            1634 Bancroft Way
   13      Robert            Lin            457 First St.
   14      Joseph            Miller         2036 Park Ave.
   15      Harriet           Noble          34 Shady Lane
   16      Andrea            Norton         2311 First St.
   17      Rosalyn           Rogers         2242 Pensylvania Ave.
   18      Samuel            Schmaltz       590 Ocean Ave.
   19      George            Silk           237 Edison st.
   20      Samuel            Smithson       203 West St.
   21      Joseph            Tuckerman      45 Arcroft Circle
   22      Jane              Walker         848 Broadway
   23      Alioo             Waltor         326 8. 31 St.
   24      Henry             Ware           1742 Dutch Elm St.
   25      John              deBonnis       2140 Shattuck Ave.
```

Figure 7.7: In an ASCII sort, uppercase always precedes lowercase

You also have the option of setting up Paradox to sort in International, Norwegian/Danish, or Swedish/Finnish order. These put certain letters that are used in other languages—such as letters with accent marks—in their proper order. The main advantage of International order, though, is that it sorts capital and small letters together, so a name like deBonnis will end up in the *D*'s, not at the end of the list, even though it begins with a small letter.

This book assumes that you use the standard American sort order. If you have trouble with small letters when you sort, you can use the Paradox Custom Configuration Program to select a different order. See Chapter 14 of the *Paradox User's Guide*, pages 276–279, for more information.

CHANGING A TABLE'S IMAGE

In this chapter, you will learn to change the way a table appears on the screen so it is more convenient for you to use. When you created the Emp-stat table in the last chapter, for example, you could not view both the name and the state at the same time, so it was hard to tell which employee belonged to which state. In this chapter, you will change the appearance of the Emp-stat table to correct this problem.

Setting and Keeping a Screen Image

There are several ways to change the image of a table so that your data is easy to see and understand. You can change the order in which the columns are arranged, change the width of individual columns, or change the display of data and number fields.

Once you have the image of a table set up in the way that is most convenient for you, you can save it. Then Paradox will automatically display the table in this way whenever you retrieve it.

How to View a Table

You will often want to view a table before you change its image. As you have seen, when you press the DO-IT! key to finish editing, the table remains on the screen, but the status message on the top of the screen changes to Viewing, and you are no longer able to change the data in the table. You can also use the menu to view a table in this way.

1. Make sure you are at the main menu and press V to select View.

2. Press Enter to see a list of tables. The list will include both Employee and the new Emp-stat table you created in the last chapter.

3. If necessary, move the cursor to Emp-stat and press Enter. The Emp-stat table appears on the screen and the status message tells you that you are viewing it.

The Clear Image key (F8), which you will use later in this chapter, does just the opposite: it removes an Image you are viewing from the screen, and returns you to the main menu.

Using the Rotate Key

The simplest way to move the columns of a table is by using the Rotate key combination (Ctrl-R). This moves the field that has the cursor in it to the far right of the table, and all of the fields to its right shift one to the left.

1. Press → three times to move the cursor to the Address field, and press Ctrl-R. The Address field disappears, and the City and State fields become visible on the screen.

2. Press Ctrl-R again. The City field disappears, and the State field is now next to the name, as shown in Figure 8.1.

```
Viewing Emp-stat table: Record 1 of 24                          Main

  ┌─First name──────────────Last name────────State─┬─Zip─┬──Date hired──────Hou┐
    Evelyn                 Adams                NY   11235    4/17/76         ****
    Sally                  Bean                 NY   10715   11/13/89         ****
    Albert                 Cruz                 NY   11226    1/15/84         ****
    Joseph                 Miller               NY   10033    3/22/81         ****
    Rosalyn                Rogers               NY   10507    7/17/82         ****
    Samuel                 Schmaltz             NY   11226    2/03/69         ****
    Samuel                 Smithson             NY   10580   12/01/83         ****
    Alice                  Walter               NY   11601   12/03/79         ****
    Joan                   Garfield             NJ   07031    2/04/86         ****
    Robert                 Lin                  NJ   07652   11/25/86         ****
    George                 Silk                 NJ   08901    3/01/85         ****
    Harriet                Noble                CT   06830    7/12/74         ****
    Jean                   Abbott               CA   94025    4/15/88         ****
    Francine               Bowen                CA   94301    7/23/84         ****
    Josephine              Buckminster          CA   94965    4/01/79         ****
    Alice                  Channing             CA   94122    7/14/90         ****
    Edward                 Channing             CA   94943   10/17/79         ****
    Edward                 Channing             CA   94122    6/15/88         ****
    William                Channing             CA   94957    2/22/81         ****
    Dianne                 Lee                  CA   94703    4/15/86         ****
    Andrea                 Norton               CA   94945    6/16/85         ****
    Joseph                 Tuckerman            CA   94406    7/06/82         ****
```

Figure 8.1: The Emp-stat table after rotating fields

3. Press Ctrl → twice to move to the far-right of the table. Notice that Address and City are now the rightmost fields.

Note that Rotate (Ctrl-R) does not work when you are looking at a table in Form View, because you can already see all the fields.

How to Move a Column

The Rotate key is handy but is not suited for all purposes. If you want more control over where you put the fields, choose Move from the Image menu. Paradox gives you a list of the fields in the table and asks you which one you want to move. After you choose a field, use the arrow keys to move the cursor to the place where you want that field positioned.

In the next example, you will begin by viewing the table again to delete the changes you made using the Rotate key. Then you will select Image from the menu to move a column.

1. Press the Menu key (F10) to call up the main menu. Press Enter once to select View and again to get a list of tables. The cursor should be on Emp-stat; press Enter to select it, and you will see the table in its original form once again.

2. Press the Menu key (F10) to call up the main menu. Press I to select Image and M to select Move. A list of the fields appears as a menu on the top of the screen. Notice the arrow on the right indicating that there are more fields than can be listed on one screen.

3. Press → four times to move the cursor to State and press Enter. Paradox displays a message telling you to use the right and left arrow keys to move the cursor to the new position for the field and then to press Enter to move the field there.

4. Press → once to move the cursor to the first field of the table (First name) and press Enter. State is now the first field, and the other fields shift one to the right.

*H*ow to Change Column Size

You now have the State field where you want it, but you still cannot see as much of each record as you might like.

If you displayed each employee's first initial, instead of the entire first name, you would be able to see more of the table. You can also narrow the Last name and Address fields, and still have enough of those fields to see their contents in almost every record, with just a bit cut off the right edge in a few records. This way you can see the name, address, city, and state on a single screen.

You can use the Image menu to change the width of the column. When you select ColumnSize from that menu, Paradox tells you to move the cursor to the record whose width you want to change and then to use the arrow key to make that change. The cursor becomes a blinking box when you are selecting the record, and moves to the far-right edge of the field when you are changing its width.

1. Press Menu (F10) to call up the main menu. Then press I to select Image and C to select ColumnSize. Notice that the cursor becomes a blinking box. Paradox displays the message that you should use the arrow keys to move the cursor to the column whose size you want to change and then press Enter to select it.

2. Press → once to move the cursor to the First name field, and press Enter. Paradox displays the message that you should use → to increase the column width and ← to decrease it, and then press Enter when you are finished. Notice that the cursor has moved to the far-right edge of the field.

3. Press ← 14 times to reduce the size of the field to one character, as shown in Figure 8.2. Then press Enter. Notice that each time you press the key, the cursor moves to the left and drags the right border of the field along with it, so it always remains at the far-right of the field.

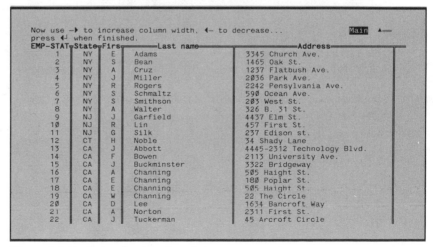

Figure 8.2: Reducing the size of a column

4. Press Menu (F10) to call up the main menu. Then press I and C to select Image and ColumnSize again. Press → to move the cursor to the Last name field and press Enter. Then press ← six times to narrow the field and press Enter.

5. Press Menu (F10) to call up the main menu. Then press I and C to select Image and ColumnSize once more.

6. Press → to move the cursor to the Address field, and press Enter. Press ← eight times to narrow the Address field, and press Enter again.

You have now changed the image of the Emp-stat table so you can see the name (with first initial) and address of each employee on the screen. Your screen should look like Figure 8.3.

```
Viewing Emp-stat table: Record 1 of 24                          Main
EMP-STAT State Firs      Last name              Address              City
      1    NY    E    Adams          3345 Church Ave.       Brooklyn
      2    NY    S    Bean           1465 Oak St.           Yonkers
      3    NY    A    Cruz           1237 Flatbush Ave.     Brooklyn
      4    NY    J    Miller         2036 Park Ave.         New York
      5    NY    R    Rogers         2242 Pensylvania Ave.  Mt. Vernon
      6    NY    S    Schmaltz       590 Ocean Ave.         Brooklyn
      7    NY    S    Smithson       203 West St.           Rye
      8    NY    A    Walter         326 B. 31 St.          Far Rockaway
      9    NJ    J    Garfield       4437 Elm St.           Hoboken
     10    NJ    R    Lin            457 First St.          Paramus
     11    NJ    G    Silk           237 Edison st.         New Brusnwick
     12    CT    H    Noble          34 Shady Lane          Greenwich
     13    CA    J    Abbott         4445-2312 Technology B Menlo Park
     14    CA    F    Bowen          2113 University Ave.   Palo Alto
     15    CA    J    Buckminster    3322 Bridgeway         Sausalito
     16    CA    A    Channing       505 Haight St.         San Francisco
     17    CA    E    Channing       180 Poplar St.         Mill Valley
     18    CA    E    Channing       505 Haight St.         San Francisco
     19    CA    W    Channing       22 The Circle          Ross
     20    CA    D    Lee            1634 Bancroft Way      Berkeley
     21    CA    A    Norton         2311 First St.         Mill Valley
     22    CA    J    Tuckerman      45 Arcroft Circle      San Mateo
```

Figure 8.3: The Emp-stat table with its new image

There are a few limitations on the changes you can make in the column size displayed on the screen:

- The minimum width of a field is 1 character.

- The maximum width of a date field is 14 characters, unless the field name is longer.

- The maximum width of a number field (either N or $) is 25 characters.

- The maximum width of an alphanumeric field is the number of characters in that field. In addition, no field may be wider than the screen, which is 76 characters wide in Table View.

You may have noticed that the Comments field in your tables, which was defined as 100 characters long, is displayed to fit into a single screen: 76 characters can be viewed, the maximum length for alphanumeric fields.

If you try to make a field's image larger than any of these limits, Paradox beeps to tell you it is not possible.

*D*ata That Does Not Fit

As you have seen, alphanumeric data that does not fit into the display width of the column is simply cut off at its right edge. The great advantage of changing the column size of the image—rather than changing the actual size of the field—is that you do not have any problems with lost data, as you did when you were restructuring a table in Chapter 6. All the data is still there; you simply cannot see it all on the screen.

When you move to a field whose data is truncated in this way, the cursor appears on the left of the field instead of the right, to indicate that you are not actually at the end of the data.

You can view the field's entire contents by toggling to Field View and using the arrow keys to scroll through it.

1. Use the arrow keys to move to the address of record 13, which is displayed as 4445-2312 Technology B. Notice that the cursor is at the end of the data in each field you pass through until you reach your destination. Then it moves to the beginning of the data.

2. Press Field View (Alt-F5). The cursor becomes a box with a blinking line in it.

3. Press → until you reach the end of the field. The beginning of the street number disappears beyond the left edge of the field, and the end of the street name appears on the right, as shown in Figure 8.4.

```
 Viewing Emp-stat table: Record 13 of 24                          Main  ▲

 EMP-STAT┬State┬Firs┬──────Last name────────────Address────────────────City═══════
       1   NY    E   Adams           3345 Church Ave.         Brooklyn
       2   NY    S   Bean            1465 Oak St.             Yonkers
       3   NY    A   Cruz            1237 Flatbush Ave.       Brooklyn
       4   NY    J   Miller          2036 Park Ave.           New York
       5   NY    R   Rogers          2242 Pensylvania Ave.    Mt. Vernon
       6   NY    S   Schmaltz        590 Ocean Ave.           Brooklyn
       7   NY    S   Smithson        203 West St.             Rye
       8   NY    A   Walter          326 B. 31 St.            Far Rockaway
       9   NJ    J   Garfield        4437 Elm St.             Hoboken
      10   NJ    R   Lin             457 First St.            Paramus
      11   NJ    G   Silk            237 Edison st.           New Brusnwick
      12   CT    H   Noble           34 Shady Lane            Greenwich
      13   CA    J   Abbott          -2312 Technology Blvd.█  Menlo Park
      14   CA    F   Bowen           2113 University Ave.     Palo Alto
      15   CA    J   Buckminster     3322 Bridgeway           Sausalito
      16   CA    A   Channing        505 Haight St.           San Francisco
      17   CA    E   Channing        180 Poplar St.           Mill Valley
      18   CA    E   Channing        505 Haight St.           San Francisco
      19   CA    W   Channing        22 The Circle            Ross
      20   CA    D   Lee             1634 Bancroft Way        Berkeley
      21   CA    A   Norton          2311 First St.           Mill Valley
      22   CA    J   Tuckerman       45 Arcroft Circle        San Mateo
```

Figure 8.4: Using Field View to see the hidden part of a field

4. Press Enter to end Field View and → to move the cursor. The field you were in scrolls back to its original position.

You can also see the contents of truncated fields by simply toggling into Form View. You generally change the way a table is displayed in order to fit more fields onto the screen in Table View. There is really no need for them to be displayed differently in Form View. Toggle into Form View, and you will see the fields in their original position and size, with all their data visible, as shown in Figure 8.5. Press the Form Toggle key (F7) again when you want to return to Table View.

Truncating alphanumeric data in this way is unlikely to cause misunderstandings, and the beginning of the data is often enough to let you guess what is in the field. If a number field is cut off, though, it can be misleading. For example, you might think that the number in a field is actually 200 rather than 2000, with potentially disastrous results.

For this reason, Paradox does not truncate numeric fields as it does alphanumeric fields. Instead, it fills the entire field with asterisks if a number is too long to fit into it.

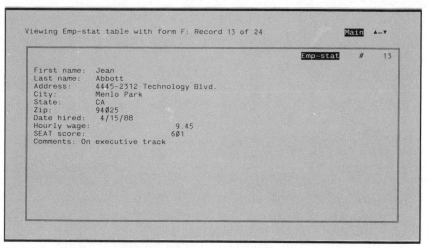

```
Viewing Emp-stat table with form F: Record 13 of 24          Main  ▲—▼

                                                    Emp-stat   #    13

   First name:  Jean
   Last name:   Abbott
   Address:     4445-2312 Technology Blvd.
   City:        Menlo Park
   State:       CA
   Zip:         94025
   Date hired:  4/15/88
   Hourly wage:                   9.45
   SEAT score:               601
   Comments: On executive track
```

Figure 8.5: The unchanged image in Form View

1. Press Menu (F10) to call up the main menu. Then press I and C to select Image and ColumnSize.

2. Press → four times to move to the Hourly wage field, and press Enter to select it.

3. Press ← nine times to narrow the field. Your screen should now look like Figure 8.6. Notice that all the numbers larger

```
Now use →  to increase column width, ◄—  to decrease...        Main  ▲—
press ◄┘ when finished.
┌──City──────┬──Zip──┬──Date hired──┬─Hourly wa─┬─SEAT score─┐
│  Brooklyn    11235    4/17/76      ******       466        Long-ter
│  Yonkers     10715    11/13/89     ******       715        Excellen
│  Brooklyn    11226    1/15/84      ******       540
│  New York    10033    3/22/81      ******       503        May be p
│  Mt. Vernon  10507    7/17/82      ******       723        Occasion
│  Brooklyn    11226    2/03/69      8.32         321        No poten
│  Rye         10580    12/01/83     ******       599
│  Far Rockaway 11601   12/03/79     8.65         488
│  Hoboken     07031    2/04/86      ******       600        Was very
│  Paramus     07652    11/25/86     ******       588
│  New Brusnwick 08901  3/01/85      8.65         322
│  Greenwich   06830    7/12/74      ******       622
│  Menlo Park  94025    4/15/88      9.45         601        On execu
│  Palo Alto   94301    7/23/84      ******       432
│  Sausalito   94965    4/01/79      ******       533        In speci
│  San Francisco 94122  7/14/90      4.45         348
│  Mill Valley 94943    10/17/79     ******       403
│  San Francisco 94122  6/15/88      4.45         325        Frequent
│  Ross        94957    2/22/81      ******       641
│  Berkeley    94703    4/15/86      9.50         602        Retestin
│  Mill Valley 94945    6/16/85      ******       722
│  San Mateo   94406    7/06/82      ******       421
```

Figure 8.6: Numbers greater than ten turn to asterisks as the field narrows

than ten have turned into asterisks, because they cannot fit into the field. Numbers less than ten are still displayed in their normal format.

4. Press → once to widen the field and all the numbers reappear. Press Enter to select this setting.

*H*ow to Reformat a Field

You can reformat numeric or date fields in a variety of ways. You simply select Image and Format from the menu, move the cursor to the field you want to reformat, and Paradox lets you choose the changes you want to make in the display.

The options for numeric fields are

- *General,* which displays as many decimal places as you need to show the value. This is the default display for the field type N.

- *Fixed,* which displays a certain number of decimal places (between 0 and 15) no matter what the value. This is the default display for the field type $, with two decimal places displayed.

- *Comma,* which uses a comma to separate groups of three numbers and displays negative numbers in parentheses. This is the default display for the field type $.

- *Scientific,* which uses exponential notation (expressing each number as a multiple of some power of ten). This format is not generally used in business applications.

You will choose just one of these ways to reformat numbers now, but you can use the same method to choose any of them.

1. Press Menu (F10) to call up the main menu. Then press I to select Image and F to select Format. Your cursor should already be in the Hourly wage field; if it is not, move it there, and press Enter to select that field.

2. Press F to select Fixed. Paradox asks how many decimal places to display and suggests the value 2. Press Backspace to erase the 2; then type **0** and press Enter. Only the dollar amounts of the wage are now displayed; the cents have disappeared.

3. Press Menu (F10) to call up the main menu. Press I and C to select Image and ColumnSize.

4. Press Enter to select Hourly wage as the column whose size you want to change. Press ← four times to narrow the column, and press Enter.

Because you have eliminated the decimal points from the wage column, you can make it narrower without the values changing into asterisks. Now you have a compact display of just the dollar part of the wage, as shown in Figure 8.7.

```
Now use → to increase column width, ← to decrease...        Main ▲—
press ↵ when finished.
─City───────Zip───────Date hired──Hourly wag──SEAT score──
  Brooklyn       11235    4/17/76      10.33      466      Long-te
  Yonkers        10715    11/15/89     11.15      715      Excelle
  Brooklyn       11226    1/15/84      10.50      540
  New York       10033    3/22/81      10.25      503      May be
  Mt. Vernon     10507    7/17/82      14.56      723      Occasio
  Brooklyn       11226    2/03/69       8.32      321      No pote
  Rye            10580   12/01/83      15.60      599
  Far Rockaway   11601   12/03/79       8.65      488
  Hoboken        07031    2/04/86      11.00      600      Was ver
  Paramus        07652   11/25/86      11.23      588
  New Brusnwick  08901    3/01/85       8.65      322
  Greenwich      06830    7/12/74      14.05      622
  Menlo Park     94025    4/15/88       9.45      601      On exec
  Palo Alto      94301    7/23/84      12.00      432
  Sausalito      94965    4/01/79      14.25      533      In spec
  San Francisco  94122    7/14/90       4.45      348
  Mill Valley    94943   10/17/79      12.50      403
  San Francisco  94122    6/15/88       4.45      325      Frequen
  Ross           94957    2/22/81      15.55      641
  Berkeley       94703    4/15/86       9.50      602      Retesti
  Mill Valley    94945    6/16/85      15.05      722
  San Mateo      94406    7/06/82      12.75      421
```

Figure 8.7: Decimals have been eliminated from the Hourly wage column

You can also change the format of date fields. When you do, Paradox asks you to choose among its three date displays.

1. Press Menu (F10) to call up the main menu. Then press I and F to select Image and Format.

2. Press ← to move the cursor to the Date hired field, and press Enter to select it. Use the cursor to move among the three date displays and read the help line for each.

3. Move the cursor to the second choice, DD-Mon-YY, and press Enter.

As you can see, the format of the dates changes to match your selection.

How to Keep Display Settings

Now that you have set up this convenient format, you would probably like to make it available permanently. All you have to do is choose KeepSet from the Image menu to keep the display you have set up.

1. Press Menu (F10) to call up the main menu. Then press I to select Image and K to select KeepSet. Paradox displays a message at the lower-right of your screen to tell you the settings have been recorded.

2. To check the settings press Clear Image (F8) to clear the workspace and call up the menu.

3. Press Enter once to select View and again to get a list of tables.

4. Make sure the cursor is on Emp-stat and press Enter.

Now that you are viewing Emp-stat again, you can see that it still appears on the screen in the way you set it up.

Since any display setting that you save appears automatically whenever you use a table, you can have only one setting for each table. If you create a new setting for the Emp-stat table, it will override the one you've just saved. However, settings that you create for other tables will not affect this table or its settings.

Other Features of the Image Menu

You have looked at all the features of the Image menu you can use to set up a new display and save it. There are a few other features of the Image menu that are also useful.

How to Change the Size of a Table

The TableSize option of the Image menu determines how many records of a table will be displayed; that is, how many lines of the screen it will fill up. You can display as few as 2 rows of the table or as many as 22 rows, so that it takes up the entire screen.

Generally you will use TableSize to fit additional tables on the screen when you want to view more than one table at a time. This occurs most frequently with multitable databases, but there are also times when TableSize is useful with a single-table database. You might, for example, want to edit a table while the Problems table that applies to it is on screen.

Using TableSize is similar to changing a column's size, which you did earlier in this chapter. When you choose TableSize, Paradox lets you use ↑ to shorten the display and ↓ to lengthen it. The cursor moves to the final record on the screen, and becomes a blinking box. When you use the arrow keys to move the cursor, it pulls up or pushes down the bottom edge of the table as it moves—just as the cursor moved the right edge of the column when you were changing column size.

You can also use the Home and End keys to display instantly the minimum and maximum number of records allowed. Press Enter to finalize the change, or Esc to cancel the change and return to the menu.

In this example, you will reset the size of the table, and then view it again to see that this setting is not saved.

1. Press Menu (F10). Then press I to select Image and Enter to select TableSize. Notice that the cursor is a blinking box in the last record, as it was when you changed column size.

2. Press ↑ five or six times to make the image smaller. Then press End and the image of the table fills the screen again. Now press Home. As you can see in Figure 8.8, only two lines of the table are displayed.

3. Press Enter to finish. The status message tells you that you are viewing the table again. Now you can confirm that this setting is not saved by pressing Menu (F10), and then K to select KeepSet. Paradox displays a message that says Settings recorded.

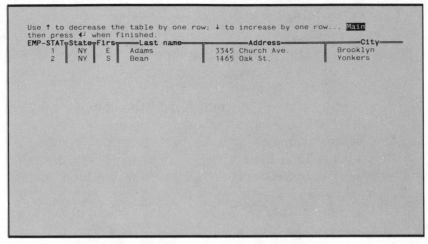

Figure 8.8: Changing the table size

4. Press Clear Image (F8), and then Enter to select View from the menu.

5. Press Enter again to get a list of tables. With the cursor on Emp-stat, press Enter once more.

Though you saved the settings when only two rows of the table were displayed, you can see that the table fills the screen when you view it again.

The settings you choose for column size, column location, and format are useful whenever you view the table. The setting you choose for table length, though, is most often useful just for one session—when you happen to be viewing more than one table—so it is not saved.

Using the Zoom Option

There is also a Zoom option on the Image menu, which works the same way as the Zoom key combination (Ctrl-Z), discussed in Chapter 5. When you choose Zoom from the Image menu, you are given three options:

• *Field* displays a menu of all the fields in the database and moves the cursor to whichever field you choose. This is usually no easier than using the left and right arrow keys (with Ctrl, if necessary) to move to the field.

- *Record* asks you to enter the number of the record you want to move to. This can be useful for getting around a large database. If you know, for example, that the record you want is somewhere in the middle of a database with 5000 records, you can zoom to record 2000 and then use PgDn to keep searching.

- *Value* is like the Zoom key combination (Ctrl-Z) but it gives you a little extra help. It prompts you to move the cursor to the field you are searching and press Enter. Then it asks you for the value you want to find. For example, you can move to the Last name field, press Enter, type **Smith**, and press Enter, and Paradox will take you to the first person named Smith in the list—just as Ctrl-Z would, but with a few extra steps. You can then use Zoom Next (Alt-Z) to find the next occurrence of the same name. Like the Zoom key, this option can be used with wildcards.

In general, it is easier to do these things directly from the keyboard than to use menu options.

Besides ColumnSize, Format, Zoom, Move, and KeepSet, you may have noticed these two additional choices on the Image menu:

- *PickForm* is used only if you have created custom forms to display your data, in addition to the standard form that Paradox automatically creates when you toggle to Form View. It lets you choose among available forms. (Custom forms are used mainly by programmers and are not discussed in this book.)

- *Graph* lets you display data in graphic form. For example, it is possible to create a pie or bar graph in Paradox. We will not discuss graphs in this book because creating them usually involves advanced query techniques.

The Image Menu in Form View

Some of the choices on the Image menu are not relevant in Form View, so they do not appear if you call up the menu when you are in

Form View. In Form View, the Image menu includes only these options: Format, Zoom, PickForm, KeepSet, and Graph.

1. Press the Form Toggle key (F7). Though you were looking at the Image menu before you pressed it, the menu disappears and you are simply viewing the table when you toggle to Form View.

2. Press Menu (F10), and then press I to select Image. Your screen should look like Figure 8.9. Notice the limited number of menu choices offered.

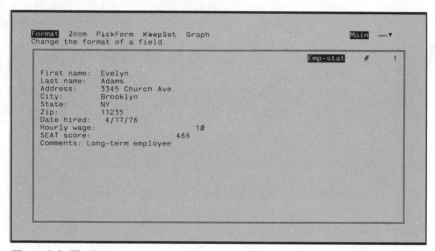

Figure 8.9: The Image menu in Form View

The only choice on this menu that actually changes the appearance of the record on the screen is the Format option, which determines how dates and numbers are displayed. The options to move records and change the field size are not available.

When you look at a record in Form View, you will notice that the order and length of the fields has not changed; State does not come first, and you can see the entire first name rather than just the initial. These changes are useful in Table View to let you see more fields of the record, but they are not needed in Form View.

Notice, though, that the format of the date and wage have been changed, as in Table View. The choices that appear on the Image menu in Form View are the only ones that affect the display in Form View.

You might want to take a break now. If so, press Ctrl-Break twice to return to the main menu, and then press E and Y to exit.

CREATING TABULAR REPORTS

THE STANDARD
REPORT

THE REPORT
SPECIFICATION
SCREEN

MODIFYING
COLUMNS AND
FIELDS

USING THE
EDITOR

PLACING FIELDS

Creating printed reports is one of the most important uses you will make of any database program. Once you have entered all your data, you will want to print it in a form you can use, such as a list of names and telephone numbers, or names and addresses for mailing labels. Any printed output that you produce with a database program is called a report.

Paradox lets you create three types of reports:

- *Standard reports:* The Instant Report key (Alt-F7) creates a standard report based on the table currently displayed on the screen—in much the same way that F7 creates a standard data entry form for the table that is displayed.

- *Free-form reports:* When you create a free-form report, you can move the fields anywhere you want. This option is useful for mailing labels and form letters. You will learn about it in Chapter 11.

- *Tabular reports:* When you create a tabular report, the data remains in table form, but you can move the columns, change their size, include only the data you want, add headers, footers, and page numbers, and so on.

The Standard Report

Unfortunately, Paradox's standard report is not as useful as its standard form is. It simply prints out all the fields in the table, with their names above them as headings. Since most tables are too wide to fit on a single sheet of paper, it breaks them into several pages, which you must tape together. Try using this feature to print a report on the Employees table.

1. Start Paradox, if necessary, and call up the main menu.

2. Press V to select View.

3. When Paradox prompts you for the name of the table, type **employee** and press Enter, to display the Employee table.

4. Make sure your printer is turned on and then press the Instant Report key combination (Alt-F7).

The standard report takes up four pages. The first page has a neat heading, including the date, the page number, and the title Standard Report. The underlined field names are listed across the tops of the pages, and all the records are listed below them, as shown in Figure 9.1.

As you can see, most of the city name is on the first page, but the last letters of some cities are on page two. The beginning of the Comments field is on page two, but the rest is on page three; and page four just has the space for the last four characters of the Comments field, though no comment is actually long enough to extend to page four.

The standard report is most useful for tables narrow enough to fit on one page. For most tables, you will want to create a custom report, if only to prevent pages from breaking in the middle of a field.

The Instant Report key (Alt-F7) does have another handy use. If you are working on a report, rather than viewing a table, the Instant Report key immediately prints the report you are currently working on.

Tabular Reports: The Basics

For most tables, you will want to use Paradox's tabular report feature to rearrange the data, at least a bit, before printing it. This is relatively easy to do: Paradox's report generator simply displays the report on the screen in standard form, and lets you change it until it suits your purposes.

How to Use the Report Specification Screen

You call up the report specification screen by simply choosing Report Design from the menu.

1. Press Clear Image (F8) to clear the screen and call up the Paradox main menu. Press R and then D to select Report Design.

2. When Paradox asks you for the name of the table you want to report on, type **employee** and press Enter. Paradox displays a list beginning with the letter *R* and including the numbers from 1 to 14, as shown in Figure 9.2. R is highlighted, and the help line indicates that is the standard report. Apart from

```
9/12/90                    Standard Report                Page    1


First name        Last name              Address                      City
---------------   --------------------   ------------------------     ---------
Alice             Channing               505 Haight St.               San Franc
Sally             Bean                   1465 Oak St.                 Yonkers
Edward            Channing               505 Haight St.               San Franc
Jean              Abbott                 4445-2312 Technology Blvd.   Menlo Par
Jane              Walker                 848 Broadway                 San Rapha
Robert            Lin                    457 First St.                Paramus
Dianne            Lee                    1634 Bancroft Way            Berkeley
Joan              Garfield               4437 Elm St.                 Hoboken
Andrea            Norton                 2311 First St.               Mill Vall
George            Silk                   237 Edison st.               New Brusn
Francine          Bowen                  2113 University Ave.         Palo Alto
Albert            Cruz                   1237 Flatbush Ave.           Brooklyn
Samuel            Smithson               203 West St.                 Rye
Rosalyn           Rogers                 2242 Pensylvania Ave.        Mt. Verno
Joseph            Tuckerman              45 Arcroft Circle            San Mateo
Joseph            Miller                 2036 Park Ave.               New York
William           Channing               22 The Circle                Ross
Alice             Walter                 326 R  31 St                 Far Rocka
Edward            Cha
Josephine         Buc
Henry             Wai
Evelyn            Ada
Harriet           Nob
Samuel            Sch
```

```
                  State  Zip     Date hired  Hourly wage      SEAT score  Comments
           ------  -----  -----   ----------  -------------    ----------  --------------
     isco  CA     94122   7/14/90          4.45             348
           NY     10715  11/13/89         11.15             715           Excellent test s
     isco  CA     94122   6/15/88          4.45             325           Frequent absente
     k     CA     94025   4/15/88          9.45             601           On executive tra
     el    CA     94901   2/12/87         14.15             560           Steady progress
           NJ     07652  11/25/86         11.23             588
           CA     94703   4/15/86          9.50             602           Retesting may be
           NJ     07031   2/04/86         11.00             600           Was very impress
     ey    CA     94945   6/16/85         15.05             722
     wick  NJ     08901   3/01/85          8.65             322
           CA     94301   7/23/84         12.00             432
           NY     11226   1/15/84         10.50             540
           NY     10580  12/01/83         15.60             599
     n     NY     10507   7/17/82         14.56             723           Occasional custo
           CA     94406   7/06/82         12.75             421
           NY     10033   3/22/81         10.25             503           May be promoted
           CA     94957   2/22/81         15.55             641
     way   NY     11601  12/03/79          8.65             488
     ey    CA     94943  10/17/79         12.50             403
     el    CA     94965   4/01/79         14.25             533           In special train
           NY     11
           CT     068
           NY     112
```

```
                   core
                   eism
                   ck
                   in training program

                    necessary
                   ive at personal interview.  Possible advancement




                   mer complaints about service

                   again soon


                   ing program
                   yee
                   ee

                       ad
```

```
                       ----
```

Figure 9.1: The standard report

the standard report, Paradox will let you create up to 14 custom reports. Press → once to move the cursor to 1. The help line says this is an unused report, so you can use this number for your new report.

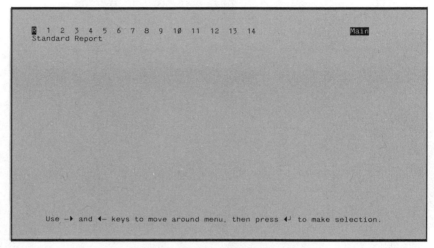

Figure 9.2: Choosing a report number

3. Press Enter to select 1. Paradox prompts you to enter the report description. In the future, when you actually use the reports you have created, Paradox will let you choose the standard report, R, or the reports numbered 1 to 14. When you move the cursor among the numbers, the help line for this report will be the description that you enter now. (This report description will also be the title of the report when it is first displayed on the screen, but you can easily change the title.)

4. Type **All Employee Data** and press Enter.

5. Paradox will ask if this is a Tabular or a free-form report. Press Enter to select Tabular.

Now Paradox displays the report specification screen, shown in Figure 9.3. As you can see, the screen is divided into horizontal bands, with the *table band* at the center, and the word *table* (with an arrow pointing at it) written above and below the band. The table band includes the headings that will be written above each column of the table, an underline, and a field *mask,* which represents the data in the field. The A's in the fields you can see indicate that the data in them is alphanumeric; the number of A's indicates the maximum number of characters each field can hold. Although they appear only once on the report specification screen, it is important to remember that these field masks represent the entire list of records in the table.

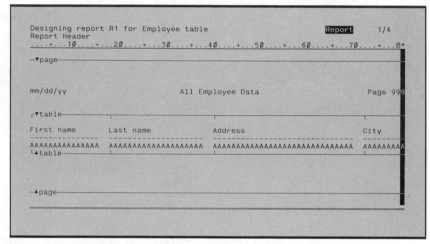

Figure 9.3: The report specification screen

Above and below the table band are the *page bands,* representing the header and footer that will appear on each page of the report. The word *page* and an arrow appear above the header and below the footer. The standard header at the top of the report includes the date on the left, the page number on the right, and a title in the center, which you entered when you created the report. Unless you change them, all of these will appear on each page of the report.

Above and below the page bands are the report bands. Unlike the other bands, these are not labeled, but the help line at the top of the screen tells you when you are in one of them. Notice that the cursor is above the word *page,* in the thin band above the band that contains the page header. The help line near the upper-left corner of the screen that says "Report Header," tells you where the cursor is now. Anything you type into this band appears only once, at the beginning of the report.

Press ↓ to move the cursor to the bottom of the page. Notice that, after you enter the page band, the help line says "Page Header." When you get down to the letters *mm/dd/yy,* another help line appears on the upper-right that says "Current date" to tell you what these letters represent.

When the cursor enters the table band, the help line on the upper-left says so, and when you get down to the field mask, the help line on the upper-right reappears, to tell you that the cursor is now in the letters that represent the First name field. Keep moving the cursor until you get through the page footer to the report footer; these are now blank, but anything you type in them will appear at the bottom of each page and at the end of the report.

The other very important help line you should notice at the top-right of the page shows the numbers 1/4. These indicate that this report is four pages wide and that you are now in the first page width.

The thick line at the right edge of the screen indicates the edge of a page. The numbers and dots at the top of the screen act as a ruler to show you where your cursor is within a page, which has room for 80 characters. You can press Ctrl→ to move across the report a half screen at a time.

1. Press Ctrl→, and you can see how the edge of the page divides the City field in two, as shown in Figure 9.4. This is how the field was divided when you printed your standard report. Notice that the ruler at the top of the page indicates the positions on page 2 starting from zero.

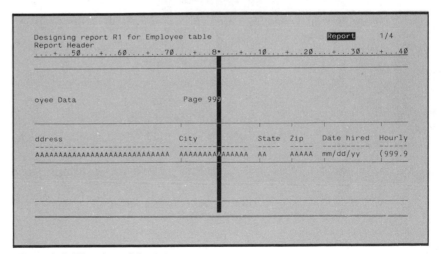

Figure 9.4: *The edge of the page*

2. Press Ctrl→ again to see all of page 2. Notice that the number fields are represented by 9's. The Hourly wage field has commas between the 9's and is in parentheses; this is the default display for a currency field. The Date field is represented by *mm/dd/yy,* to show how it is displayed.

3. Press Ctrl-Home to move back to the left edge of the report, and press Home to move back to the top of the page.

As you can see, the way you move the cursor around the report specification screen is very much like the way you move it around a table.

In addition to using Home and End to move the cursor to the top and bottom of the report, you can also use Ctrl-Home and Ctrl-End to move the cursor to the left and right edge of a line of text. If there is no text on the line, Ctrl-End does not move the cursor at all; if the line extends to the fourth page width, Ctrl-End moves it all the way there. Ctrl-Home moves the cursor to the left edge of the report regardless of whether anything is on the line.

Now that you are oriented within the report generator, you will not find it difficult to modify the Paradox standard report to fit your own needs. You will learn three important ways to modify the report specification:

- By choosing TableBand from the Report menu, you can erase, insert, move, or resize the columns of the table band.

- By choosing Field from the Report menu, you can modify the field masks displayed in the table band to change the way the fields are displayed in the final report.

- You can modify almost everything else by simply moving the cursor and making changes in the specification that appears on the screen. Type what you want and delete what you do not want. You cannot change the field masks or the locations and sizes of the columns in this way, but you can change the page header, report header, headings above the columns, and so on.

Later you will learn to make other changes using the menus, but these three basics will take you a long way toward creating exactly the reports you want.

Beginners often confuse the TableBand and Field features of the menu, so it is worth repeating the difference between them. Table-Band changes the columns themselves; for example, you would use it to widen or narrow a column. Field changes the field masks that represent the data displayed in the columns, and is used to widen or narrow the field. As you will see, you will have to change both to narrow the address display, first reducing the Address field itself and then the column it is in.

How to Modify Columns in Reports

The first report you are creating, which contains all employee data, is like the standard report, except that you will modify the columns to fit it onto the paper a bit more neatly.

Begin by assuming that you do not need the Comments field in the printed report, so you can delete this column. Let's say you also want the report with the last name first, so you will also move the First name column to follow the Last name column. Finally, you can widen the First name column, so the edge of the page does not cut the report apart. This will leave a space between the name and the other data, which will make the report easier to read.

1. From the report specification screen, press the Menu key (F10) to call up the Report menu.

2. Press T to select TableBand and E to select Erase. Paradox prompts you to move to the column to be erased and press Enter to delete it. You must move the cursor to the table band and to the column within it that you want.

3. Press ↓ until the cursor is somewhere in the table band, then press Ctrl→ to move to the Comments field, and press Enter. The column disappears.

4. Press Ctrl-Home to move back to the left edge of the report.

5. Press the Menu key (F10), then press T to select TableBand, and M to select Move.

6. Press Enter to select the First name column, (where you already moved the cursor, in step 2), press → until the cursor is

somewhere in the Last name column, and then press Enter. The first name column moves there.

7. Press the Menu key (F10). Press T and then R to select Table-Band Resize.

8. Use → to move the cursor to the right edge of the First name column and press Enter to select it. If the cursor is in the field that is displayed in that column, Paradox tells you that you cannot split a field during resizing. The cursor must be within the First name column but to the right of the field mask. After you have selected the field, the cursor becomes a blinking box, as it did when you resized fields using the Image menu.

9. Press → nine times so that the First name column pushes the City column beyond the edge of the page. Press Enter to select this width.

10. Press Ctrl→ twice to see what page 2 looks like. Two page-widths now hold all the fields, as you can see in Figure 9.5.

11. If you want to print this report, make sure your printer is turned on, and press Instant Report (Alt-F7) to send it to the printer. Press DO-IT! (F2) to save this report specification and return to the main menu.

The report now fits on two pages instead of four. Since the edge of the page does not divide a field in half, it requires less skill with the Scotch tape to assemble the pages than it would for the standard report.

There are two other options under Report TableRange. Copy copies a column to another location, so the report has the same column twice. Although this option is rarely called for, you will find it simple to use if you ever need it. Insert inserts a blank column. You will use this option later in this chapter.

Creating a Name and Address Report

It was easy to fit the report on employee data onto two pages. Often, though, you will want to create a report that is only one page wide, and this may require more sophisticated techniques. To learn

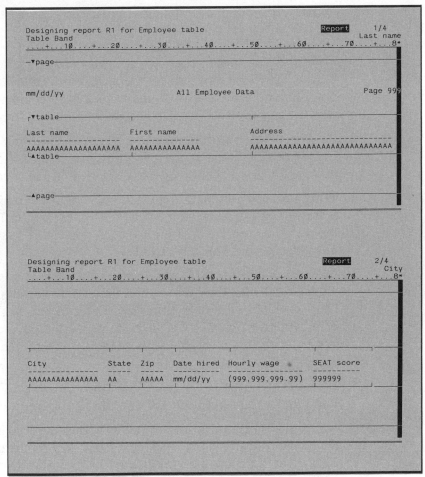

```
Designing report R1 for Employee table                    Report     1/4
Table Band                                                         Last name
....+...10....+...20....+...30....+...40....+...50....+...60....+...70....+...8*

  ▼page

  mm/dd/yy                        All Employee Data                  Page 999

  ▼table

  Last name              First name              Address
  --------------------   -----------------       --------------------------------
  AAAAAAAAAAAAAAAAAAAA   AAAAAAAAAAAAAAAA        AAAAAAAAAAAAAAAAAAAAAAAAAAAAAAAA
  ▲table

  ▲page
```

```
Designing report R1 for Employee table                    Report     2/4
Table Band                                                              City
....+...10....+...20....+...30....+...40....+...50....+...60....+...70....+...8*

  City           State  Zip    Date hired  Hourly wage       SEAT score
  -------------  -----  -----  ----------  ----------------  ----------
  AAAAAAAAAAAAA  AA     AAAAA  mm/dd/yy    (999,999,999.99)  999999
```

Figure 9.5: The first and second page-widths of the report

these, you will create another report, with employees' names and
addresses squeezed into the width of a single page.

*H*ow to Narrow a Column

First, you will erase the columns you do not need, such as Hourly wage
and Date hired. Then you will try to narrow the address column. You will
find that it is not as easy to narrow columns as it was to widen them; you
cannot make a column narrower than the field mask or the heading that

it contains. You have to use the Field option to make the field mask narrower, and you also need to delete part of the heading.

1. From the main menu, press R and then D to select Report DESIGN Define. When Paradox asks for the table, type **employee** and press Enter. Paradox displays the menu of report numbers, with the cursor on R. The help line reads "Standard Report."

2. Press → twice. Report number 1 will have the help line "All Employee Data"; this is the report you just created. Report number 2 will say "Unused Report." Press Enter to select it.

3. When Paradox asks for the report description, type **Employee Address List** and press Enter. Then press Enter to select Tabular, and the report specification screen appears. Press ↓ to move the cursor to the table band.

4. Press the Menu key (F10), then press T and then E to select TableBand Erase. Press Ctrl→ three times to move the cursor to the Hourly wage field, and press Enter to erase it. The columns to the right of the erased column will all move to the left to fill the empty space, so the cursor is now on the Test score field.

5. Press the Menu key (F10); press T and then E to select Table-Band Erase; then press Enter to erase the Test score field.

6. Repeat step 5 to erase the Comments field. Then use ← to move the cursor to the Date hired field and repeat step 5 to erase it. Notice that the report still extends almost halfway across the second page.

7. Press Ctrl-Home to move back to the left edge of the report to reorient yourself. Now you will try to squeeze the report a bit by narrowing the Address field. First, to learn the error you must avoid, try to do it in the same way that you widened the field.

8. Press the Menu key (F10). Press T and then R to select Table-Band Resize. Paradox prompts you to move to the column to be resized. Use → to move the cursor to the end of the Address field, as you did when you were widening it, and press Enter.

9. Press ← to narrow the field. As soon as you hit the end of the field mask, Paradox beeps and stops you. Before you can go any further, you must narrow the field mask itself.

10. Press Esc three times to return to the Report menu. Press F and then R to select Field Reformat.

11. Use the arrow keys to move the cursor onto the Address field mask and press Enter to select it. (The cursor must be on the field mask itself, or Paradox will display an error message.) The cursor moves the last letter of the field mask. Paradox prompts you to change the size of the field and then press Enter, as shown in Figure 9.6. Notice that the way you reformat a field in a report is similar to the way you change a table's image.

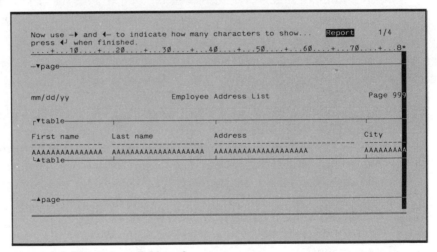

Figure 9.6: *Narrowing a field mask*

12. Press ← 11 times to shorten the field mask; press → once to make it only ten spaces shorter. Press Enter to select this length. If you try to narrow the column again, Paradox will beep and not let you do so, because you cannot make it narrower than the line under the word *address*.

13. Press Esc to back out of the menu system so you can shorten this line. If you press Esc too many times Paradox tells you that you must choose Cancel to leave the report specification screen.

14. Press ↑ once to move the cursor to the underline above the Address field mask. If it is not already there, place the cursor on the dash just to the right of the final *A* of the field mask.

15. Press Del until all the dashes to the right of the cursor and the dash the cursor is on disappear. Notice that each column is independent of the others; pressing Del moves the dashes within this column but does not affect those in the next column. Now that you have narrowed its contents, you can finally narrow the column itself.

16. Repeat steps 8 and 9. Make sure the cursor is at the far right of the column—not just of the field mask—before you press Enter. This time Paradox will not beep when you press ← to narrow the column, unless you keep pressing until you hit the field mask. Leave two blank spaces after the field mask, as in the other columns, and press Enter to select this column width.

How to Use Word Wrap

In the last chapter, when you narrowed the fields of a table's screen image, some of the data was no longer visible. In printed reports, you can make sure all the data is displayed by using the WordWrap option. When you select this option, any data that is too wide to fit onto one line is continued on the next line. In general, the data will be broken between words, so individual words are not divided; if a single word is too wide to fit in a column, that word will be broken.

To use this feature, you just select Field WordWrap from the Report menu:

1. Press the Menu key (F10). Press F and then W to select Field WordWrap. Paradox tells you to move the cursor to the field you want wrapped.

2. Use the arrow keys to move the cursor to the Address field and press Enter. The cursor must be on the field mask itself, or Paradox displays an error message.

3. Paradox asks you the number of lines to output, and suggests 1, the current number of lines. Press Backspace to delete the 1.

4. Type **2** and press Enter. Paradox displays a message to tell you that the word wrap value has been recorded, as shown in Figure 9.7.

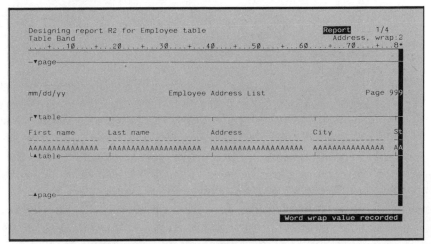

```
Designing report R2 for Employee table            Report    1/4
Table Band                                       Address, wrap:2
....+...10....+...20....+...30....+...40....+...50....+...60....+...70....+...8*

  ─▼page──────────────────────────────────────────────────────────


  mm/dd/yy                    Employee Address List              Page 999


  ┌▼table────────────────────────────────────────────────────────
  First name        Last name          Address          City         St
  ─────────────     ──────────────     ──────────────   ───────────  ─
  AAAAAAAAAAAAAA    AAAAAAAAAAAAAAAAAA  AAAAAAAAAAAAAAAA AAAAAAAAAAAAA AA
  └▲table────────────────────────────────────────────────────────


  ─▲page──────────────────────────────────────────────────────────

                                          Word wrap value recorded
```

Figure 9.7: A narrowed address column, just after WordWrap has been selected

Paradox will now use up to two lines to display an address. The column should be wide enough to accommodate any address.

How to Use the Editor

As you have seen, the report specification screen also acts as a full-screen editor. You can use the arrow keys to move the cursor, use Del or Backspace to delete characters, and the other keys to type in anything you want. You cannot edit the field masks themselves this way, but you can edit anything else in the report, including the headings above the field masks.

When you first call up the Report screen, the editor is in Typeover mode. What you type replaces the character where the cursor is, and deleting a character leaves a blank space.

To toggle into Insert mode, press the Ins key. The Ins message appears near the upper-right corner of the screen and any characters you type will move existing characters to the right. When you delete characters in Insert mode, everything to the right is pulled left to fill the gap.

When you use the editor within the table band, each column functions independently. Characters beyond the edge of a column are not affected by insertions and deletions. Anywhere else, the entire width of the screen is affected.

If you press Enter in Insert mode, you add an extra line where the cursor is and any characters to the right of the cursor move to the new line. If there are no characters to the right of the cursor, the new line is blank.

Pressing Ctrl-Y deletes everything to the right of the cursor. If the cursor is at the left margin when you press Ctrl- Y, the entire line will be removed. This is a good way to remove blank lines. Ctrl-Y is a bit dangerous, because it can erase the field masks themselves—unlike Del and Backspace, which only erase text. If you erase a field by mistake, you can use Field Place (which you will learn about in the next section) to put it back where it was, or you can press Ctrl-Break to cancel everything you have done and start over.

Knowing these basic facts about the report specification editor, you can change the appearance of your report in most any way you want. Let's say you want the title to appear only at the beginning of the report, you want the header to be smaller, and you want blank lines between the records on the report.

1. Press Home to move the cursor to the report header band at the top of the screen, and Ctrl-Home to move it to the left margin. Type **Employee Names and Addresses** at the left margin.

2. Press Ins to toggle into Insert mode, then press Enter twice to add two blank lines. Press ↑ twice to move the cursor to the first letter of the title you just typed.

3. Still in Insert mode, press the spacebar to push the title to the right until it is centered. If you go too far, press Backspace to pull it back. Use the numbers on the ruler to align the title properly.

4. Press ↓ four times to move to the page header band, and Ctrl-Home to move to the left margin.

5. Press Ctrl-Y twice to delete two blank lines so the header will be closer to the top of each page, then use the arrow keys to move the cursor so it is just to the right of the final *t* of the header title, Employee Address List.

6. Press Ins to toggle back to Typeover mode, and press Back-space until you delete the entire header title. Notice that the page number to its right remains where it was.

7. Press ↓ until the cursor is on a field mask, then press Enter to move the cursor to the left margin of the line below the field masks, just to the left of the word *table*. Now press Ins to toggle into Insert mode.

8. Press Enter twice to add two blank lines in the table band below the field mask. When you add blank lines at the bottom of the table band, they appear after each record in the printed report. The report specification screen should now look like Figure 9.8.

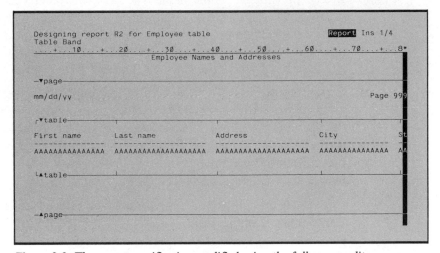

Figure 9.8: The report specification modified using the full-screen editor

How to Place a Field

There is a good reason for adding those blank lines in the table band. We now have room to place the First name field under the Last name field, and we can delete the First name column to fit the report onto a single page.

To place a field, select Field Place from the Report menu. But first make sure there is enough room in the column to hold the field. As always, each column functions independently, and a field cannot cross the edge of a column.

1. Press the Menu key (F10). Press F and then P to select Field Place. You must now choose the kind of field you want to place.

2. Press Enter to select Regular, which means that you want to place one of the existing fields in the table. Paradox displays a menu that lists all of the fields in the table. Because you choose from this menu rather than moving the cursor to the field you want, you can place a field even if you have erased it earlier.

3. Press Enter to select First name. Paradox tells you to use the arrow keys to indicate where the field should begin. Press ↑ twice and → 20 times. This moves the cursor to a position one line below the Last name field mask, indented three characters to the right of where the mask begins.

4. Press Enter to place the field. Its field mask appears under the Last name field mask, indented three characters from the beginning of the last name. Paradox now lets you use the arrow keys to format the field, so fewer characters are displayed. Since there is plenty of room to display the whole first name, press Enter to select its current width.

5. Press the Menu key (F10). Then press T and E to select Table-Band Erase from the menu. Now press Ctrl← to move the cursor to the First name column, and press Enter to erase it.

6. Press ↑ to move the cursor to the initial *L* of Last name, and press Del six times to delete Last n. Then type **N** (be sure to use uppercase) to change the column heading to Name.

Congratulations. You have succeeded in fitting the names and addresses into the width of a single page—with room to spare, as you can see in Figure 9.9.

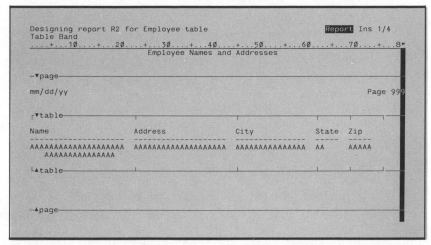

```
Designing report R2 for Employee table                    Report  Ins 1/4
Table Band
....+...10....+...20....+...30....+...40....+...50....+...60....+...70....+...8*
                      Employee Names and Addresses

 —▼page————————————————————————————————————————————————————————————————
 mm/dd/yy                                                         Page 999

 ┌▼table———————————————————————————————————————————————————————————————
 Name                  Address                City              State  Zip
 -------------------   --------------------   ---------------   -----  -----
 AAAAAAAAAAAAAAAAAAAA  AAAAAAAAAAAAAAAAAAAAA  AAAAAAAAAAAAAA    AA     AAAAA
   AAAAAAAAAAAAAAA
 L▲table———————————————————————————————————————————————————————————————



 —▲page————————————————————————————————————————————————————————————————
```

Figure 9.9: Names and addresses squeezed into the width of one page

When you place a number or date field, rather than an alphanumeric field, Paradox lets you format it in other ways, which you are already familiar with. You can choose a variety of date displays, choose the number of decimal places displayed for numbers, choose whether numbers have commas, and whether negative numbers are displayed in parentheses, just as you can when you change a field's image.

You probably noticed when you were using the Report menu that Paradox lets you place several other types of fields apart from the regular fields that are part of the table. You can place the date, time, or page number anywhere on the report by selecting Date, Time, or Page instead of Regular from the menu. For example, if you wanted the date and page number to appear in the footer of each page, you could simply use the editor to delete them from the header, and then use Field Place to place them in the footer band.

You can also choose #Record from this menu to include the record number in the report, although this feature is rarely useful. You would have to add a new column first, probably at the left of the report, and then use Field Place to put the record number in it.

You will learn about Summary and Calculated fields, the two additional options for placing fields, in Chapter 10.

Output for Reports

In addition to sending your report to the printer, you can use the Output option of the Report menu to send it to a DOS file or to the screen of your computer.

You will save yourself time and paper if you get in the habit of sending reports to the screen before printing them, to make sure they are correct.

1. Press the Menu key (F10), then press O to select Output.

2. Press S to select Screen. Paradox displays the beginning of the report on your screen, as it will be printed. The message at the top of the screen tells you where you are in the report. Notice that the first names are indented under the last names, that some of the longer addresses are wrapped onto a second line, and that blank lines appear between records, as shown in Figure 9.10. Press Enter several times to look through the entire report.

3. After you have finished looking at the output and have returned to the report specification screen, press DO-IT! (F2) to save this report specification and return to the main menu. If you would like to take a break, you can exit from the program now.

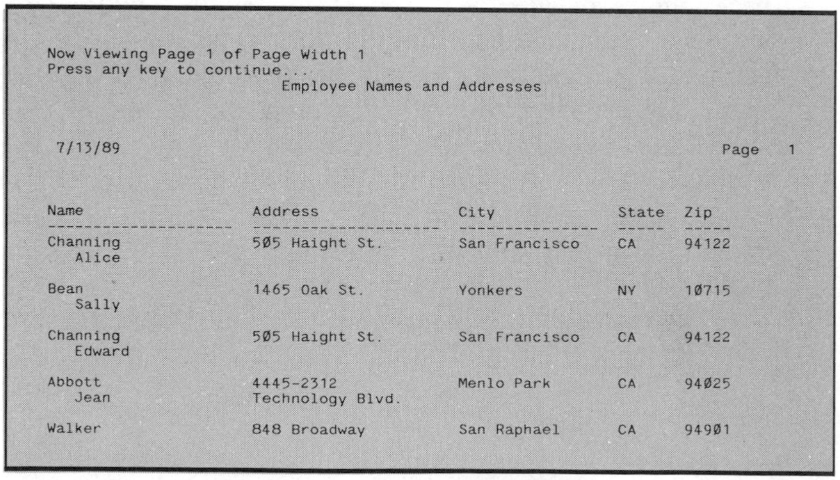

```
Now Viewing Page 1 of Page Width 1
Press any key to continue...
                    Employee Names and Addresses


   7/13/89                                                     Page    1


   Name                Address              City            State  Zip
   ------------------- -------------------- --------------- -----  -----
   Channing            5Ø5 Haight St.       San Francisco   CA     94122
      Alice

   Bean                1465 Oak St.         Yonkers         NY     1Ø715
      Sally

   Channing            5Ø5 Haight St.       San Francisco   CA     94122
      Edward

   Abbott              4445-2312            Menlo Park      CA     94Ø25
      Jean             Technology Blvd.

   Walker              848 Broadway         San Raphael     CA     94901
```

Figure 9.10: Screen output of the name and address report

You can use Output File to send the report to a DOS text file in much the same way that you used Output Screen. Paradox prompts you to enter a name for the file. Then you can use any word processor that will read DOS text files (that is, plain ASCII files) to enhance the report and print it. You can use your word processor to print the headers in bold type, for example, or to print the report in different font sizes if your word processor is capable of it.

Changing Reports

Modifying an existing report is virtually identical to creating a new one. After pressing R to select Report from the main menu, press C to select Change (instead of D to select Design). Paradox asks you for the table name, as it does when you are designing a report, and then gives you a menu that lists the numbers of the reports that already exist for that table. When you move through this menu, the help lines that describe the reports are the report descriptions that you entered when you created them. After you select a report, Paradox gives you a chance to change the description, or to press Enter to keep the existing description, and displays the report specification screen again. Then you can make changes in the same way you can when you are creating a report.

You have learned all the basics of working with the report editor and of placing, deleting, inserting, and reformatting both columns and table bands. In the next chapter, you will learn a few more sophisticated report techniques.

MORE
ADVANCED
REPORT
TECHNIQUES

**GROUPING
RECORDS**

**ADDING
CALCULATED/
SUMMARY
FIELDS**

**CREATING PAGE
BREAKS AND
BLANK LINES**

**REPORT
SETTINGS**

The basic techniques you learned in the last chapter will probably let you create most of the tabular reports you need. This chapter offers a few more advanced techniques for creating reports that help you analyze your data. First, you will learn to create a grouped report—for example, a report that groups employees by state or test score. Then you will learn to add calculated and summary fields to reports—so you can, for example, add a line to the report telling you the total weekly wages or the average test score for all the employees.

Creating a Wage and Test Score Report

You will begin by creating a report on employees' wages and test scores. To start, simply design a new report specification and erase unnecessary fields.

1. From the Paradox main menu, press R and then D to select Report Design. When Paradox asks you the name of the table, type **employee** and press Enter.

2. Move the cursor to 3, the first unused report, and press Enter. When Paradox asks for the report description, type **Employee Wages and Test Scores** and press Enter, then press Enter to select Tabular.

3. When the report specification screen appears, use the arrow keys to move the cursor to the Address column.

4. Press the Menu key (F10), and then press T and E to select TableBand Erase. Press Enter to erase the Address column.

5. Using the arrow keys move the cursor, repeat step 4 to erase the City, Zip, Date hired, and Comments columns. Be careful not to erase the State, Hourly wage, and SEAT score columns.

6. Press Ctrl-Home to move back to the left edge of the report.

Now, just the fields that you want to work with are left on the report specification screen, as shown in Figure 10.1.

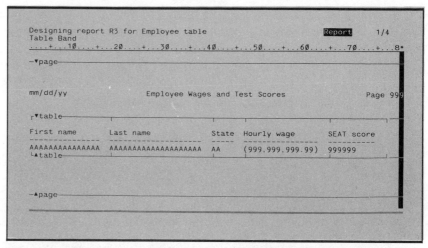

```
  Designing report R3 for Employee table                  Report    1/4
  Table Band
  ....+...1Ø....+...2Ø....+...3Ø....+...4Ø....+...5Ø....+...6Ø....+...7Ø....+...8*
   —▼page—

   mm/dd/yy                   Employee Wages and Test Scores        Page 999

   ┌▼table
   First name       Last name            State  Hourly wage      SEAT score
   ---------------  --------------------  -----  ---------------  ----------
   AAAAAAAAAAAAAAA  AAAAAAAAAAAAAAAAAAAA  AA     (999,999,999.99) 999999
   └▲table

   —▲page—
```

Figure 10.1: *The report specification screen with unneeded fields removed*

*H*ow to Group Records

Now, let's say you want the salaries and test scores of employees from different states listed separately, for purposes of analysis. You can do this simply by choosing Group Insert from the Report menu.

1. Press the Menu key (F10), then press G and I to select Group Insert.

2. Press Enter to select Field. Paradox presents a menu of all the fields and asks you which field you want to group on, as shown in Figure 10.2. The arrow to the right of the menu indicates that there are more choices, which are not shown on the screen.

3. Press → four times to move the cursor to State and press Enter. Paradox asks you to use the arrow keys to show where you want the group inserted. Use the arrow key to move the cursor to the upper page band, and press Enter.

A new band is inserted that says "group State" above and below the table band, as illustrated in Figure 10.3.

Because Paradox gives you a menu from which to choose the field you want the report grouped on, rather than asking you to move your cursor to that field, you can group on fields that you have already erased. For example, you could place the name of the state only in the group header, rather than in each record. You will learn more about group headers and footers later in this chapter.

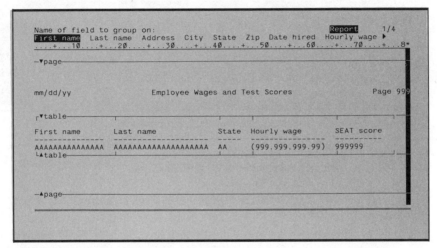

Figure 10.2: Choosing which field to group on

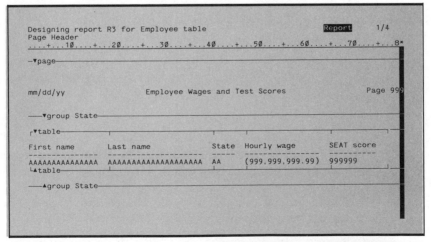

Figure 10.3: The report specification screen after choosing to group on State

How to Group by Range

Paradox asked you to locate the cursor to place the group, because you can have groups within groups. Let's say that you want the records for each state further grouped into wage categories.

1. Press the Menu key (F10) to call up the Report menu. Press G and then I to select Group Insert.

2. Press R to select Range. When you make this choice, Paradox lets you select a field to group on (as it did previously, when you selected Field), and it also gives you more control over how the grouping is done, as you will see.

3. Paradox displays a menu of the fields. Move the cursor to Hourly wage and press Enter.

4. Paradox asks you for the Size of Range. You want to group records to separate employees who earn less than $5, $5 to $10, $10 to $15, and so on. Type **5** and press Enter.

5. Paradox asks you where to place the group. Use the arrow keys to move the cursor to somewhere above the table band and under the group State line, and press Enter. A new band appears that says "group Hourly wage, range = 5," as shown in Figure 10.4.

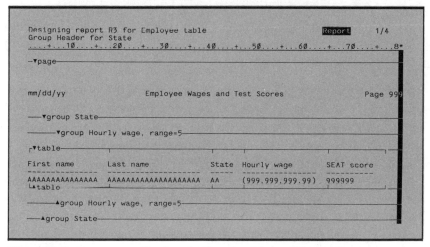

Figure 10.4: A report specification that has one group within another

Because you placed the Hourly wage group within the State group, the primary grouping in your report will be by state, and within each state, the employees will be grouped by wage.

You probably noticed that Group Insert also had a third option, NumberRecords. This lets you skip a line occasionally to make the report easier to read. For example, you could make the report skip a line after each group of five records.

Selecting Group Delete lets you get rid of a grouping. You can change the type of a grouping (for example, from Field to Range) by choosing Group Regroup, which is equivalent to deleting a group and then inserting a group of a different type in the same place. When you group records, the groups are automatically sorted in ascending order: for example, states are listed alphabetically, and wages are listed with those under $5 first. If you choose Group SortDirection, you can sort in descending order. In all of these cases, Paradox tells you what to do, just follow the self-explanatory prompts.

Now that you have placed one group within another, let's see what the report looks like. Although the idea of groups within one another seems a bit confusing, its meaning becomes obvious when you look at the actual output. Follow these steps to send this report to the screen so you can see for yourself:

1. Press the Menu key (F10).

2. Press O and then S to select Output Screen.

3. Press Enter repeatedly until you have looked through the entire report and have returned to the report specification screen.

Notice that records are grouped by state: records from the different states are separated, and the states are in alphabetical order. Within each state, the records are divided by wage, as shown in Figure 10.5, where you can see the California workers with wages under $5, from $5 to $10, and $10 to $15.

This illustration should make it clear what grouping by range means; if you had not chosen Range, each employee would be in a separate group, since all have different wages.

You can also use Group Insert Range with date or alphanumeric fields. You can group by range on a date field to separate records from

```
Now Viewing Page 1 of Page Width 1
Press any key to continue...


   7/14/90              Employee Wages and Test Scores              Page    1


   First name        Last name             State  Hourly wage       SEAT score
   ---------------   --------------------   -----  ----------------  ----------


   Alice             Channing              CA            4.45        348
   Edward            Channing              CA            4.45        325


   Jean              Abbott                CA            9.45        601
   Dianne            Lee                   CA            9.50        602


   Francine          Bowen                 CA           12.00        432
   Edward            Channing              CA           12.50        403
   Henry             Ware                  CA           12.50        664
```

Figure 10.5: *The report with one group within another*

different years, months, or weeks. If you group on an alphanumeric field, Paradox asks how many letters of the field you want to group on. You could group by one letter, to place all the employees whose names begin with C (for example) in a separate group; on two letters, to place all whose names begin with Ch in a separate group, and so on.

The illustration should also make clear what it means to place one group inside another. The outer group is the more important one: the main division in this report is by state. The inner group is less important: employees *within* each state are grouped by wage. That is all it means to put one group within another.

Calculated and Summary Fields with Arithmetic Operators

There are two situations where you might want to calculate a value in a field. You might want a calculated value for each record: for example, if you know each employee's Hourly wage and the number of hours worked each week, you could calculate the weekly wage for each employee. On the other hand, you might want a calculated value for all the records: for example, the average wage for all employees.

Paradox uses two different types of fields for these records. The first is a called a calculated field. It is used *only* when you want to calculate a value for each record. The second is called a summary field. As the name indicates, it is used for calculations that summarize the values in all the records of a table or group.

To make calculations, you use these familiar arithmetic operators:

+   Addition

−   Subtraction

*   Multiplication

/   Division

You can also group terms in a mathematical expression by enclosing them in parentheses as you do in algebra, so that some calculations take precedence over others.

In calculations, field names are placed in square brackets. For example, if you had an Hours worked field, you could calculate each employee's total weekly earnings by typing **[Hours worked] * [Hourly wage]** as the value of a new field. In the next example, you will assume that everyone works 40 hours per week and will add a calculated field for weekly earnings.

*H*ow to Add a Calculated Field

To add this field, you need to insert a new column, type its heading, and then select Field Place Calculated from the menu.

1. Press the Menu key (F10). Press T and then I to select Table-Band Insert.

2. When Paradox prompts you, use the arrow keys to move the cursor to the SEAT score column within the table band and press Enter. Paradox inserts a blank column, with the cursor at its left edge.

3. Use ↑ and ↓ to move the cursor so it is on the same line as the column headings, still at the left edge of the column, and type **Weekly wage**.

4. Press ↓ once and use the ← key to move back to the left edge of the column. Type ------------- (13 hyphens).

5. Press the Menu key (F10). Press F, P, and then C to select Field Place Calculated.

6. Paradox prompts you to enter an expression. Type **40 * [Hourly wage]**. Be sure to use square brackets around the field name. Your screen should look like Figure 10.6. Press Enter. If you make a typographical error and the expression is invalid, Paradox will not accept it. Use the Backspace key to erase the error; then make the correction and press Enter.

7. Paradox prompts you to position the cursor where the field should begin. Press ↓ once and ← 13 times to move to the left edge of the column, on the same level as the fields, and press Enter.

8. Paradox prompts you to adjust the number of digits displayed. Press ← six times to shorten the field to (9,999), since no one earns $10,000 per week, and press Enter.

9. Paradox prompts you to adjust the number of decimal places and suggests two places, as shown in Figure 10.7. Press Enter to accept two decimal places.

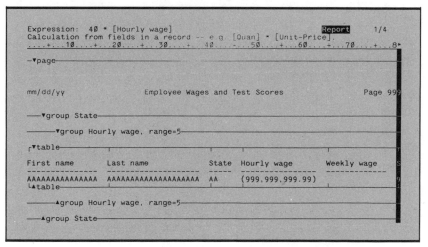

Figure 10.6: *Entering the expression for a calculated field*

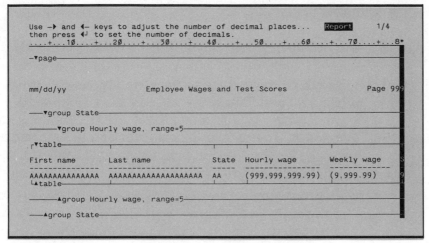

Figure 10.7: *Placing and formatting the calculated field*

Like virtually all calculated fields, this one will obviously have a different value in each record. If a field used in the expression is blank in a record, the calculated field will also be blank in that record.

Though it may sound odd, you can also create calculated alphanumeric fields. For example, if you wanted to highlight the name of the state by placing asterisks next to it, you could create a new column with the value **** + [State] + **** in it.

How to Add a Summary Field

Summary fields use five summary operators to summarize the data of all the records in a group or table. Some of these operators do not apply to all field types.

- *Sum* adds all the values in a field. (This operator is not applicable to alphanumeric or date fields.)

- *Average* averages all the values in a field. (The operator is not applicable to alphanumeric fields.)

- *Count* shows how many values there are in a field.

- *High* shows the highest value in a field.

- *Low* shows the lowest value in a field.

In a summary field, blank values are simply ignored—that is, they are not included in the average.

To insert summary fields, select Field Place Summary from the Report menu. Let's say, for example, that you want to know the average test score for the people in each of the wage groups that you have created, so you can see if wages and test scores are correlated.

1. Use the arrow keys to move the cursor to the group Hourly wage band below the table band; the help line in the upper-left should say, "Group footer for Hourly wage, range = 5." Press Ctrl-Home to move the cursor to the left edge of the screen. Summary fields must always be in the lower group band, below the group they are summarizing.

2. Type **Average aptitude test score for this group:**.

3. Press the Menu key (F10). Press F, P, and then S to select Field Place Summary. Press Enter to select Regular, because you are summarizing a regular rather than a calculated field.

4. Paradox displays a menu of all the field names. Press → eight times to move the cursor to SEAT score and press Enter. Paradox now displays a menu of the five summary operators. Press A to select Average.

5. Press Enter to select PerGroup, because you want the average for each group. (The other choice, Overall, gives an average for all field values so far. You will use it later.) Paradox tells you to place the field. Press → once, to leave a space, and press Enter.

6. Paradox tells you to adjust the number of digits displayed. Since the test score only goes into the thousands, press ← eight times, to shorten the field mask to 9999, and press Enter.

7. Paradox tells you to adjust the number of decimal places. Since the field being averaged is displayed without decimal places, Paradox begins by displaying no decimal places on the summary field. To get a more precise average, you can display two decimal places. Press → three times (first to add the decimal point and then to add two decimal places), and press Enter.

8. Make sure you are in Insert mode (the Ins message should appear on the upper-right of the screen). Press → once to move the cursor off the field mask, and press Enter to add a blank line.

You have not only placed the summary field, but also created a group footer and added an extra blank line between it and the next group to make the report more readable, as shown in Figure 10.8.

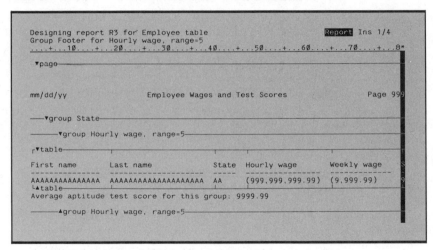

Figure 10.8: A summary field in a group footer

As you saw when you went through the menu, you can also summarize a calculated field. Suppose you want to know the total weekly wages for the employees who live in each state.

1. Press ↓ twice to move the cursor to the left edge of the group State band, and type **Total weekly wages:**.

2. Press the Menu key (F10). Press F, P, S, and then C to select Field Place Summary Calculated.

3. When Paradox asks for an expression, type **40 * [Hourly wage]** and press Enter. Then press Enter to select Sum.

4. Press Enter again to select PerGroup.

5. Press → once to leave a space and then Enter to place the field. Press Enter once to accept the suggested display, and again to accept the suggested two decimal places.

6. Press ↓ seven times to move the cursor beyond the page band to the report footer. The help line on the upper-left of your screen should say Report Footer.

7. Press Enter three times to add three blank lines, and type **Total Weekly Payroll:**. Repeat steps 2 and 3 to begin placing a summary field here.

8. Press O to select Overall, because this is a summary for the entire report, not just for a group. Press → and press Enter three times (as in step 5) to finish placing the field.

9. Press → three times, type **for**, and press → again.

10. Press the Menu key (F10). Press F, P, S, and then R to select Field Place Summary Regular. Press → seven times to move the cursor to Hourly wage, and then press Enter.

11. Press C to select Count and then O to select Overall. Press Enter three times to place and format the field, then press → twice and type **employees.** Your screen should look like Figure 10.9.

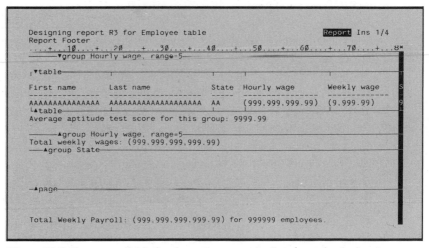

Figure 10.9: Summary fields for the entire report in the report footer band

Now there will be a footer at the bottom of the report, which would (assuming you had a larger number of employees) say something like "Total weekly payroll: 123,231.78 for 238 employees."

Since this is a complex report, you should probably print it to see what it looks like. In a real report, you might want to place the first name under the last name to fit it onto the width of each page; to save time here, you can just delete the First name column instead.

1. Press the Menu key (F10). Press T and then E to select Table-Band Erase.

2. Use the arrow keys to move the cursor to the First name column within the table band and press Enter.

3. Make sure your printer is on and press Instant Report (Alt-F7) to print the report. The result should look like Figure 10.10.

If you do not want to print the report, you can ignore step 3, and instead select Output Screen from the menu to look at the report on your screen. Figure 10.11 shows the first screen of output, and Figure 10.12 shows the last screen, with the summary of the total weekly payroll.

When you look at this report—either printed or on the screen—notice how the groupings you chose affect it. The employees are listed by state, with the states in alphabetical order. Within each state, the employees are grouped by hourly wage, with the wages arranged from lowest to highest and further grouped by $5 increments, with an average aptitude test score provided for each of these groups. This report lets you see, for example, that employees from California who earn between $5 and $10 per hour have higher test scores than those who earn from $10 to $15 per hour. You can also see that most employees are in the middle salary range.

How to Use PAGEBREAK and BLANKLINE

In the report you just created, the total weekly wages are listed for each state, but they are a bit hard to find, because all the states run together on the page. To print the states on separate pages, you can use the key word PAGEBREAK. When you type this word using your editor, it does not appear in the final report. Instead, it acts as a code that

```
7/14/90                 Employee Wages and Test Scores


Last name              State  Hourly wage      Weekly wage    SEAT score
--------------------   -----  ----------------  -------------  ----------


Channing               CA            4.45       178.00            348
Channing               CA            4.45       178.00            325
Average aptitude test score for this group:  336.50


Abbott                 CA            9.45       378.00            601
Lee                    CA            9.50       380.00            602
Average aptitude test score for this group:  601.50


Bowen                  CA           12.00       480.00            432
Channing               CA           12.50       500.00            403
Ware                   CA           12.50       500.00            664
Tuckerman              CA           12.75       510.00            421
Walker                 CA           14.15       566.00            560
Buckminster            CA           14.25       570.00            533
Average aptitude test score for this group:  502.17


Norton                 CA           15.05       602.00            722
Channing               CA           15.55       622.00            641
Average aptitude test score for this group:  681.50

Total weekly  wages:             5,464.00


Noble                  CT           14.05       562.00            622
Average aptitude test score for this group:  622.00

Total weekly  wages:              562.00


Silk                   NJ            8.65       346.00            322
Average aptitude test score for this group:  322.00


Garfield               NJ           11.00       440.00            600
Lin                    NJ           11.23       449.20            588
Average aptitude test score for this group:  594.00

Total weekly  wages:            1,235.20


Schmaltz               NY            8.32       332.80            321
Walter                 NY            8.65       346.00            488
Average aptitude test score for this group:  404.50


Miller                 NY           10.25       410.00            503
Adams                  NY           10.33       413.20            466
Cruz                   NY           10.50       420.00            540
Bean                   NY           11.15       446.00            715
Rogers                 NY           14.56       582.40            723
Average aptitude test score for this group:  589.40


Smithson               NY           15.60       624.00            599
Average aptitude test score for this group:  599.00

Total weekly  wages:            3,574.40


Total Weekly Payroll:          10,835.60  for     24 employees.
```

Figure 10.10: The report in printed form

```
Now Viewing Page 1 of Page Width 1
Press any key to continue...


   7/14/90              Employee Wages and Test Scores                Page   1


   Last name             State  Hourly wage       Weekly wage      SEAT score
   --------------------- -----  ----------------  -------------    ----------


   Channing              CA              4.45         178.00          348
   Channing              CA              4.45         178.00          325
   Average aptitude test score for this group:  336.50


   Abbott                CA              9.45         378.00          601
   Lee                   CA              9.50         380.00          602
   Average aptitude test score for this group:  601.50


   Bowen                 CA             12.00         480.00          432
```

Figure 10.11: The beginning of the report on screen

```
Now Viewing Page 2 of Page Width 1
Press any key to continue...


   Last name             State  Hourly wage       Weekly wage      SEAT score
   --------------------- -----  ----------------  -------------    ----------


   Adams                 NY             10.33         413.20          466
   Cruz                  NY             10.50         420.00          540
   Bean                  NY             11.15         446.00          715
   Rogers                NY             14.56         582.40          723
   Average aptitude test score for this group:  589.40


   Smithson              NY             15.60         624.00          599
   Average aptitude test score for this group:  599.00

   Total weekly  wages:           3,574.40


   Total Weekly Payroll:         10,835.60  for     24 employees.
```

Figure 10.12: The end of the report on screen, showing the report footer

makes the printer begin a new page. To work properly, PAGEBREAK must be typed in uppercase at the left edge of the report.

1. Use the arrow keys in order to move the cursor to the line in the group State band that says "Total weekly wages: (999,999,999,999.99)," and press Ctrl-End to move it to the right of any characters on that line.

2. Make sure you are in Insert mode and press Enter to insert a blank line under the total. The cursor will be at the left margin on the new line.

3. Type **PAGEBREAK**, as shown in Figure 10.13.

4. To print the report, press the Instant Report key combination (Alt- F7).

5. To save this report specification, press DO-IT! (F2).

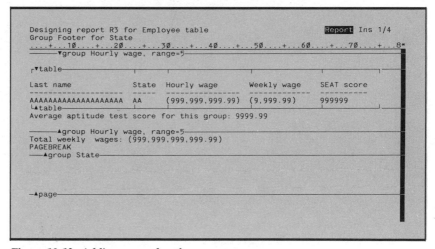

```
Designing report R3 for Employee table                    Report  Ins 1/4
Group Footer for State
....+...1Ø....+...2Ø....+...3Ø....+...4Ø....+...5Ø....+...6Ø....+...7Ø....+...8*
          ▼group Hourly wage, range=5
  ┌▼table
  │
  Last name              State  Hourly wage        Weekly wage       SEAT score
  ------------------     -----  ------------------ --------------    ----------
  AAAAAAAAAAAAAAAAAAAA   AA     (999,999,999.99)   (9,999.99)        999999
  └▲table
  Average aptitude test score for this group: 9999.99

          ▲group Hourly wage, range=5
  Total weekly  wages: (999,999,999,999.99)
  PAGEBREAK
          ▲group State


  ─▲page
```

Figure 10.13: Adding a page break

You will see that the figures for each state are printed on a separate page, as shown in Figure 10.14, which makes it easier to read the report.

Another key word you can use in reports is BLANKLINE. Like PAGEBREAK, this key word must be typed in uppercase at the left margin, and it does not appear in the actual report.

BLANKLINE preserves a blank line between records, and is generally used with word-wrapped fields. The name and address report you created in the last chapter, for example, added two lines after each record; one of these contained the first name and possibly the ending of the address, and the second was blank. Suppose you had very long addresses, including some that might require three lines, but you still wanted a blank line after each record. You could type the word BLANKLINE at the left edge of the third line. It would be printed as a blank line, as always, even if the field did not wrap onto the third line.

```
7/14/90                    Employee Wages and Test Scores


Last name               State  Hourly wage      Weekly wage     SEAT score
--------------------    -----  ----------------  -------------   ----------


Channing                CA              4.45       178.00          348
Channing                CA              4.45       178.00          325
Average aptitude test score for this group:  336.50


Abbott                  CA              9.45       378.00          601
Lee                     CA              9.50       380.00          602
Average aptitude test score for this group:  601.50


Bowen                   CA             12.00       480.00          432
Channing                CA             12.50       500.00          403
Ware                    CA             12.50       500.00          664
Tuckerman               CA             12.75       510.00          421
Walker                  CA             14.15       566.00          560
Buckminster             CA             14.25       570.00          533
Average aptitude test score for this group:  502.17


Norton                  CA             15.05       602.00          722
Channing                CA             15.55       622.00          641
Average aptitude test score for this group:  681.50

Total weekly  wages:             5,464.00


Last name               State  Hourly wage      Weekly wage     SEAT score
--------------------    -----  ----------------  -------------   ----------


Noble                   CT             14.05       562.00          622
Average aptitude test score for this group:  622.00

Total weekly  wages:              562.00


Last name               State  Hourly wage      Weekly wage     SEAT score
--------------------    -----  ----------------  -------------   ----------


Silk                    NJ              8.65       346.00          322
Average aptitude test score for this group:  322.00


Garfield                NJ             11.00       440.00          600
Lin                     NJ             11.23       449.20          588
Average aptitude test score for this group:  594.00

Total weekly  wages:             1,235.20


Last name               State  Hourly wage      Weekly wage     SEAT score
--------------------    -----  ----------------  -------------   ----------


Schmaltz                NY              8.32       332.80          321
Walter                  NY              8.65       346.00          488
Average aptitude test score for this group:  404.50
```

Figure 10.14: The printed report with page breaks separating the states

```
Miller              NY             10.25      410.00        503
Adams               NY             10.33      413.20        466
Cruz                NY             10.50      420.00        540
Bean                NY             11.15      446.00        715
Rogers              NY             14.56      582.40        723
Average aptitude test score for this group:   589.40


Smithson            NY             15.60      624.00        599
Average aptitude test score for this group:   599.00

Total weekly  wages:               3,574.40


Total Weekly Payroll:              10,835.60  for     24 employees.
```

Figure 10.14: The printed report with page breaks separating the states (continued)

In addition, records where the field did wrap onto the third line would have an extra blank line added after them, to preserve the blank line where the key word was used.

Other Features of the Tabular Report Menu

So far, you have learned about the Field, TableBand, Group, and Output options of the Report menu. The Tabular Report menu has a few other features that you should know about.

Report Settings

Choosing Setting from the Report menu lets you control the way a report appears on the printed page.

Setting Format lets you choose how the column headings appear above groups. The default format is called TablesOfGroups, which causes the heading to appear once at the beginning of each page. You can also choose a format called GroupsOfTables, which prints the column heading after each group header. These names may seem cryptic at first, but when you think about them they make sense. TableOfGroups (the default display) produces a single table that is divided into groups. GroupsOfTables makes each group look like a table in itself, with its own header.

Setting GroupRepeats lets you choose whether to suppress repeated group values. In the example in this chapter, where you grouped employees by state, you might have chosen Setting GroupRepeats

Suppress so that the name of the state would be printed only once instead of being repeated in each record.

Setting PageLayout is important if you have an unusual printer. It lets you choose the length and width of your paper. If you have a wide-carriage printer or one that uses legal-sized paper, for example, you would use this option. You can also enter the letter C as the page length, instead of a number of lines, and the report will be printed continuously, as if it were one long page. This option also lets you insert and delete page widths from the report.

Setting Margin lets you add a left margin to the report. Initially, the margin is zero, and you can enter the number of characters that you want blank at the left margin: ten characters would give you a one-inch margin. This is useful if the report is going to be bound. In the next chapter, you will use this feature with a free-form report to create a form letter.

Setting Setup lets you choose which printer to send a report to, if you have more than one printer. It also lets you add a setup string to print in boldface, large type, and so on. These setup strings are cryptic and difficult to use. If you want a report printed in special ways, it is easier to use Output File to send the report to a disk file; then use your word processor to edit the file and print it out in the style you want.

Setting Wait is useful if you need to insert a new piece of paper in your printer after each page is printed. By default, Paradox prints one page after another without pausing.

*H*elp, DO-IT!, and Cancel

Like all Paradox submenus, the Tabular Report menu also contains three familiar options that you can access through the keyboard. Choosing Help from the menu is the same as pressing the Help key (F1). Choosing DO-IT! is the same as pressing the DO-IT! key (F2). And choosing Cancel is the same as pressing Ctrl-Break.

You have now looked at the most important features of tabular reports; in the next chapter, you will go on to work with free-form reports. The Free-Form Report menu is similar to the Tabular Report menu, and much of what you learn in the next chapter will reinforce and expand on your present experience.

FREE-FORM
REPORTS

eaturing

---

CREATING
MAILING
LABELS

CONTINUOUS-FORM
LABELS

MULTICOLUMN
LABELS

CREATING FORM
LETTERS

Now that you have learned about tabular reports, you should be able to produce free-form reports easily. They are simpler to manipulate than tabular reports because they don't have columns. Also, many of the menu options for free-form reports are the same ones you used to create tabular reports.

When you create free-form reports, you just move the fields around the screen, place them where you wish, and use the editor to type the text you want around them.

Creating Free-Form Reports

First, call up the free-form report specification screen. When Paradox asks for a report description, enter "Mailing Labels," because this is the most common use of free-form reports and the one you will use as your first example.

1. From the Paradox main menu, press R and then D to select Report Design.

2. When Paradox prompts you to enter a table name, type **employee** and press Enter.

3. Press → four times to move the cursor to report 4, the first unused report, and press Enter.

4. When Paradox asks for the report description, type **Mailing Labels** and press Enter.

5. Press F to select Free-form.

Paradox displays the free-form report specification screen, shown in Figure 11.1. This screen should look familiar. It resembles the tabular report specification screen except that, instead of a table band with the fields arranged in columns, it has a *form band,* with the fields arranged one above the other, as they are in the standard data entry form.

```
Designing report R4 for Employee table                Report    1/2
Report Header
....+...1Ø....+...2Ø....+...3Ø....+...4Ø....+...5Ø....+...6Ø....+...7Ø....+...8*

 —▼page

 mm/dd/yy                        Mailing Labels                 Page 99Ø

 —▼form
 First name: AAAAAAAAAAAAAAA
 Last name: AAAAAAAAAAAAAAAAAAAA
 Address: AAAAAAAAAAAAAAAAAAAAAAAAAAAAAA
 City: AAAAAAAAAAAAAAA
 State: AA
 Zip: AAAAA
 Date hired: mm/dd/yy
 Hourly wage: (999,999,999.99)
 SEAT score: 999999
 Comments: AAAAAAAAAAAAAAAAAAAAAAAAAAAAAAAAAAAAAAAAAAAAAAAAAAAAAAAAAAAAAAAAAA
 —▲form
```

Figure 11.1: The free-form report specification screen

Creating Mailing Labels

Creating free-form reports is so similar to creating tabular reports that you can learn how it's done by simply creating some mailing labels.

How to Rearrange the Fields

First, you have to erase the fields you do not need—at least, not in their current position. Then delete the field names, which you do not need on mailing labels, and use the Backspace key to place fields on the same line. Finally, since mailing labels do not need headers or footers, you delete everything from these bands.

1. Press ↓ 16 times to move the cursor to the line that contains the Date hired field. The cursor must be at the left edge of the screen. Press Ctrl-Y to erase the line; all the lines below it move up one. Then press Ctrl-Y three more times to erase the Hourly wage, SEAT score, and Comments lines.

2. To erase the field names, press ↑ once to move the cursor to the Z in Zip. Then press Del until you delete the word Zip as well as the colon and blank space following it, so the Zip field mask is at the left edge of the screen. Do not worry about deleting part of the field mask itself. If you press Del with the cursor on the initial A of the field mask, Paradox just beeps. Notice that when the cursor is on the field mask, the field name, Zip, appears in the upper-right corner of the screen. This help line becomes important when you have deleted the field name from the report.

3. Repeat step 2 five times to delete the names of the State, City, Address, Last name, and First name fields, and to pull their field masks over to the left margin. Instead of pressing Del repeatedly, you can just hold it down until Paradox beeps to tell you that you have reached the field mask, which you cannot delete. Figure 11.2 shows how the screen looks after the unneeded fields and all the field names have been deleted.

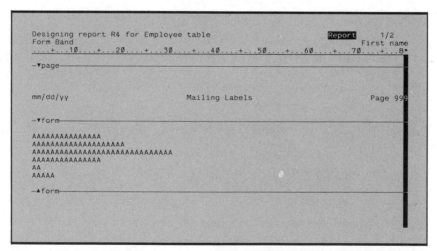

Figure 11.2: The report specification screen with only needed fields remaining

4. To put the First and Last name fields on the same line, press ↓ once to place the cursor at the beginning of the Last name field mask, then press Ins to toggle into Insert mode. Press Backspace to delete the line between the two fields, and the

field mask of Last name moves up to the same line as First name. You can delete a line in this way only when you are in Insert mode. Press the spacebar once to put a blank space between the first and last names.

5. Press ↓ three times, and then Ctrl-Home to move the cursor to the left margin, at the beginning of the State field. Press Backspace to move the State field mask to the same line as the City field mask. Type a comma followed by a blank space, to separate the City and State fields.

6. Press ↓ once, then Ctrl-Home to move the cursor to the left margin, at the beginning of the Zip field. Press Backspace to move the Zip field mask to the same line as the City and State. Type one blank space to separate it from the State.

7. Now that you have the fields in place, you can erase the report header. Press Home to move to the report header band. Press ← until the cursor is at the left edge of the screen. Then press Ctrl-Y, and the blank line in this band disappears.

8. Press ↓ once to move to the page header band. Press Ctrl-Y six times to delete the entire page header.

9. Press ↓ seven times to move to the page footer band. Press Ctrl-Y four times to eliminate all the lines in the page footer.

10. Press ↓ once to move to the report footer band. Press Ctrl-Y to eliminate the report footer. Your screen should look like Figure 11.3.

With this table, you were able to get all the fields in the right place simply by deleting unneeded lines. If you were creating mailing labels with another table—say, one that had the last name first—you might also need to select Field Place from the menu to place fields where you need them. This option works the same way in free-form reports as it does in tabular reports.

Now you have a report form that looks like it could be repeated indefinitely to create mailing labels, with the field masks representing the first and last name on one line, the address on the next line, and the city, state, and zip code on the next line. As you'll see in the next section, though, this form is not yet complete.

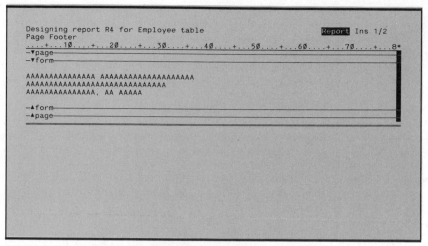

```
Designing report R4 for Employee table               Report  Ins 1/2
Page Footer
....+...10....+...20....+...30....+...40....+...50....+...60....+...70....+...8*
 —▼page————————————————————————————————————————————————————————————
   —▼form——————————————————————————————————————————————————————————

 AAAAAAAAAAAAAAA AAAAAAAAAAAAAAAAAAAAA
 AAAAAAAAAAAAAAAAAAAAAAAAAAAAAAA
 AAAAAAAAAAAAAAA, AA AAAAA

   —▲form——————————————————————————————————————————————————————————
 —▲page————————————————————————————————————————————————————————————
```

Figure 11.3: The fields arranged in the form of a mailing label

*H*ow to Squeeze Out Blank Spaces and Blank Lines

One problem with the mailing label form is that the content of the fields is generally not as large as the field masks. Since the field mask reserves 15 spaces for the first name, for example, this form would leave 11 blank spaces after the first name "John" before printing the space you added and then the last name. Likewise, it would leave spaces between the city and state.

This problem does not arise in tabular reports, where each field is in a separate column; but in free-form reports, you often want to squeeze out the extra spaces the field mask allows, so that words are right next to each other. You can do this by selecting Setting Remove-Blanks from the Report menu.

1. Press the Menu key (F10). Press S and then R to select Setting RemoveBlanks.

2. Press → once to move the cursor to FieldSqueeze and read the help line for this option. Then press Enter to select it.

3. Press Y to select Yes and confirm your choice. Paradox displays a message that says "Settings changed."

That is all there is to it. The labels will now be printed without extra spaces between words.

As you may have noticed, in addition to the FieldSqueeze option you chose, Setting RemoveBlanks also offers a LineSqueeze option, which removes blank lines.

This is useful if you have fields that only exist in some records. For example, many mailing lists include a line for a company name after the person's name. For records with no company name, though, you do not want a blank line between the person's name and address on the label. Selecting Setting RemoveBlanks LineSqueeze removes these unwanted blank lines.

How to Print Continuous-Form Labels

With one minor alteration, the layout that you have now will work with single-column labels, which are generally used with dot-matrix printers. These labels come in a continuous form; they are not divided into separate pages. To make Paradox print a continuous single column of labels without spaces between pages, you need to select Setting PageLayout Length from the Report menu. When Paradox asks how many lines to the page, press C, which stands for continuous, and then press Enter.

Labels come in different sizes, and you might have to add extra blank lines above or below the record in the report form to space the records properly on your label paper. You can insert these by pressing Enter when you are in Insert mode. If you have a wide label, you might also want to choose Setting Margin from the Report menu to add a margin of ten or fifteen spaces (an inch or an inch and a half) so the records print in the center of the labels, instead of at their left edge.

How to Print Labels Across the Page

On the other hand, you might need to adjust this report for the label paper that is usually used with laser printers, which has multiple columns and is on separate pages rather than on a continuous form.

To print multicolumn labels, set the page width to the width of one column of labels on your paper. Then choose Setting Labels from the

Report menu. This choice makes Paradox print the page widths next to each other on a single page, rather than on separate pages.

An example will make this clear. Assume you have labels that are two across on the page. In that case, the width of each column on your label paper is 40 spaces—half of the total spaces across the page.

1. Press the Menu key (F10). Press S, P, and then W to select Setting PageLayout Width; then Backspace twice to delete the suggested page width of 80.

2. Type **40** and press Enter. Notice that Paradox places the dark line representing the page edge in the center of the screen, as shown in Figure 11.4. The screen now contains two page widths, each numbered from 0 to 40, across the top of the screen.

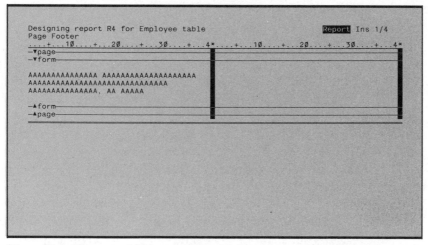

Figure 11.4: The page width narrowed to 40 characters

3. Press the Menu key (F10). Press S and then L to choose Setting Labels, then press Y to confirm the choice. Paradox displays a message saying "Label status has been recorded."

4. Press the Menu key (F10). Press O and then S to select Output Screen. Notice that the names and addresses are displayed two across on the screen, as two-column mailing labels should be printed (see Figure 11.5). Keep pressing Enter until you return to the report specification screen.

```
Alice Channing                    Sally Bean
505 Haight St.                    1465 Oak St.
San Francisco, CA 94122           Yonkers, NY 10715

Jane Walker                       Robert Lin
848 Broadway                      457 First St.
San Raphael, CA 94901             Paramus, NJ 07652

Andrea Norton                     George Silk
2311 First St.                    237 Edison st.
Mill Valley, CA 94945             New Brusnwick, NJ 08901

Samuel Smithson                   Rosalyn Rogers
203 West St.                      2242 Pensylvania Ave.
Rye, NY 10580                     Mt. Vernon, NY 10507

William Channing                  Alice Walter
22 The Circle                     326 B. 31 St.
Ross, CA 94957                    Far Rockaway, NY 11601

Henry Ware                        Evelyn Adams
1742 Dutch Elm St.                3345 Church Ave.
San Raphael, CA 94904             Brooklyn, NY 11235
```

Figure 11.5: Two-column mailing labels

Notice that the field masks just fit into half of the screen. If you were using three-across labels, you would have to narrow the field masks to fit three onto the width of the page. You would select Field Reformat to narrow the field masks, just as you do with tabular reports. In this case, you might find that the ends of the longer names and addresses have been cut off.

Some multicolumn label paper has a half-inch margin at the top of each page. Other brands have no margins; the labels extend from the top to the bottom of the page. You can adjust the top and bottom margins by adding or removing blank lines in the page header and footer. As you know, you add lines by pressing Enter when you are in Insert mode, and delete them by pressing Ctrl-Y with the cursor at the left margin. There is also continuous-form multicolumn label paper. To use this, select Setting PageLayout Length from the menu and Enter C, as you would for continuous single-column labels.

Of course, you will have to do some experimenting with the number of blank lines between records to fit the labels on your own paper. When you are experimenting, it is best to print on plain paper, to avoid wasting expensive label paper. Put this printout behind your label paper, and hold it up to the light to make sure the report fits your labels.

You might need to tinker with this report for a while to fit it on your own labels. When you are done, press DO-IT! (F2) to save the report and return to the main menu.

Creating Form Letters

The other major use of free-form reports is to create form letters. Say, for example, that you are giving each employee a bonus equal to 20 hours of wages. You can use the free-form report screen as a simple word processor to write a personalized letter to each person.

1. If you are not already at the Paradox main menu, press the Menu key (F10). Press R and then D to select Report Design. When Paradox asks you for the name of a table, type **employee** and press Enter.

2. Move the cursor to 5, the first unused report, and press Enter. When Paradox asks for the Report description, type **Form Letter Announcing Bonus** and press Enter, then press F to select Free-form.

3. Since business letters begin with the recipient's name and address and do not need a header or footer on each page, repeat all the steps you used in the section at the beginning of this chapter titled "How to Rearrange the Fields." Delete the unneeded fields and all the field names. Place the first and last name on the first line, the address on the next, and the city, state and zip code on the third line. Then delete the headers and footers. When you are done, you will again have a form that looks like the single-column mailing label form illustrated in Figure 11.3. You should be in Insert mode, and your cursor should be at the bottom of the screen.

4. Since this is a letter, add a left margin, so the text does not print flush against the left edge of the page. The standard margin in a letter is one inch (ten spaces). Press the Menu key (F10). Press S and then M to select Setting Margin. Paradox asks for the width of the left margin and suggests 0, the current width. Press Backspace to delete the 0. Type **10** and press

Enter. The field masks move ten spaces to the right, and a message confirms the report margin has been changed, as in Figure 11.6.

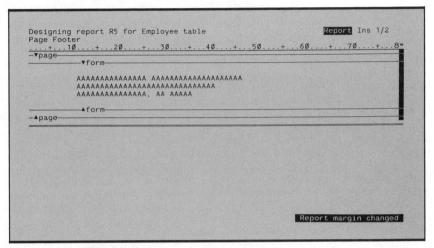

```
Designing report R5 for Employee table                          Report  Ins 1/2
Page Footer
....+...1Ø....+...2Ø....+...3Ø....+...4Ø....+...5Ø....+...6Ø....+...7Ø....+...8*
—▼page—————————————————————————————————————————————————————————————————————
—————————▼form—————————————————————————————————————————————————————————————

          AAAAAAAAAAAAAAA AAAAAAAAAAAAAAAAAAAAA
          AAAAAAAAAAAAAAAAAAAAAAAAAAAAAAAAAA
          AAAAAAAAAAAAAAA, AA AAAAA

—————————▲form—————————————————————————————————————————————————————————————
—▲page—————————————————————————————————————————————————————————————————————




                                                          Report margin changed
```

Figure 11.6: *Adding a left margin*

5. Press ↑ twice to move the cursor to the form band, on the line below the field masks. Make sure you are in Insert mode and press Enter to add an extra line to the form band.

6. Type **Dear Employee:** and press Enter twice. Type **It is our pleasure to announce that, because we have increased** and press Enter. Then type **efficiency and cut costs by installing our new computer system,** and press Enter. Type **we are able to offer our employees a bonus this year,** and press Enter twice to start a new paragraph. Then type **Your bonus will be $.**

7. Press the Menu key (F10). Press F, P, and then C to select Field Place Calculated. When Paradox asks for an expression, type **20 * [Hourly wage]** and press Enter. Press Enter again to indicate that the field mask should begin where the cursor is now positioned.

8. Since no one's bonus will be more than $1,000, press ← nine times to shorten the field mask to three digits and press Enter.

Press Enter again to confirm the suggested two decimal places.

9. Press Ctrl-End to move the cursor to the end of the line. Type a period to end the sentence, press Enter twice to start a new paragraph, and then type **We are pleased that you are a long-term employee who has been** and press Enter. Type **with our company ever since**.

10. Press the Menu key (F10). Press F, P, and then R to select Field Place Regular. A menu appears, listing the names of all the table's fields. Press → six times to move the cursor to Date hired and press Enter. Press → once to move the cursor to the *M o n t h dd, yyyy* format and press Enter. (Paradox stretches the word *month* so the field mask is long enough to hold the name of any month.)

11. When Paradox asks you to place the field, press → once to begin the field one space to the right of the last word you typed, and press Enter. Type **, and we hope** and press Enter, then type **you stay with us for many more years.** and press Enter twice.

12. Hold the spacebar down until the cursor is about two-thirds of the way across the screen, where you want the closing to be. Type **Very sincerely yours,** and press Enter three times. Press the spacebar until the cursor is lined up under the *V* of Very Sincerely, Type **Harden Grypp, President** and press Enter.

13. Since you want each form letter to be printed on a separate page, type **PAGEBREAK** in capital letters at the left margin.

14. To insert the current date at the beginning of the letter, lined up above "Very sincerely yours," first use the arrow keys to move the cursor to the *V* of "Very sincerely yours." Then press Home to move to the top line of the screen, above the *V.* Press ↓ twice to move the cursor into the form band.

15. Press the Menu key (F10). Press F, P, and then D to select Field Place Date. Press → once and press Enter to choose the fully written out format. Press Enter again to place the date where the cursor is and once more to add a blank line between the date and the address. Your screen should now look like Figure 11.7.

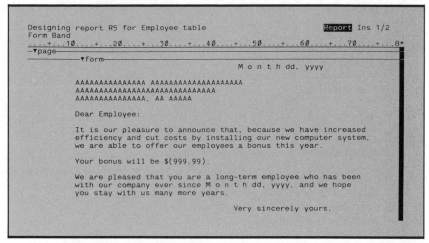

```
Designing report R5 for Employee table                    Report  Ins 1/2
Form Band
....+...1Ø....+...2Ø....+...3Ø....+...4Ø....+...5Ø....+...6Ø....+...7Ø....+...8*
 ─▾page─────────────────────────────────────────────────────────────────────
              ─▾form──────────────────────────────────────
                                           M o n t h dd, yyyy

              AAAAAAAAAAAAAAA AAAAAAAAAAAAAAAAAAAAA
              AAAAAAAAAAAAAAAAAAAAAAAAAAAAAAA
              AAAAAAAAAAAAAA, AA AAAAA

              Dear Employee:

              It is our pleasure to announce that, because we have increased
              efficiency and cut costs by installing our new computer system,
              we are able to offer our employees a bonus this year.

              Your bonus will be $(999.99).

              We are pleased that you are a long-term employee who has been
              with our company ever since M o n t h dd, yyyy, and we hope
              you stay with us many more years.

                                           Very sincerely yours,
```

Figure 11.7: The report specification for a form letter (blank lines must be added to allow space for the letterhead)

16. Press the Menu key (F10). Press S, R, F, and then Y to select Setting RemoveBlanks FieldSqueeze Yes.

17. To see the output, press the Menu key (F10), press O, and then S. Unfortunately, the screen display does not show the blank lines at the end of each page; it places the date of one page directly below the signature of the previous page. If you sent this report to the printer, though, it would print each form letter on a separate page, assuming that you put PAGEBREAK in the right place. Figure 11.8 shows a typical form letter.

18. Press DO-IT! (F2) to save this report, and if you want to take a break, press E and then Y to exit from Paradox.

If the screen output looks good, the personalized letters are ready to be printed and sent to Mr. Grypp for his signature.

The Paradox report editor is not a very sophisticated word processor. For example, you have to press Enter at the end of each line of text; it does not automatically move to the next line as most editors do. This can cause trouble if you need to make changes in the letter, because you have to justify the lines by hand. If you try to add or widen a margin after you have entered the letter, Paradox will not change the margin and justify the text automatically, as virtually any

```
                                    July 14, 1990

Alice Channing
505 Haight St.
San Francisco, CA 94122

Dear Employee:

It is our pleasure to announce that, because we have increased
efficiency and cut costs by installing our new computer system,
we are able to offer our employees a bonus this year.

Your bonus will be 89.00.

We are pleased that you are a long-term employee who has been
with our company ever since July 14, 1990, and we hope
you stay with us for many more years.

                                Very sincerely yours,

                                Harden Grypp, President
```

Figure 11.8: A typical form letter

word processor would do. It will not change the margin at all unless you first change the length of all of the lines to make them fit.

Because of these limitations, you should do a rough draft on your ordinary word processor before typing the finished letter into Paradox. With this precaution, Paradox is quite adequate for generating form letters.

Other Features of Free-Form Reports

Apart from what you have already learned, the Free-Form Report menu is virtually identical to the Tabular Report menu. It is possible, for example, to group records in free-form reports and to include summary fields for each group, as you did when you created tabular reports. You could create the report on employees' wages and test scores that you created in the last chapter with the same groups and group footers, but with the fields arranged free-form instead of in columns.

In fact, there are only three differences between the Free-Form and the Tabular Report menus. The TableBand option is missing from the

Free-Form Report menu. The Setting option of the Free-Form Report menu offers the RemoveBlanks and Labels options, which don't apply to tabular reports; you don't need to squeeze out blanks when fields are in separate columns, and you cannot create tabular mailing labels. Finally, the Tabular Report menu offers two relatively unimportant choices that are not available on the Free-Form Report menu: Setting Format and Setting GroupRepeat.

With the tools you have learned in the last three chapters, you can do virtually anything you want to do with either tabular or free-form reports.

RETRIEVING

DATA WITH

QUERIES

**USING THE
QUERY FORM**

**USING A
CRITERION TO
SELECT
RECORDS**

**COMPLEX
QUERIES WITH
LOGICAL AND
AND
LOGICAL OR**

**CREATING
REPORTS FROM
QUERIES**

One of the biggest advantages of storing your database in a computer is that you can quickly pull out only the data you want. When you ask for only the records that meet certain criteria, you are *querying* the database.

Most queries have simple criteria. It is common to ask for all the records that have a certain value in a field—for example, to list all the employees who live in California. It is also common to query for a range of values, say, to find all the employees with an aptitude test score over 700.

You can also make more complex queries to find records that meet more than one criterion. For example, if you are looking for someone to promote in the California office, you might want to see all the records of employees who live in California and also have an aptitude test score greater than 700.

The Basics of Using the Query Form

Many database management programs require you to write elaborate statements in a special query language to make complex queries, but Paradox lets you make even the most complex queries by simply filling out its Query form. This method of querying is called *query by example* (QBE). Rather than learning a query language and entering commands to tell the program what data you want, you simply place an example of the data you're after in the Query form.

To call up the Paradox Query form you select Ask from the main menu, as follows.

1. Make sure you are at the Paradox main menu, and press A to select Ask.

2. When Paradox asks you for the name of the table, type **employee** and press Enter. Paradox displays the screen illustrated in Figure 12.1.

The Query form lists all the fields in the specified table across the screen. Note that the form extends beyond the screen's right edge. It looks a bit like a table in Table View. In fact, you can move among the fields of the Query form in the same way you did in Table View. The

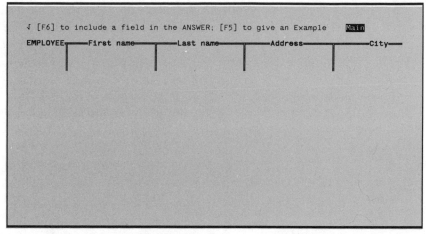

Figure 12.1: The Paradox Query form

help line at the top of the screen tells you to press the F6 key to include a field in the answer and the F5 key to give an example. You will learn about F6 in a moment. You don't have to worry about F5 at this point; the example the help line refers to is a special kind that is only used in multitable databases. You'll learn about this special type of example in Chapter 17.

As you will see, you can type entries in the fields of the Query form and edit them with the Backspace key, just as you edit table entries. You can even edit the queries in Field View by pressing the Field View key combination (Alt-F5), although the editing you do with Query forms will rarely be elaborate enough to justify this choice.

*H*ow to Select the Fields to Include in the Answer

You generally do not need to include all of the fields in a table in the answer to your query. When you fill out the Query form, put a checkmark in the fields that you want included in the answer. To do this, place the cursor in the field and press the Check key (F6).

The Check key is a toggle: if there is already a checkmark in a field and you want to remove it, put the cursor in that field and press the Check key (F6) again to make it disappear.

There is a shortcut you can use if you do want to display all the fields in the answer: press the Check key when the cursor is in the left-most field of the Query form—the field under the name of the table that is being queried—and a checkmark will appear in all the fields. This feature is also a toggle: to make all the checkmarks disappear, press the Check key again with the cursor in the leftmost field.

Suppose that you want a listing of just the names and the test scores of all the employees. Let's fill out the Query form to extract this answer.

1. Press → once to move the cursor to First name.

2. Press the Check key (F6) and a checkmark appears in that field.

3. Press → again to move the cursor to Last name, and press the Check key (F6) to place a check mark in that field.

4. Press Ctrl→ twice and → once to move the cursor to the SEAT score field and press the Check key (F6) to place a check mark there.

5. Press DO-IT! (F2).

Paradox displays a message to tell you it is processing the query. First it displays both the Query form and the Answer table; then, after a moment, it displays just the Answer table, as shown in Figure 12.2.

```
Viewing Answer table: Record 1 of 24                              Main  ▲━━
 ANSWER━┰━━First name━━━━━━━━━━━Last name━━━━━┳━SEAT score━━━
      1 ┃  Albert             Cruz             ┃     540
      2 ┃  Alice              Channing         ┃     348
      3 ┃  Alice              Walter           ┃     488
      4 ┃  Andrea             Norton           ┃     722
      5 ┃  Dianne             Lee              ┃     602
      6 ┃  Edward             Channing         ┃     325
      7 ┃  Edward             Channing         ┃     403
      8 ┃  Evelyn             Adams            ┃     466
      9 ┃  Francine           Bowen            ┃     432
     10 ┃  George             Silk             ┃     322
     11 ┃  Harriet            Noble            ┃     622
     12 ┃  Henry              Ware             ┃     664
     13 ┃  Jane               Walker           ┃     560
     14 ┃  Jean               Abbott           ┃     601
     15 ┃  Joan               Garfield         ┃     600
     16 ┃  Joseph             Miller           ┃     503
     17 ┃  Joseph             Tuckerman        ┃     421
     18 ┃  Josephine          Buckminster      ┃     533
     19 ┃  Robert             Lin              ┃     588
     20 ┃  Rosalyn            Rogers           ┃     723
     21 ┃  Sally              Bean             ┃     715
     22 ┃  Samuel             Schmaltz         ┃     321
```

Figure 12.2: The Answer table

The Answer table is another temporary Paradox table. It is like any ordinary Paradox table, except that it disappears when you exit from Paradox, unless you rename it. It also disappears when you make another query. There can only be one Answer table, and the one created by the latest query replaces any existing one.

How to Use Up Image and Down Image

Remember that, after you pressed DO-IT! in the last example, both the Query form and the Answer table were displayed simultaneously for a moment, before the Answer table filled the entire screen.

Both appeared because both are available to you. In fact, if you had a smaller Answer table, both would remain on the screen. In most cases, the Answer table is large enough to fill the entire screen and crowd out the Query form, but you can still move between them by using the Up Image key (F3) and the Down Image key (F4).

1. Press the Up Image key (F3). The Answer table moves down a bit to make room for the Query form, which appears above it. Notice that the lines around the Query form are now brighter than the lines around the Answer table to show that the Query form is active and the Answer table is not. Also, the cursor is in the Query form.

2. Press Ctrl-Home to move the cursor to the left edge of the Query form. Now, you can clearly see both the form and the table at once, as shown in Figure 12.3.

3. Press the Down Image key (F4), and the Answer table again fills the entire screen.

Being able to use the Up and Down Image keys makes it easier to edit your queries. If the Answer table does not come out right, you can press the Up Image key and edit the Query form while looking at the Answer table to remind you of where the original query went wrong.

You will find that you often use this process to improve your queries. After making a query and seeing the Answer table, you will think of other criteria to add to it that will make the answer more useful.

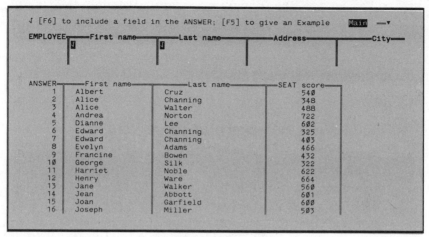

Figure 12.3: The Query form and the Answer table

How to Manipulate the Answer Table

Notice that the Answer table is listed in alphabetical order by first name. The Answer table is always sorted by its first field, with the fields to the right used as tie-breakers.

You can also sort a field in descending order, by pressing the Check Descending key combination (Ctrl-F6) instead of the Check key alone (F6) to include each field in the answer. When you do this, a check-mark with a small downward-pointing arrow to its right appears in the fields.

Of course, none of this automatic sorting does you much good when you have the First name field in the left column, but want the listing alphabetized by last name. There is an advanced Paradox feature that makes the queries sensitive to rotation of the fields on the Query form, so that the list would be alphabetized properly if you made Last name the leftmost field in the Query form; but this is a fairly sophisticated procedure that involves using the Paradox Custom Configuration program.

Fortunately, there is a much simpler way to deal with the problem: the Answer table produced by a query is like any other table, and that means you can sort it.

1. Press the Menu key (F10). Then press M and S to select Modify Sort.

2. When Paradox asks for the name of the table to sort, press Enter to get a list of the tables. You will see that Answer is included in the list, along with the Employee and Emp-Stat tables that you've created. Press Enter again to select Answer.

3. Press Enter once more to place the results in the same table. The Sort form, which you learned about in Chapter 7, appears, with the cursor next to the First name field.

4. Press 2 to make First name the tie-breaker and press ↓ to move the cursor to the Last name field. Now press 1 to make Last name the main field for your sort. The screen should look like Figure 12.4.

5. Press DO-IT! (F2).

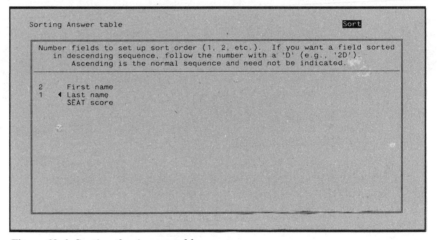

Figure 12.4: *Sorting the Answer table*

After a moment, the Answer table reappears, alphabetized by last name. (First, both the Query form and the Answer table are displayed for a second, to remind you that both are available.)

You can see the extra power you get by treating the Answer table as an ordinary table. This power also makes it possible to change the Answer table so it is no longer identical to the table you queried; you have to be cautious when you work with this table.

How to Include Repetitious Records

If you use a checkmark to indicate the fields you want to include, the Answer table will skip records that repeat the same data. If you want repetitious records included, use the Check Plus key combination (Alt-F6) instead of the Check key (F6) alone.

An example will make the difference obvious. Try both ways to produce a list of the cities and states where your employees live.

1. Press Up Image (F3) to move the cursor to the Query form. The cursor should be in the far left column, under the word EMPLOYEE, where you left it the last time you used the form.

2. Press the Check key (F6) to place a checkmark in every field. Then press the Check key again to remove the checkmark from every field. You now have a blank form to work with.

3. Press Ctrl→ to move the cursor to the City field, and press the Check key (F6) to include this field in the Answer.

4. Press → once to move the cursor to the State field, and press the Check key (F6) to include it in the Answer.

5. Press DO-IT! (F2)

Notice that the new Answer table has only 19 records, as you can see in Figure 12.5. It does not have a record for each employee, because duplicate records are not included. (In fact, this Answer table is small enough that you can still see part of the Query form at the top of the screen.)

In general, this is the way you want your answer. If you need a list of the cities and states where your employees live, you usually want each city listed only once.

In the event that you need to see how many employees live in each city, you will want to repeat the city name each time there is another employee in it. To do this, use the Check Plus combination (Alt-F6).

1. Press the Up Image key (F3) to move the cursor from the Answer table up to the Query form. It will be in the State field, where you left it.

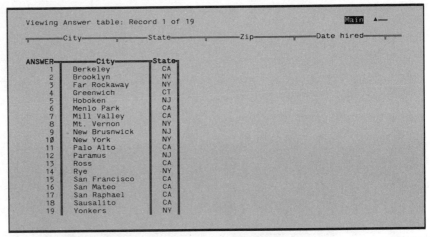

```
Viewing Answer table: Record 1 of 19                          Main ▲—
┬———City———————┬———State———————┬———Zip———————┬———Date hired———┬
 ANSWER┬————————City————————┬————State┐
     1 │ Berkeley           │ CA
     2 │ Brooklyn           │ NY
     3 │ Far Rockaway       │ NY
     4 │ Greenwich          │ CT
     5 │ Hoboken            │ NJ
     6 │ Menlo Park         │ CA
     7 │ Mill Valley        │ CA
     8 │ Mt. Vernon         │ NY
     9 │ New Brusnwick      │ NJ
    1Ø │ New York           │ NY
    11 │ Palo Alto          │ CA
    12 │ Paramus            │ NJ
    13 │ Ross               │ CA
    14 │ Rye                │ NY
    15 │ San Francisco      │ CA
    16 │ San Mateo          │ CA
    17 │ San Raphael        │ CA
    18 │ Sausalito          │ CA
    19 │ Yonkers            │ NY
```

Figure 12.5: The answer to a query using the checkmark

2. Press ← to move the cursor to the City field.

3. Press the Check key (F6) to remove the checkmark currently in the field.

4. Press the Check Plus combination (Alt-F6). A checkmark with a plus next to it will appear in the field.

5. Press DO-IT! (F2).

The Answer table produced when you use the Check Plus key combination is shown in Figure 12.6. It has has 24 records, one for each employee, so you can see which cities have more than one employee in them.

When you use Check Plus, the Answer table is not sorted. If you were really trying to analyze how many employees were in each city, you would probably want to choose Modify Sort to sort this Answer table by city.

You can take advantage of this feature of the Check Plus combination if you are querying a table that is already sorted in the order you want the Answer table in. Use all check pluses instead of all checks, and the original order will not be changed.

```
 Viewing Answer table: Record 1 of 24                    Main  ▲━━━

   ANSWER━━━━━━City━━━━━━━State━
         1      San Francisco      CA
         2      Yonkers            NY
         3      San Francisco      CA
         4      Menlo Park         CA
         5      San Raphael        CA
         6      Paramus            NJ
         7      Berkeley           CA
         8      Hoboken            NJ
         9      Mill Valley        CA
        10      New Brusnwick      NJ
        11      Palo Alto          CA
        12      Brooklyn           NY
        13      Rye                NY
        14      Mt. Vernon         NY
        15      San Mateo          CA
        16      New York           NY
        17      Ross               CA
        18      Far Rockaway       NY
        19      Mill Valley        CA
        20      Sausalito          CA
        21      San Raphael        CA
        22      Brooklyn           NY
```

Figure 12.6: The answer to a query using a check and a plus

Using Simple Criteria to Select Records

Now that you have learned the basics, you can begin to take advantage of the power of Paradox queries by selecting only the records that you want to see.

First, you will look at queries that use only one criterion to choose records. This criterion could be a single value, such as all the records from a certain state, or a range of values, such as all the workers with test scores greater than a certain number. As you will see, Paradox even lets you select records with values that are similar to, but not necessarily identical to, some value.

How to Select Records that Match a Value

If the criterion is a single value, all you have to do is type that value in the appropriate field. The Answer table will include only the records that match it.

Let's say that you want a list of cities and states where employees live, like the one that you just created, but containing only the cities in New York State.

1. Press the Up Image key (F3) to move the cursor to the Query form. The cursor should be in the City field, where you left it.

2. Press → once to move the cursor to the State field, to the right of the checkmark.

3. Type **NY** to select only records with that value in their State field.

4. Press DO-IT! (F2).

Now you have a listing of only the cities in New York State, as illustrated in Figure 12.7. Because you left the check plus in the City field, repetitious city names are included.

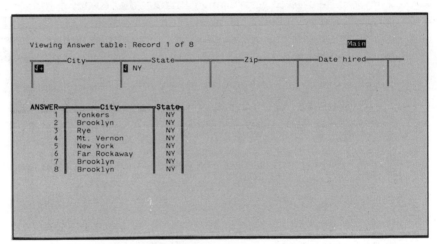

Figure 12.7: The answer to a query that matches a single value

You can do the same with any field; just type a value in that field on the Query form, and only records that match that value will be included in the Answer table.

*H*ow to Select Records with a Range of Values

Selecting records with a range of values is no more difficult than selecting records with an exact value. You simply type a criterion that includes one of the following range operators:

>	Greater than
<	Less than
> =	Greater than or equal to
< =	Less than or equal to

You can easily see how these range operators could be used with number fields. If you wanted to list employees with test scores of 600 or more, for example, you would type > = **600** in the SEAT score field.

Range operators can also be used for alphanumeric and date fields. They can be used to get a listing of names that comes before or after the criterion in alphabetical order, although this is rarely useful. They can also be used to get records with certain dates, and this often is useful. For example, you might need the names of all employees hired since 1985.

1. Press the Up Image key (F3) to move the cursor to the Query form. The cursor should be in the State field, where you left it.

2. Press Backspace twice to delete NY from this field and press the Check key (F6) to remove the checkmark.

3. Press ← once to move the cursor to the City field and press the Check key (F6) to remove the check plus from it.

4. Press Ctrl← and then press → once to move to the First name field.

5. Press the Check key (F6). Then press → once to move the cursor to the Last name field, and press the Check key again.

6. Press → five times to move the cursor to the Date hired field. Then press the Check key (F6) to include this field in the result.

7. Remain in the Date hired field and type > = **1/1/85**.

8. Press DO-IT! (F2).

The Answer table will include the names of the ten employees hired since 1985, as shown in Figure 12.8.

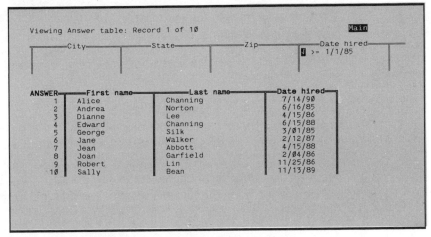

Figure 12.8: The answer to a query for a range of values

Remember that you must be precise when you use the range operators. In common speech, when you say that you want the people hired since 1985, you usually mean to include those hired during 1985; when you say you want people with a test score greater than 600, you also want to include those whose score is exactly 600. Speaking colloquially, you say greater than, but you must actually use the greater-than-or-equal-to operator to include records that are right on the boundary.

*H*ow to Make Fuzzy Queries

There are times when you cannot remember exactly what value you are searching for. In this situation, Paradox's *like* operator is invaluable.

Let's say you know there are a few employees with the same name. It is something like Caning, but you cannot remember it exactly.

1. Press the Up Image key (F3) to move the cursor to the Query form.

2. Press Ctrl-Backspace to delete the entire criterion in the Date hired field, and press the Check key (F6) to delete the checkmark in the field.

3. Press ← five times to move the cursor to the Last name field, and type **like caning**.

4. Press DO-IT! (F2). Paradox lists the three Channings in the table.

The like operator is a boon to poor spellers.

You can also make "fuzzy" queries by using the same wildcard characters in Query forms that you've already used with the Zoom and Zoom Next keys. The at sign (@) stands for any single character, and two periods (..) stand for any number of characters from zero up. Thus, if you put the criterion Sm@th.. in the Last name field, it would match Smith, Smyth, Smythe, Smathers, Smithson, Smothers, and so on.

Creating Complex Queries

Although they are not as common as simple queries, you will find that there will be times when you want to make complex queries, with more than one criterion. The criteria can be related to each other in several ways.

For example, to find a trainee for a difficult job opening in your California office, you might want to query for all employees who live in California and have an aptitude test score of more than 700. These criteria are related by what is called a logical AND. That is, both conditions must be true for the record to be included. The employee must be a California resident, and also have a high test score.

On the other hand, you might want to list all the employees who work in your New York office; these people either live in New York or commute from New Jersey or Connecticut. To do this, you use criteria that are related by a logical OR. If any of the conditions is satisfied, the record is included. The employee may either live in either New York, New Jersey, or Connecticut.

Once you know how to use the logical AND and the logical OR, it is easy to combine them. For example, to find a trainee for a difficult job in your New York office, you would look for an employee whose test score is over 700 and who lives in either New York, New Jersey, or Connecticut.

*H*ow to Use the Logical AND

To use the logical AND—that is, to find records that meet more than one criterion—you simply type both criteria on the same line.

Try finding the employees who live in California and have a test score over 700.

1. Press the Up Image (F3) key to move to the Query form.

2. The cursor should already be on the Last name field. Press Ctrl-Backspace to remove the criterion you put there last time, but leave the checkmark in the field.

3. Press → three times to move the cursor to the State field, and then type **CA**. Do not press the Check key.

4. Press → four times to move the cursor to the SEAT score field, and press the Check key (F6) to include that field in the Answer table.

5. Leaving the cursor in that field, type > **700**.

6. Press DO-IT! (F2).

You will find that there is only one employee who lives in California and has a test score over 700. Notice that you did not need to include the State field in the Answer table to select records by state. But you have to rely on your memory to tell you that all the employees in this table are from California—usually not a good idea in practice.

The logical AND is also used to combine two range operators in order to get values within a certain range. For example, if you want the employees with test scores between 600 and 700, then you must combine two criteria for the SEAT score field. The score must be greater than or equal to 600 and must also be less than 700 (assuming that the colloquial "between 600 and 700" actually means 600 through 699.)

When you enter two criteria in the same field, separate them with a comma, so Paradox knows where one ends and the next begins. Apart from the comma, using two criteria in a single field is just like using two criteria in two fields.

Finding the California employees with test scores from 600 through 699 requires three criteria, all related by the logical AND.

1. Press the Up Image key (F3) to move back to the Query form. The cursor should still be in the SEAT score field.

2. Press Ctrl-Backspace to delete the criterion that is there now.

3. Type **> = 600, < 700**. Remember to include the comma.

4. Press DO-IT! (F2).

The four California employees with test scores in the 600s are displayed under the Query form, as shown in Figure 12.9.

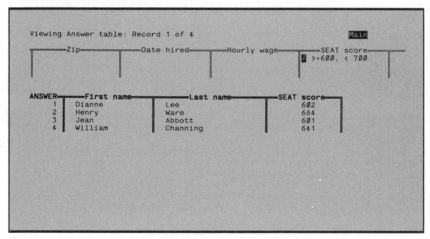

Figure 12.9: Using the logical AND to find a range of values

*H*ow to Use the Logical OR

There are two ways to indicate a logical OR in Paradox queries. The easy way is to use the OR operator, which you do in the same way you use the comma for the logical AND: just put the word *or* between the two criteria. Try finding the employees who have a test score over 600 and who live in either New York, New Jersey, or Connecticut.

1. Press the Up Image key (F3) to move the cursor to the Query form. It should still be in the SEAT score field.

2. Press the Backspace key until you have deleted the comma and the second criterion in that field. Only the criterion >= 600 should remain.

3. Press ← four times to move to the State field, and press Ctrl-Backspace to delete the criterion that is now in that field.

4. Type **NY or NJ or CT**. Press the Check key (F6) to include the State field in the Answer table. Notice that the checkmark appears before the states' names, even though you pressed the Check key after typing them.

5. Press DO-IT! (F2).

Paradox displays the four people who meet these criteria, as you can see in Figure 12.10.

Notice that this query combines a logical AND with a logical OR. It shows employees who have a score over 600 and live in New York, New Jersey, or Connecticut. Paradox makes it so easy to create this sort of complex query that you can do it almost without thinking.

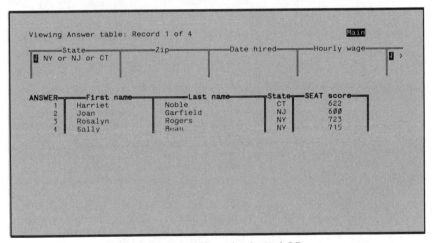

Figure 12.10: Combining a logical AND with a logical OR

There are times when the criteria you want to use are complex enough that the logical OR cannot be entered on a single line. For example, suppose you are looking for trainees on both the East and West Coasts, but that you have lower standards in the California office. You might want the records for employees who have a test score over 500 and live in California, or who have a test score over 600 and live in New York, New Jersey, or Connecticut.

In this case, you can indicate the logical OR by adding a second line to the query.

1. Press the Up Image (F3) key to move the cursor to the Query form. Then press Ctrl← to move the cursor to the First name field.

2. Press ↓ once to move the cursor to the second line, and press the Check key (F6) to place a checkmark on the second line of the First name field.

3. Press → once to move the cursor to the Last name field and press the Check key (F6).

4. Press → three times to move the cursor to the State field. Press the Check key (F6), and then type **CA** in the State field.

5. Press → four times to move the cursor to the SEAT score field. Press the Check key (F6), and then type > = **500** in the SEAT score field.

6. Press DO-IT! (F2).

Notice in the Answer table, shown in Figure 12.11, that all the employees from the East Coast have scores over 600, and all those from the West Coast have scores over 500.

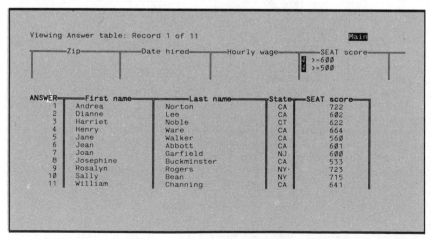

Figure 12.11: The Answer table for a complex query

You can see that it is more trouble to use a second line to represent a logical OR than it is to use the OR operator, because you have to duplicate all the checkmarks on both lines. In fact, you will rarely have occasion to use queries with more than one line. The criteria for the previous query are obviously contrived. In reality, you would probably do separate queries for the two offices. You are reaching the point where Paradox's power exceeds your ordinary needs.

Combining Reports with Queries

In most cases, you will want to print the results of your query. You already know how to do this. As you have seen, the Answer table can be manipulated like any other Paradox table, so that you can produce reports on the answers to your queries just as you do with any other table.

Instant reports are often all you need to print the answers to your queries. Since you select the fields you want to include in it, the Answer table is often narrow enough to fit onto one page, and you can print it in a usable form by simply pressing the Instant Report key combination (Alt-F7).

For more formal presentations, you can create tabular or free-form reports on the Answer table. Just select Report Design and, when Paradox asks for the name of the table, type Answer and press Enter. Then design the report as you would any other.

Remember, though, that the Answer table is temporary and disappears when you exit Paradox. If you want to do the query today and write the report tomorrow, you must change the name of the Answer table, using the Tools Rename option, which you will learn about in Part III of this book. When you leave the program and lose the Answer table, you also lose any associated report tables, so you would have to create the report from scratch if you needed it again. For this reason, it is usually best to make the Answer table permanent by changing its name before you create reports on it. In Chapter 20, you will learn how to save a query and repeat it again automatically, without filling out the Query form each time. You'll also find out how to use an existing report with data obtained from a repeated query.

Other Features of Paradox Queries

Paradox queries can be very powerful. As you have already seen with two-line queries, they can be more powerful than you will commonly need. This book does not cover the advanced features of queries, which are rarely required for day-to-day work with Paradox.

Queries can use many operators that merely duplicate the functions of reports. You can include calculated fields in queries, but if you are doing anything so elaborate, you will want to use a report specification to create more polished output, so that you can use calculated fields in the report to perform the calculations you want. Queries with calculated fields are useful in combination with Paradox graphics, an advanced feature that is not covered in this book.

There is even an *as* operator, that gives a field a different name in the Answer table than it has in the original table. Again, it is likely that, if you need output so perfect that you cannot get by with the field's original name, you will probably want to use a report specification, which lets you give the field whatever heading you want.

If you feel, after you have used Paradox for a while, that you want to make more powerful queries, read Chapter 4 in the *Paradox User's Guide*. By that time, you will be able to see which features you might find useful, and which you can skip.

Until then, you will do quite well with what you have learned plus a few extra operators listed here:

- NOT finds values that do not match. For example, if you want a list of the employees who live in any state *except* California, you can perform a query with **not CA** in the State field.

- BLANK finds fields with no value entered. If you want to find all the employees who have not taken the aptitude test, perform a query with **blank** in the SEAT score field.

- TODAY indicates today's date. If you have a table of accounts receivables with one field named Date due, and you want to know which receivables are overdue, perform a query with < **today** in the Date due field.

If you want to use one of the query key words literally, you must place it in quotation marks. For example, if you have an employee named Mrs. Blank, you can find her record by doing a query with **"Blank"** in the Last name field. If you put the word *blank* in the field without the quotation marks, you would be requesting a listing of the records with no last name.

To use special characters literally, precede them with a backslash. If you are searching for records that actually have an @ sign in one of their fields, put \@ in the field, so Paradox knows that you mean @ literally and not as a wildcard character.

You will find there are many queries that you must repeat regularly—for example, you may need to find out which payments are overdue each month. Therefore, it is useful to save queries, rather than filling out the Query form each time. As mentioned previously, the chapter on Scripts in Part III will teach you how to save queries and to automate the query process. When you repeat the same query regularly, you can also use the QuerySpeedup feature, described in Chapter 20.

Part II

MULTITABLE
DATABASES

BREAKING DOWN
YOUR DATA

ONE-TO-MANY
AND
MANY-TO-MANY
DATABASE
DESIGNS

In Part I, you learned enough to create and work with single-table databases, which are sufficient for many business applications.

After reading this chapter and learning when multitable databases are used, you may decide that you do not have any immediate need for them and are ready to apply what you have already learned. If so, you can skip the rest of this section for now, and get down to work setting up your own database application. Look at Part III of this book while you are setting up your own application. You will find Chapter 18, "Tools for Managing Files," indispensable; and Chapter 20, "Using Paradox Scripts," will save you time. Apart from these extra topics, though, you may have already learned everything you need for your work.

Before you decide to skip Part II, however, at least look through this chapter to learn when multitable databases are used. Reading it will help you decide whether a single-table database is enough for your needs. Even if it is, you will probably need a multitable database for some application in the future. When that time comes, you will be better off if you recognize immediately that an application demands a multitable database, because trying to squeeze a multitable application into a single table can create endless difficulties. Then you can come back to this book and learn to set up multitable databases using Paradox.

Understanding Database Design

Working with multitable databases involves data *normalization*— that is, breaking complex data into several tables. More advanced books include detailed discussions of database normalization theory. What you need to know in practice, though, is mostly a matter of common sense. You simply have to remember that the goal is to eliminate unnecessary repetition of data.

One-to-Many Database Design

Let's say that you want to expand the employee database you have been working on up to this point in order to keep a record of how many hours the employees worked each week. Your first impulse might be to add extra fields to the Employee table to hold the number of hours worked and the date the week ends. Just adding these extra fields to the same table, though, would require repeating the entire record each week. Figure 13.1 shows a simplified version of what the table would look like if you set it up this way.

You can see that you would need 12 records to record four weeks of work-hours for just three of your employees, and that most of the data is simply repeated. Imagine how much unnecessary data there would be in this table if you had to record years of weekly work-hours for all your employees. Apart from the disk space needed to store the extra data, think of the time it would take to enter it.

You might consider adding 52 additional fields to each record, one for each week's work-hours, but this would also create problems. The table would be so large that it would become unwieldy to work with. If new employees were hired, they would have blank spaces in all the earlier weeks. And after the 52 weeks ended, you would have to add another 52 fields to the table for the next year's work-hours.

These problems arise because there are many weeks of work-hours to record for each employee. This is called a *one-to-many* relationship.

The way to break down the data is to separate the one from the many—that is, separate the data that you need to record only once, such as the employee's name and address, from the data that changes and needs to be recorded each week, such as the hours worked and the

```
Viewing Employee table: Record 1 of 12                              Main

EMPLOYEE   Date      Hours      Name            Address          City
       1   8/03/90     41   Harriet Noble    34 Shady Lane     Greenwich
       2   8/03/90     46   Robert Lin       457 First St.     Paramus
       3   8/03/90     42   Evelyn Adams     3345 Church Ave   Brooklyn
       4   8/10/90     32   Harriet Noble    34 Shady Lane     Greenwich
       5   8/10/90     41   Robert Lin       457 First St.     Paramus
       6   8/10/90     40   Evelyn Adams     3345 Church Ave   Brooklyn
       7   8/17/90     38   Harriet Noble    34 Shady Lane     Greenwich
       8   8/17/90     40   Robert Lin       457 First St.     Paramus
       9   8/17/90     38   Evelyn Adams     3345 Church Ave   Brooklyn
      10   8/24/90     43   Harriet Noble    34 Shady Lane     Greenwich
      11   8/24/90     42   Robert Lin       457 First St.     Paramus
      12   8/24/90     48   Evelyn Adams     3345 Church Ave   Brooklyn
```

Figure 13.1: Incorrect database design

date that the week ends. Then you can place these two types of data in separate tables.

In order to break the data into two tables, you need a way to relate the records in one table to those in another, so you know which work-hours go with which employee. The two tables are related by using a *key field,* which is shared by both tables. Because the tables must be related to each other, this is a *relational* database.

Figure 13.2 shows a simplified example of related tables that will make it clear how the key field is used. Here, the same data that was recorded in Figure 13.1 is broken down into two tables, which are related by using Emp No (short for Employee Number) as a key field. To see how many hours Harriet Noble worked each week, first look on the Employee table to find her employee number, which is A1. Then look at the Hours table to see how many hours employee A1 worked each week. The computer can relate the two tables to each other in this way almost instantly.

The amount of space and data-entry time you save is not obvious when you look at Figures 13.1 and 13.2, because only a few weeks are recorded. To appreciate the use of multitable databases, imagine several years' worth of employee records. Placing the database in one table, as in Figure 13.1, would mean repeating each employee's name and address (and any other data that you have) hundreds of times. Breaking the data-base into two tables means that you only need to repeat each employee

```
 Viewing Employee table: Record 3 of 3                          Main

 EMPLOYEE┬Emp No┬────Name────┬─────Address─────┬───City───┬State┐
      1  │  A1  │ Harriet Noble │ 34 Shady Lane    │ Greenwich │ CT
      2  │  A2  │ Robert Lin    │ 457 First St.    │ Paramus   │ NJ
      3  │  A3  │ Evelyn Adams  │ 3345 Church Ave  │ Brooklyn  │ NY


 HOURS┬Emp No┬───Date───┬Hours┐
     1 │  A1  │ 8/03/90  │  41
     2 │  A2  │ 8/03/90  │  46
     3 │  A3  │ 8/03/90  │  42
     4 │  A1  │ 8/10/90  │  32
     5 │  A2  │ 8/10/90  │  41
     6 │  A3  │ 8/10/90  │  40
     7 │  A1  │ 8/17/90  │  38
     8 │  A2  │ 8/17/90  │  40
     9 │  A3  │ 8/17/90  │  38
    10 │  A1  │ 8/24/90  │  43
    11 │  A2  │ 8/24/90  │  42
    12 │  A3  │ 8/24/90  │  48
```

Figure 13.2: Correct database design

number hundreds of times. Over the course of a few years, you will avoid entering a tremendous amount of repetitious data.

Of course, you save even more time if there are several one-to-many relations to keep track of, as there often are in a business. You have to keep track not only of the number of hours each employee works but also of other data, such as benefits used and training courses taken. As the Introduction to this book pointed out, an employee's moving could create a major chore if you had to change the employee's address in a dozen different files. That is the way it was when records were kept on paper. On computer, though, you need only change the address in the Employee table: all the other tables use the employee number, which relates them to the Employee file and lets them use the address stored there.

It is hard to believe that anyone would set up a database like the table illustrated in Figure 13.1, where the repetition is so obvious. But there are less obvious cases where the same principle applies, and people do make this error if they are not deliberately looking for one-to-many relationships between data. I once redesigned a mailing list and contribution program set up by a computer consultant, which had just this error. The original database had a single table with fields for the name and address of each person on the mailing list and for the date and amount of the contribution.

The user was still doing the first mailing using this list, so it was not yet obvious how much trouble this database design would cause. You can imagine, though, that when somebody gave a second contribution, the data-entry person would be puzzled for a moment and then would probably decide to create an entire new record for that person. Then, when the mailing labels were generated again, there would be two mailing labels for that person. After a few mailings, the program would have so much repetition that it would be unworkable.

To avoid this sort of problem, you have to look in advance for possible one-to-many relationships and break down the data to avoid repetition.

*M*any-to-Many Database Design

The great majority of the relational databases you create will involve the one-to-many relationship. If you run a membership organization, for example, each member will pay many years' dues. If you run a wholesale business, each customer will make many purchases. If you want to record your purchases of supplies, each supplier will make many sales. In all of these cases, you have repeated transactions with each person you deal with. You will want to break down your database into one table to hold some kind of identification number (member number, customer number, or something similar) and the name and address of each person you deal with, and a second table to hold the identification number, and the date and amount of each transaction.

You should be aware, though, that databases can also involve many-to-many relationships. A typical example is the enrollment of students in classes. Each student can take many classes, and each class can have many students enrolled.

A database with a many-to-many relationship is not hard to deal with in practice. Before you work with it, you simply have to break it up into two different one-to-many relationships.

In the case of students and classes, for example, you would create a database like the simplified one shown in Figure 13.3, where there is one table with data about the students, one table with data about the classes, and one table of enrollments, which links the other two.

You can see in Figure 13.3 that students are in a one-to-many relationship with enrollments: each student can be enrolled in many classes. Likewise, classes are in a one-to-many relationship with

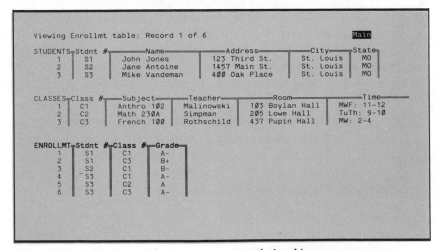

Figure 13.3: A database with a many-to-many relationship

enrollments: each class can enroll many students. The many-to-many relationship between students and classes is contained in these two one-to-many relationships.

In Figure 13.3, you can find all the classes that any student is enrolled in. For example, to find John Jones's classes, you first look on the Student table to find that he is student S1. Then you can see on the Enrollmt table that he is enrolled in classes C1 and C3. Finally, looking at the Classes table, you can see that the two classes he is enrolled in are Anthropology 102 and French 100, and you can also see who their instructors are, where they meet, and so on.

Likewise, you can see all the students who are enrolled in any class. French 100, for example, is Class C3, as you can see from the Classes table. Looking in the Enrollmt table, you can see that students S1 and S3 are enrolled in it. And you can look at the Student table to find the names and addresses of these two students.

At the minimum, a "linking" table must have two fields: the key fields of the two tables it is linking. The Enrollmt table must have Stdnt # and Class # to link the tables of students and classes. In many cases, it also has other fields. The Enrollmt table has one for the Grade, for example, since there is one grade for each student enrolled in each class.

Since you must break it down into two separate one-to-many relationships, managing a database with a many-to-many relationship does not require any skills beyond those you need to manage one-to-many relationships. It is just a more complex variation on the same theme. Since this book is for beginners, it will only deal with multi-table databases that have one-to-many relationships.

It is important that you know the difference between the two in advance, in order to avoid confusion in case you do run across a database with a many-to-many relationship. Though they are less common than one-to-many relationships, they do come up. In fact, a seemingly minor change in company policy could turn a database from one to the other.

If your company assigns one salesperson to each of its customers, for example, then you have a typical one-to-many relationship. Each salesperson deals with many customers, but each customer deals with just one salesperson. Each salesperson could keep his or her own database: one table would have the customers' numbers and their names, addresses and so on, and a second table would have the customers' numbers and the date and amount of each sale.

On the other hand, if your company lets any salesperson deal with any customer, then you are working with a many-to-many relationship. Each salesperson deals with many customers and each customer deals with many salespeople.

Because this is a many-to-many relationship, you would have to break this database into three tables. As shown in Figure 13.4, one table would hold the salespeople's social security numbers, names, addresses, and all the other data that you need to keep for each salesperson. One would hold the customers' numbers, names, addresses, the contact person, and other data that you need just once for each customer. Finally, one table would record sales: each record would contain just the social security number of the salesperson, the customer number of the customer, the amount of the sale, and the date of the sale. (Notice, incidentally, that this database uses social security numbers instead of employee numbers, as many real applications do.)

When you used this database, you would probably want to look at the two one-to-many relationships separately. For example, you might want a report to calculate the commissions you owe. For this report you would need the name and address of each salesperson plus the dates and amounts of that person's sales for the month. To generate this report, you would only need to use the Salesppl table and the Sales table, and you would list many sales for each employee.

```
Viewing Sales table: Record 1 of 10                           Main

SALESPPL┌Soc Sec Num┬──────────Name─────────┬──────Address──────┬────City────
      1 │ 051-22-6063 │  Charles Goldberger   │  434 Poplar St.   │ Columbus
      2 │ 233-41-7742 │  Mary Harris          │  503 Third St.    │ Columbus
      3 │ 458-22-5682 │  Barry Hones          │  800 Main St.     │ Columbus


CUSTOMRS┬Cust no┬──────Contact──────┬────────Name────────┬──────Address──────
      1 │  Z22  │  Albert Herman     │  AAA Acme Garage    │ 457 Maple St.
      2 │  Z23  │  Samuel Smith      │  Cheap Charlies Parts │ 631 Frontage
      3 │  Z24  │  Melvin Roderigo   │  Mel's Grease Pit   │ 800 Highway 1


SALES──┬─Soc Sec Num──┬─Cust num─┬───Date──┬────Amount────
     1 │ 458-22-5682  │   Z22    │ 6/10/90 │    337.82
     2 │ 458-22-5682  │   Z23    │ 6/11/90 │  1,165.94
     3 │ 051-22-6063  │   Z22    │ 6/12/90 │    128.52
     4 │ 233-41-7742  │   Z23    │ 6/14/90 │    214.56
     5 │ 458-22-5682  │   Z24    │ 6/16/90 │    298.67
     6 │ 051-22-6063  │   Z24    │ 6/18/90 │    430.00
     7 │ 233-41-7742  │   Z22    │ 6/21/90 │    303.00
     8 │ 458-22-5682  │   Z23    │ 6/22/90 │     97.00
     9 │ 233-41-7742  │   Z24    │ 6/25/90 │    112.02
    10 │ 051-22-6063  │   Z22    │ 6/29/90 │    202.12
```

Figure 13.4: A many-to-many database that keeps track of sales

Looking at Figure 13.4, you can begin to appreciate the work you save by computerizing. It would be impossible to break down the data in this way and keep track of this complex a database without the help of a computer: imagine trying to track all of Mary Harris' sales by looking through a long Sales file for every occurrence of her social security number. If you were still keeping records on paper, you would have to duplicate the entry of some data. You might have to enter each sale once in the file of the salesperson who made the sale, so that you could produce a report to determine the employee's commission. Then you might want to enter the same sale in the file of the customer who made the purchase, so that you could produce a report to track the trends of your sales to each of your customers.

With a computer, though, it is easy to produce a report on your employee's sales from a multitable database such as this. You would simply fill out a report form to generate a report from the Salesppl and Sales tables.

Many-to-many relationships sound complicated when you describe them, but they are clearer in practice—when they apply to your own salespeople and customers, for example. It is best not to add this extra complication when you are first learning to use multitable databases. But once you have experience working with multitable databases that have one-to-many relationships, you should not have much trouble applying the same skills to many-to-many relationships.

SETTING UP A MULTITABLE DATABASE

Now that you have learned the basic idea of breaking down data to avoid repetition, it should not be difficult to set up and work with a multitable database. You will use many of the same skills you learned for single-table databases, with slight variations.

In this chapter, you'll modify your employee database to record the number of hours employees work each week—like the one-to-many relationship you learned about in the last chapter. This requires a multitable database, so you will add a second table, the Hours table, to record the number of hours the employees worked each week. The Hours table will need an employee number field, so you will also add numbers to your Employee table to relate it to the Hours table.

*H*ow to Use Key Fields in Paradox

As a general rule, it is best to use some arbitrary value, such as an employee number, for a key field. An arbitrary value is better than a meaningful value (such as the employee's name) for two important reasons.

First, an arbitrary value does not change. If you use a meaningful value such as the employee's name as the key field, you have a major data-entry problem if the employee changes his or her name: the name must be changed in every table in the database. Typographical errors when the names are being changed might cause the name in the Hours table to vary from the one in the Employee table. The slightest difference would mean the database management program could not relate the two tables and would garble your data.

Second, you can assign an arbitrary value as the key field of each record in a way that avoids repetition. A key field must be unique. The possibility of hiring a new employee with the same name as an existing employee, makes it unwise to use names as key fields. Social security numbers are often used in a key field, because they are unique and unchanging, and must be recorded anyway. The examples you'll work on in this book will use a three-digit employee number instead of a social security number to save time on data entry.

Think about why a key field must be unique. If you understand the reason, you will understand the use of key fields in Paradox.

If two tables have a one-to-many relationship, like the Employee and Hours tables you'll be working with, then Paradox must be able to look at the employee number in a record in the Hours table and find only *one* record with the same employee number in the Employee table. If there were two records in the Employee table with that same employee number, then Paradox would have no way of knowing which one contained the name and address of the employee it was looking for.

Though there can be no repetition of the key field in the Employee table, there obviously can be repetition of the key field in the Hours table. In fact, we expect that there will be many weeks of work-hours recorded for each employee in the Hours table.

The essential thing to remember about key fields in tables that have a one-to-many relationship is that the key field cannot be repeated in more than one record of the table that is on the "one" side of the one-to-many relationship, but that it can be repeated in the table that is on the "many" side of the one-to-many relationship.

The table on the "one" side of the relationship is sometimes called a *lookup* table. Its key fields must be unique, because the program must be able to take the key field of any record from the table on the "many" side of the relationship, and look it up in the table on the "one" side of the relationship. In this example, Paradox must be able to take the employee number from any record in the Hours table and look it up in the Employee table in order to find the name and address of the employee that number refers to.

*C*reating a Key Field

When you were learning to define the structure of a Paradox table, the help screen said to place an asterisk next to the field type in order to designate it as a key field. Another point to remember when you are creating a table is that the key field must be the first field of the table. And when you are working on a table that already has a key field, remember that Paradox always keeps a table sorted on its key field: if you want to sort the table on another field, you must sort it into another table (by selecting Modify Sort New instead of Modify Sort Same from the main menu.

You now have enough background to see when to use a key field. Just remember that putting an asterisk next to the field type to designate a key field makes it impossible to put any repetitive contents into that field. Use an asterisk to designate the key field only in the lookup table—the table that is on the "one" side of the one-to-many relationship.

In this chapter, you will add an Emp No field to the Employee table and will designate it as a key field with an asterisk. You will also include a field for the employee number in the Hours table you create, but you will not designate it with an asterisk. If you did use an asterisk, you would not be able to enter more than one week's worth of work hours for each employee.

Other database management programs confuse the issue by talking about "primary keys" and "secondary keys," but the use of key fields in Paradox is very simple. You must put an asterisk next to the key field in the lookup table, where there cannot be any duplication of key fields. In the other table, you must include a field that is identical in field type to the key in the lookup table, but you cannot put an asterisk next to it. As you will see, though the employee number fields in the two tables must have the same field type, they need not have the same name, because you must relate them explicitly every time you use them together.

Using the Keyviol Table

The best way to verify that a key field in Paradox does not allow repetition is to make an error. Let's designate the Last name field as a key field in the Emp-stat table, which you created in Chapter 6. (Be careful not to use the Employee table, which you have been using throughout this book.) To do so, you have to make Last name the first field in the table and then add an asterisk next to its field type. As you'll see, Paradox puts records with repeated key fields in a temporary table called Keyviol.

1. From the Paradox main menu, Press M and then R to select Modify Restructure.

2. When Paradox asks you for the table name, type Emp-stat and press Enter. BE SURE TO TYPE EMP-STAT AND *NOT* EMPLOYEE. Paradox displays the restructure screen, with

the message "Restructuring the Emp-stat table" in the upper-left corner.

3. Press Ins to insert a new field as field 1. Press → to move the cursor to the Field Name column of field 1; then type **Last name** and press Enter. Paradox displays a message to tell you it is moving the Last name field.

4. The cursor should already be in the Field Type column of the Last name field. Type * after the field type to make it a key field. Your screen should now look like Figure 14.1. Press DO-IT! (F2).

After spending a bit of time to update the table, Paradox displays the new table plus the Keyviol table it has created, as shown in Figure 14.2.

Notice that the table is sorted on Last name, and that there are no repetitions. In the original Emp-stat table, there were four Channings. In the new table, there is only one Channing: the other three have been removed from the Emp-stat table and placed in the temporary Keyviol table instead. Press the Up Image key (F3) to view the Emp-stat table, and you will see that there are only 21 records in it now, rather than the 24 that you started with.

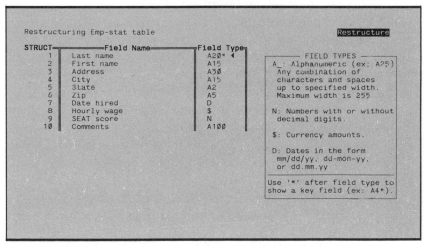

Figure 14.1: Using an asterisk to designate a key field

```
Viewing Keyviol table: Record 1 of 3                          Main  ▲—
EMP-STAT      Last name     Firs        Address              City        Sta
     6     Channing          E     180 Poplar St.         Mill Valley     C
     7     Cruz              A     1237 Flatbush Ave.     Brooklyn        N
     8     Garfield          J     4437 Elm St.           Hoboken         N
     9     Lee               D     1634 Bancroft Way      Berkeley        C
    10     Lin               R     457 First St.          Paramus         N
    11     Miller            J     2036 Park Ave.         New York        N
    12     Noble             H     34 Shady Lane          Greenwich       C
    13     Norton            A     2311 First St.         Mill Valley     C
    14     Rogers            R     2242 Pensylvania Ave.  Mt. Vernon      N
    15     Schmaltz          S     590 Ocean Ave.         Brooklyn        N
    16     Silk              G     237 Edison st.         New Brusnwick   N
    17     Smithson          S     203 West St.           Rye             N
    18     Tuckerman         J     45 Arcroft Circle      San Mateo       C
    19     Walker            J     848 Broadway           San Raphael     C
    20     Walter            A     326 B. 31 St.          Far Rockaway    N
    21     Ware              H     1742 Dutch Elm St.     San Raphael     C


KEYVIOL        Last name           First name            Address
     1    Channing              William          22 The Circle
     2    Channing              Alice            505 Haight St.
     3    Channing              Edward           505 Haight St.
```

Figure 14.2: The Keyviol table

If you had done this with a real application, you would have to edit the Keyviol table to make sure that its records no longer duplicated the key field of any record in the Emp-stat table. Then you would have to use the Tools Add option from the main menu (which you will learn about in Part III of this book) to put the records in the Keyviol table back into the Emp-stat table. If there were still duplications of the key field, Paradox would not let you add them.

Of course, it would be hard to change the last name to avoid duplication, unless you wanted to rename one employee Channing1 and another Channing2—and to refer to them by this name in all correspondence and reports generated by Paradox. You can see the advantage of using an arbitrary employee number rather than a name as a key field. If you create a duplicate by mistake, you can change an employee number without any problem.

(Incidentally, it also is possible to use multifield keys in Paradox, but doing so creates unnecessary complications. In general, they should be avoided.)

If you ever do make an error that causes Paradox to generate a Keyviol table, remember that it is another temporary table, which is discarded when you exit from Paradox or create a new Keyviol table. You must eliminate duplicate keys and add the records to the original table—or at least change the name of the Keyviol table—before you exit from Paradox, or the records in the Keyviol table will be lost. In this example, the records have been removed from the Emp-stat table, which you will be discarding later anyway, so you don't need to worry about them.

How to Create the Hours Table

As you will see, creating the Hours table for this multitable database is no different from creating any other table. In addition to fields for the date of each week and the number of hours worked, it will also need a field for the employee number, in order to relate it to the Employee table. Later you will modify the Employee table to add an employee number field, marked with an asterisk. In the Hours table, though, there will be many weeks of work hours recorded for each employee; the employee number must be repeated, so it will not be designated as a key field with an asterisk.

Is there any other field you need to add to the Hours table? Before jumping in and creating the table, analyze the database carefully. Imagine what it will be like working with this database, and try to visualize any problems that may arise.

What if you were trying to create a report at the end of the year, calculating each employee's total wages for the year. If you needed total wages for the current week, you could use the hourly wage figure from the Employee table and multiply it by the number of hours worked to figure the total wage. During the year, though, Mr. Grypp might have given some of his employees a raise, so you could not assume that the hourly wage listed in the Employee table at the end of the year was the correct one for calculating total annual wages.

Though it is not obvious at first, the employee and the hourly wage are also in a one-to-many relationship. One employee may have many different wages during his or her career. The hourly wage also belongs in the Hours table—the table that is on the many side of the one-to-many relationship.

Once you have thought out what should be in the Hours table, you will have no trouble creating it. The process is identical to the one you used to create your first table at the beginning of this book.

1. Be sure you are at the Paradox main menu, and press C to select Create. When Paradox asks you to enter the new table name, type **Hours** and press Enter.

2. The Create screen appears with the cursor in the Field Name column of field 1. Type **Emp no** and press Enter. Type **A3** as the field type, and press Enter again.

3. For the name of field 2, type **Week ends** and press Enter. Type **D** to make the field type Date, and press Enter.

4. Type **Hours worked** as the name of field 3 and press Enter. Type **N** to make the field type Numeric, and press Enter.

5. Type **Hourly wage** as the name of field 4 and press Enter. As you will see later, this field must have exactly the same name and field type as the corresponding field in the Employee table so that it can be filled in automatically.

6. Type **$** to make the field type Currency. Your screen should look like Figure 14.3. Press DO-IT! (F2) to save the structure.

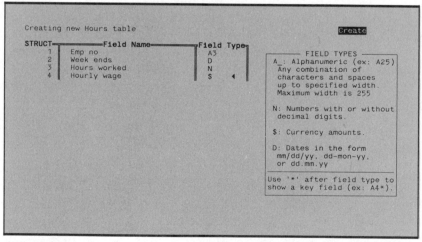

Figure 14.3: The structure of the Hours table

That's all there is to creating the Hours table.

How to Modify the Employee Table

To add the employee number as a key field to the Employee table, simply select Modify Restructure from the main menu. You must insert the key field as the first field of the table.

You will notice one minor difference from the restructuring you did before. Before it lets you restructure the Employee table, Paradox asks if you are willing to overwrite existing Problems or Keyviol tables (assuming you have not exited from the program since the last restructuring, which created the current Keyviol table). If a key violation occurred when you were restructuring this table, as one did during your last restructuring, Paradox would create a new Keyviol table, which would replace the existing one. The program asks you to confirm that you are willing to overwrite the Keyviol table to make sure that you do not lose the data in the existing Keyviol table by mistake.

Paradox forces you to add this new key field in a slightly roundabout way. If you added the employee number field and made it a key field immediately, all the records would be blank when you pressed DO-IT! to create the new structure. Paradox would interpret all these blanks as the same value, and would put all the records except one in a Keyviol table.

To avoid this problem, you must first add the employee number field as an ordinary, non-key field. Then you can add a different value to it in each record, and finally you can restructure the table a second time to make this field a key field. Of course, this problem would not come up if you were creating a multitable database from scratch, but you do have to bear it in mind when you are converting from a single-table to a multitable database.

1. Press the Menu key (F10) to call up the main menu. Press M and then R to select Modify Restructure. When Paradox asks you for the name of the table, type **employee** and press Enter.

2. You must confirm that you are willing to overwrite the Keyviol table. The cursor is on Cancel, which would abort the process of restructuring, so that you could deal with the Keyviol table. Press → to move the cursor to OK. Notice the help

line, and press Enter. When the restructure screen appears, press Ins to insert a new field 1.

3. Press → to move the cursor to the Field Name column of field one, which is now blank. Type **Emp No** and press Enter. Notice that the name of the key field here is not identical to the name of the key field in the Hours table, where it is Emp no. Though it is common to make the name of the key fields the same in the tables of a multitable database, this example uses slightly different names to emphasize the point that they do not have to be the same.

4. Type **A3** as the field type. Do not include an asterisk. Your screen should look like Figure 14.4. Note that the key fields must have the same data type in the two tables. When you relate them, Paradox will show an error if the data types are not identical.

5. Press DO-IT! (F2). Paradox makes the changes and displays the restructured Employee table. Press the Edit key (F9) so you can make entries in this table. Then press → to move the cursor to the Emp No field of record 1.

6. Type **A01** and press ↓ to move to the Emp No field of record 2, then type **A02** and press ↓ again.

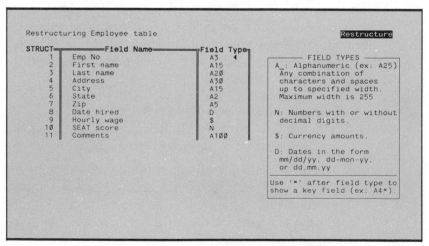

Figure 14.4: First add the Emp No field without the asterisk

7. Continue to number all the records consecutively. Since there are 24 records in the table, you should be at A24 when you reach the end. Each employee number should be the same as the record number, but with a capital A before it, as illustrated in Figure 14.5. When you are sure the numbers are correct, press DO-IT! (F2) to conclude editing.

8. Press the menu key (F10). Press M and then R to select Modify Restructure. When Paradox asks for the table name, type **employee** and press Enter. Then press O to select OK, confirming that Paradox may overwrite existing Problems or Keyviol tables.

9. When the restructure screen appears, press → twice to move the cursor to the Field Type column of field 1. Type * to designate field 1 as a key field, check that your screen matches Figure 14.6, and then press DO-IT! (F2).

If the Keyviol table that you created earlier is still in existence (if you have not exited from the program since then), Paradox displays it for an instant before showing the restructured Employee table. This does *not* mean that a new Keyviol table was created as a result of the last restructuring. The help line in the upper-left corner of your screen should say

```
Editing Employee table: Record 24 of 24                          Edit

EMPLOYEE─Emp No─      ──First name──      ──Last name──        ────Address─
      3     A03        Edward              Channing             505 Haight St.
      4     A04        Jean                Abbott               4445-2312 Technolog
      5     A05        Jane                Walker               848 Broadway
      6     A06        Robert              Lin                  457 First St.
      7     A07        Dianne              Lee                  1634 Bancroft Way
      8     A08        Joan                Garfield             4437 Elm St.
      9     A09        Andrea              Norton               2311 First St.
     10     A10        George              Silk                 237 Edison st.
     11     A11        Francine            Bowen                2113 University Ave
     12     A12        Albert              Cruz                 1237 Flatbush Ave.
     13     A13        Samuel              Smithson             203 West St.
     14     A14        Rosalyn             Rogers               2242 Pensylvania Av
     15     A15        Joseph              Tuckerman            45 Arcroft Circle
     16     A16        Joseph              Miller               2036 Park Ave.
     17     A17        William             Channing             22 The Circle
     18     A18        Alice               Walter               326 B. 31 St.
     19     A19        Edward              Channing             180 Poplar St.
     20     A20        Josephine           Buckminster          3322 Bridgeway
     21     A21        Henry               Ware                 1742 Dutch Elm St.
     22     A22        Evelyn              Adams                3345 Church Ave.
     23     A23        Harriet             Noble                34 Shady Lane
     24     A24◄       Samuel              Schmaltz             590 Ocean Ave.
```

Figure 14.5: Second, enter the values in the field

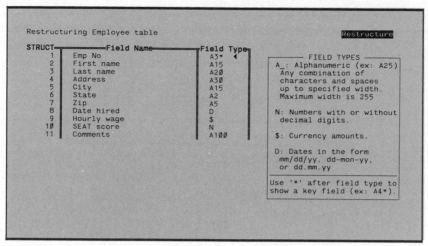

Figure 14.6: *Finally, add an asterisk to the field type*

"Viewing Employee table: Record 1 of 24." If all 24 records are still in the table, no key violation has occurred. To avoid confusion, it is probably best to get rid of any old Keyviol table before you restructure a table in a way that could create a new one. You can do this either by exiting from Paradox and starting it again, or by using the Tools option from the main menu, which you will learn about in Part III. You should at least note the number of records in an existing table before you restructure it, so you can be sure none is lost.

It is also good practice to back up a table that has data in it before restructuring. If your electrical power fails while Paradox is in the midst of restructuring, you could lose data. You will learn to back up a file in Chapter 18.

You have succeeded in setting up a multitable database in Paradox, and have learned about the minor perils to avoid along the way. As you can see, no cryptic programming commands are required to relate two tables in Paradox. You related the Employee table to the Hours table simply by giving the two tables a common field with the same data type and placing an asterisk in the key field of the Employee table, which is on the "one" side of the one-to-many relationship.

ADDING DATA TO A MULTITABLE DATABASE

USING DATAENTRY AND COEDIT

ADDING VALID RECORDS TO A "MANY" SIDE TABLE

FILLING IN FIELDS

Entering data in a multitable database is like entering data in a single-table database, but with one important difference: in a multitable database, you must be sure to protect the integrity of the key fields. Key fields can cause two problems, one in the lookup table on the "one" side of the one-to-many relationship, and another in the table on the "many" side of the relationship.

In the lookup table, you might try to add an entry with a key field that is the same as an existing one. For example, you might try to give a new employee the same employee number as an old employee. If this were possible, the program would not know which of these two employees the records in the other table applied to.

In the other table, the table on the "many" side of the relationship, there would be a problem if you mistakenly entered a value in the common field that did not exist in the lookup table. For example, you might make an entry in the Hours table but mistakenly use an employee number that did not exist in the Employee table; then the program would not be able to tell you which employee worked those hours.

This chapter begins with a review of the procedure for viewing two tables at once. This feature is especially useful when you are working with multitable databases. Then you will modify the Hours and Employee tables, and learn the pitfalls that you must avoid when you alter tables in a one-to-many relationship.

*H*ow to View More Than One Table

Though it is not always necessary, there will probably be many occasions when you want to see both tables of a multitable database.

In general, when Paradox needs to display a new table, it uses only as much space as necessary. If the table is bigger than the screen, Paradox removes any other tables from the screen to display as much of the new table as possible. On the other hand, if the new table is smaller than the screen, Paradox continues to show as much as it can of the table already on the screen.

It is easy to display more than one table, then. All you have to do is view the tables and adjust their size, using the Image TableSize option that you learned about in Chapter 8.

1. From the Paradox main menu, press V to select View. When Paradox asks you the name of the table, type **employee** and press Enter.

2. Press the Menu key (F10) to call up the main menu again. Then Press V to select View, and when Paradox asks you the name of the table, type **hours** and press Enter. Because the Hours table is empty, there is plenty of room to display the Employee table on the screen with it, as Figure 15.1 shows.

```
Viewing Hours table: Table is empty                          Main ▲—

EMPLOYEE┬Emp No┬─────First name─────────┬────Last name─────┬────────Address═
     5  │  AØ5  │ Jane                    │ Walker            │ 848 Broadway
     6  │  AØ6  │ Robert                  │ Lin               │ 457 First St.
     7  │  AØ7  │ Dianne                  │ Lee               │ 1634 Bancroft Way
     8  │  AØ8  │ Joan                    │ Garfield          │ 4437 Elm St.
     9  │  AØ9  │ Andrea                  │ Norton            │ 2311 First St.
    1Ø  │  A1Ø  │ George                  │ Silk              │ 237 Edison st.
    11  │  A11  │ Francine                │ Bowen             │ 2113 University Ave
    12  │  A12  │ Albert                  │ Cruz              │ 1237 Flatbush Ave.
    13  │  A13  │ Samuel                  │ Smithson          │ 2Ø3 West St.
    14  │  A14  │ Rosalyn                 │ Rogers            │ 2242 Pensylvania Av
    15  │  A15  │ Joseph                  │ Tuckerman         │ 45 Arcroft Circle
    16  │  A16  │ Joseph                  │ Miller            │ 2Ø36 Park Ave.
    17  │  A17  │ William                 │ Channing          │ 22 The Circle
    18  │  A18  │ Alice                   │ Walter            │ 326 B. 31 St.
    19  │  A19  │ Edward                  │ Channing          │ 18Ø Poplar St.
    2Ø  │  A2Ø  │ Josephine               │ Buckminster       │ 3322 Bridgeway
    21  │  A21  │ Henry                   │ Ware              │ 1742 Dutch Elm St.
    22  │  A22  │ Evelyn                  │ Adams             │ 3345 Church Ave.

HOURS══┬Emp no┬══Week ends══┬══Hours worked══┬══Hourly wage══┬
```

Figure 15.1: The Hours table leaves room for the Employee table

3. Press the Up Image key (F3) to move the cursor to the Employee table. Because it has more than the 22 records the screen can hold, the Employee table pushes the Hours table off the screen.

4. To view the Hours table while you have the cursor in the Employee table, you need to make the Employee table's image smaller. Press the Menu key (F10) to call up the main menu. Press I and then T to select Image TableSize.

5. Paradox tells you to use ↑ and ↓ to change the size of the table. Press ↑ 11 times, to make the Employee table smaller. The Hours table reappears below it, as you make room on the screen (see Figure 15.2). Press Enter to select this size.

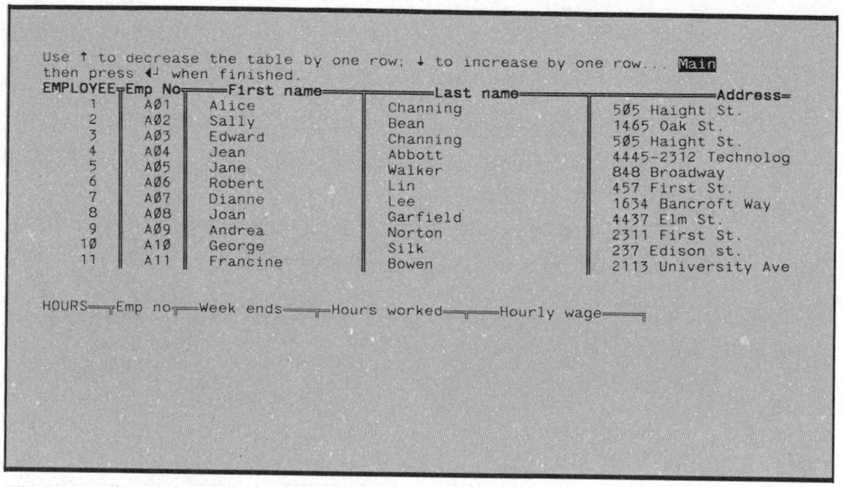

Figure 15.2: The smaller Employee table leaves room for the Hours table

You won't be using either of these tables for the moment, so let's clear the screen. Pressing the Clear Image key (F8) is a quick way to remove the table that the cursor is in from the screen.

1. Press Clear Image (F8) to get rid of the Employee table, so only the Hours table is left on the screen.

2. Press Clear Image (F8) to get rid of the Hours table and the Paradox main menu reappears.

How to Add and Edit Data

You have seen that, when you restructure an existing table by adding an asterisk to the field type of one of its fields to designate it as a key field, Paradox handles the problem of duplications by creating a Keyviol table. Unfortunately, if you modify a table using Modify Edit, Paradox does not protect your data in this way. In Edit mode, the program avoids duplication by eliminating data.

In this section you will explore the possible consequences of using Modify Edit on a keyed table, and will learn to protect your data by using Modify DataEntry or Modify Coedit instead.

The Dangers of Edit

First, let's try adding records to a keyed table using Modify Edit, so that you'll appreciate how serious the problems involved can be. (Since the records you add here will be discarded, you will not fill them out completely.)

Suppose your oldest employee has employee number A00. Add this number to the end of the Employee table to see how the table is kept sorted by key field.

1. Make sure you are in the Paradox main menu. Press M and then E to select Modify Edit. When Paradox asks for the table name, type **employee** and press Enter.

2. Press the End key to move to the last record (record 24) and press ↓ to add a blank record 25.

3. Type **A00** in the Emp No field and press Enter. Then type **oldest employee** in the First name field and press DO-IT! (F2).

The new record becomes the first record in the table, as shown in Figure 15.3, because the key field is always kept sorted.

Now, imagine that this employee has worked for you for 30 years, that you have his name and address in this table, and that you have a

EMPLOYEE	Emp No	First name	Last name	Address
1	A00	oldest employee		
2	A01	Alice	Channing	505 Haight St.
3	A02	Sally	Bean	1465 Oak St.
4	A03	Edward	Channing	505 Haight St.
5	A04	Jean	Abbott	4445-2312 Technolog
6	A05	Jane	Walker	848 Broadway
7	A06	Robert	Lin	457 First St.
8	A07	Dianne	Lee	1634 Bancroft Way
9	A08	Joan	Garfield	4437 Elm St.
10	A09	Andrea	Norton	2311 First St.
11	A10	George	Silk	237 Edison st.
12	A11	Francine	Bowen	2113 University Ave
13	A12	Albert	Cruz	1237 Flatbush Ave.
14	A13	Samuel	Smithson	203 West St.
15	A14	Rosalyn	Rogers	2242 Pensylvania Av
16	A15	Joseph	Tuckerman	45 Arcroft Circle
17	A16	Joseph	Miller	2036 Park Ave.
18	A17	William	Channing	22 The Circle
19	A18	Alice	Walter	326 B. 31 St.
20	A19	Edward	Channing	180 Poplar St.
21	A20	Josephine	Buckminster	3322 Bridgeway
22	A21	Henry	Ware	1742 Dutch Elm St.

Figure 15.3: Your oldest employee, Emp No A00

half-dozen other tables with information on how many hours he has worked, how much is in his pension fund, and so on. All these other tables, of course, do not include his name; they just have his employee number and the other data. They get his name and address from the Employee table.

Then you hire a new employee. You mean to give him the next employee number in sequence, but you make an error and press A00 instead of A25 by mistake. Let's see what happens.

1. Press the menu key (F10). Then press M and E to select Modify Edit.

2. When Paradox asks for the table name, type **employee** and press Enter. Then press the End key to move to the last record, and ↓ to add a new, blank record 26.

3. Type **A00** in the Emp No field and press Enter. Then type **new employee** in the First name field, and press DO-IT! (F2).

The new employee takes the place of your oldest employee in the first record, and your oldest employee disappears from the table without a trace. You may have noticed that the Keyviol table did not appear before the updated Employee table was displayed. In fact, when you enter data in Edit mode, no Keyviol table is created to hold duplicate data; it is simply eliminated.

Consider the possible consequences. If, for example, someone loses vital data by mistakenly adding a new customer with the same number as an existing one, it could take months, and many mistaken reports, to notice, track down, and correct the mistake. In the meantime, you would make errors in your dealings with the new customer and might well lose the old one.

*P*rotecting Your Data by Using DataEntry

Now that you've been forewarned, you can avoid this pitfall. DataEntry handles key violations much more intelligently than Edit does. Try making the same error using DataEntry.

First, return the table to the way it was before data was lost, with your oldest employee still in it. Then, try adding the record for the new employee, using DataEntry, and making the same mistake that you did last time. You will see that the consequences are not nearly as dire.

1. Press the menu key (F10). Then press M and E to select Modify Edit.

2. When Paradox asks for the table name, type **employee** and press Enter. The cursor should still be on the First name field of record 1. If it is not, use the arrow keys to move it there.

3. Press Ctrl-Backspace to erase "new employee." Then type **oldest employee** and press DO-IT! (F2).

4. Press the menu key (F10). Press M and then D to select Modify DataEntry.

5. When Paradox asks for the table name, type **employee** and press Enter. Type **A00** in the Emp No field of the Entry table and press Enter. Then type **new employee** in the First name field and press DO-IT! (F2).

Paradox docs not add the record for the new employee to the table; instead it sends it to a separate Keyviol table, as shown in Figure 15.4.

If you want to make sure that your oldest employee is still in the Employee table, press the Up Image key (F3). The cursor should still be on record 1, the oldest employee.

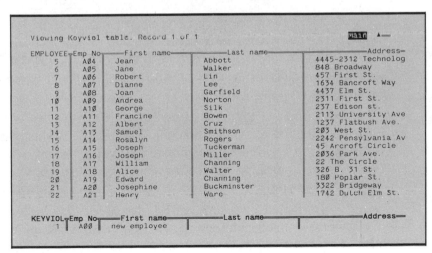

Figure 15.4: Using DataEntry to guard against data loss

*P*rotecting Your Data By Using Coedit

Using DataEntry protects you when you are adding new records. You still might have problems, though, when you want to edit existing records in the table. To change an employee's address or salary, for example, you have to move the cursor through the Emp No field, and you might inadvertently press the Backspace key and delete part of the employee number, making it identical to an existing number, so that you lose a record.

Though the possibility of this happening may be remote, it is safest to avoid the problem by using the Coedit option rather than the Edit option to edit a table with a key field designated by an asterisk.

As mentioned earlier, Coedit is intended for use on networks. It is designed to lock records, so that two people on a network cannot change the same record at the same time. If you are working on your own PC, though, you can ignore Coedit's messages about locking and posting records, and just take advantage of one of its important features: it does not destroy records that have duplicate keys without warning you first.

Try adding the new employee with a mistaken number once again, to see how Coedit handles key violations.

1. Press the menu key (F10). Then press M and E to select Modify Coedit. When Paradox asks for the name of the table to coedit, type **employee** and press Enter.

2. Press the End key to move the cursor to the last record of the table. Then press ↓ to add a new, blank record. Type **A00** in the Emp No field, press Enter, and then type **new employee** in the First name field.

3. Press DO-IT! (F2). Paradox displays a message to tell you that the key exists, as shown in Figure 15.5. If you pressed Alt-L, Paradox would eliminate the existing record with the same employee number as the new record, just as it would if you were using Edit.

4. Press Alt-K, and Paradox displays the old record in the location where you added the new record. Now press Alt-K again, and Paradox displays the new record again.

```
Coediting Employee table: Record 26 of 26                    CoEdit  ━▼
New key value conflicts with existing record
EMPLOYEE┬Emp No──────First name───────────Last name──────────────Address═
    5     A04    Jean            Abbott          4445-2312 Technolog
    6     A05    Jane            Walker          848 Broadway
    7     A06    Robert          Lin             457 First St.
    8     A07    Dianne          Lee             1634 Bancroft Way
    9     A08    Joan            Garfield        4457 Elm St.
   10     A09    Andrea          Norton          2311 First St.
   11     A10    George          Silk            237 Edison st.
   12     A11    Francine        Bowen           2113 University Ave
   13     A12    Albert          Cruz            1237 Flatbush Ave.
   14     A13    Samuel          Smithson        203 West St.
   15     A14    Rosalyn         Rogers          2242 Pensylvania Av
   16     A15    Joseph          Tuckerman       45 Arcroft Circle
   17     A16    Joseph          Miller          2036 Park Ave.
   18     A17    William         Channing        22 The Circle
   19     A18    Alice           Walter          326 B. 31 St.
   20     A19    Edward          Channing        180 Poplar St.
   21     A20    Josephine       Buckminster     3322 Bridgeway
   22     A21    Henry           Ware            1742 Dutch Elm St.
   23     A22    Evelyn          Adams           3345 Church Ave.
   24     A23    Harriet         Noble           34 Shady Lane
   25     A24    Samuel          Schmaltz        590 Ocean Ave.
      Key exists -- press [Alt][L] to confirm or [Alt][K] to see existing record
```

Figure 15.5: *How Coedit handles a key violation*

5. Press Del to delete the new record. (In a real application, of course, you would press ← to move to the Emp No field, and correct it. Then you could press DO-IT! and keep both records.)

6. Press Home to check that your oldest employee's record is still intact. Since this was just an example, press Del to delete this record and then press DO-IT! (F2).

As you can see, Alt-K is a toggle that lets you look at two records that have the same key. It is particularly useful when you are working with a large table.

Remember, if you enter a new record with the same value in the key field as an existing record, or if you change a key field so it is the same as an existing key field, Edit simply replaces the old record with the new one and deletes the old record without any warning. Coedit warns you that there is a key violation and gives you the option of deleting the old record by pressing Alt-L, or of correcting the error.

The consequences of losing a record in your lookup table can be so dire that it is probably best always to use Coedit when you are editing a table with a key field designated by an asterisk. Select Modify Coedit from the main menu, or press the Coedit key combination (Alt-F9) when you are viewing the table. Be careful not to press the Edit key (F9) by mistake.

*H*ow to Add Records to the Hours Table

Paradox has an excellent, easy-to-use method of adding records to tables on the "many" side of a one-to-many relationship. It not only protects your key fields but can also help you fill in your table.

Before you edit or add data to the Hours table—or any similar table—you should protect the integrity of your key fields by choosing ValCheck TableLookup from the Edit menu. If you choose this option, Paradox checks the validity of your entries by seeing if the value you enter also exists in the lookup table. When you enter an employee number in the Hours table, for example, Paradox makes sure that the Employee table contains that number. If you do this, you can only enter work hours for an employee who actually exists—not for a mistaken employee number that does not refer to a real employee.

Since it is hard to remember employee numbers, you will usually search for an employee's name in the Employee table first, and then enter the number in the Hours table. As you will see, ValCheck TableLookup lets you do this and then enters the number for you automatically.

In this application, you will need to fill in both the employee number and the hourly wage. (Remember that you had to add a field for the hourly wage to the Hours table, to record any changes in an employee's wage.) You can choose to automatically fill in only one field, or you can choose AllCorrespondingFields, and Paradox will automatically fill in all the fields in the table you are editing that correspond to a field in the lookup table: in this case, it will automatically fill in both the Emp no and the Hourly wage fields.

Whether you're filling one field or all corresponding fields automatically, you can choose to hide the lookup table from the user or you can let the user see the lookup table.

*V*alidating an Entry with HelpAndFill

When you set up a validity check, Paradox asks you to choose between two options: PrivateLookup and HelpAndFill. Both protect your data, but PrivateLookup hides the lookup table from the user, while HelpAndFill lets you browse through the lookup table. Private-Lookup is for programmers who are setting up data-entry systems for people who should not have access to all of the tables in the database. You'll be using the lookup table to find the values you want to enter, so you should always choose HelpAndFill. The HelpAndFill option not only checks to make sure an entry is valid; it also helps you find the values you need.

Suppose you have to enter 42 hours of work for Albert Cruz for the week ending 9/7/90—and that your boss forgot to give you his employee number.

1. Press the Clear Image Key (F8) until the screen is clear and the main menu appears. Press M and E to select Modify Edit. When Paradox asks you the name of the table to edit, type **hours** and press Enter.

2. Press the Menu key (F10). Then press V and then D to select ValCheck Define. Since the cursor is already in the Emp no field, press Enter to select it.

3. Press T to select TableLookup. When Paradox asks for the name of the table, type **employee** and press Enter.

4. Press Enter to select JustCurrentField, and then H to select HelpAndFill. Notice that Paradox tells you to press F1 for help with fill-in, as shown in Figure 15.6. Press F1 to get help. The Employee table appears, with a help line above, as shown in Figure 15.7.

5. Press ↓ to move to Albert Cruz's record. Since you will have to enter his hourly wage also, press → until you can see that his wage is $10.50. Press F2 to select the record. His employee

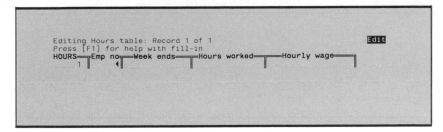

Figure 15.6: The Hours table using HelpAndFill

```
Move to the record you want to select
Press [F2] to select the record; Esc to cancel; [F1] for help
EMPLOYEE=Emp No=——First name————————Last name——————————————Address=
        1   A01   Alice        Channing        505 Haight St.
        2   A02   Sally        Bean            1465 Oak St.
        3   A03   Edward       Channing        505 Haight St.
        4   A04   Jean         Abbott          4445-2312 Technolog
        5   A05   Jane         Walker          848 Broadway
        6   A06   Robert       Lin             457 First St.
        7   A07   Dianne       Lee             1634 Bancroft Way
        8   A08   Joan         Garfield        4437 Elm St.
        9   A09   Andrea       Norton          2311 First St.
       10   A10   George       Silk            237 Edison st.
       11   A11   Francine     Bowen           2113 University Ave
       12   A12   Albert       Cruz            1237 Flatbush Ave.
       13   A13   Samuel       Smithson        203 West St.
       14   A14   Rosalyn      Rogers          2242 Pensylvania Av
       15   A15   Joseph       Tuckerman       45 Arcroft Circle
       16   A16   Joseph       Miller          2036 Park Ave.
       17   A17   William      Channing        22 The Circle
       18   A18   Alice        Walter          326 B. 31 St.
       19   A19   Edward       Channing        180 Poplar St.
       20   A20   Josephine    Buckminster     3322 Bridgeway
       21   A21   Henry        Ware            1742 Dutch Elm St.
       22   A22   Evelyn       Adams           3345 Church Ave.
```

Figure 15.7: The Employee table using HelpAndFill

number is automatically entered in the Emp no field of the Hours table.

6. Press Enter to move the cursor to the Week ends field. Type **9/7/90** and press Enter. Then type **42** in the Hours worked field, and press Enter.

7. Type **10.5** in the Hourly wage field, and press Enter. Notice that when the cursor moves to the Emp no field of record 2, the message telling you to press F1 for help with fill-in reappears.

8. Try making an invalid entry. Type **Z10** as the Emp no for record 2. Paradox refuses to accept the entry, and displays a message saying that it is not a possible value for the field. Press Ctrl-Backspace to delete this value.

9. Press the Ditto key (Ctrl-D) to enter the same Emp no in record 2 as in record 1, and press Enter.

10. Type **9/14/90** in the Week ends field, and press Enter. Then type **38** in the Hours worked field, and press Enter again.

11. Press the Ditto key (Ctrl-D) to enter the same hourly wage and press DO-IT! (F2).

With this method of data entry you can fill in the key field yourself and have Paradox reject it if it is invalid, or you can have Paradox fill in the key field for you.

*F*illing in All Corresponding Fields

It is also inconvenient to have to look up the wage and fill it in by hand. There are some cases where you would want only the key field filled in, and would use this JustCurrentField HelpAndFill option. In this case, though, you want to have the Hourly wage field filled in automatically also.

To do this, simply choose AllCorrespondingFields when you set up your validity check, and Paradox automatically fills in any field with the same name and data type as a field in the lookup table. Notice that the names of the key fields can be different, because you actually made a choice from the menu to tell Paradox which field was related to the key field in the lookup table; but the names and data types of any other corresponding fields must be identical for this option to work.

1. You should be viewing the Hours table, with the cursor in the Hourly wage field of record 2. Press the Edit key (F9) to change to Edit mode, and press Enter to move to record 3.

2. To set up the new validity check, press the Menu key (F10) to call up the Edit menu. Then press V and then D to select Val-Check Define.

3. The cursor should already be in the Emp no field. Press Enter to select it as the field that you want checked, and T to select TableLookup. Paradox suggests Employee as the table to check values against, because you selected it previously. Press Enter to select it again.

4. Press A and then H to select AllCorrespondingFields HelpAndFill. You are now ready to edit the table.

5. Try making an error. Type **Q10** in the Emp no field and press Enter. Paradox refuses to advance to the next field and again displays a message to tell you that this is not one of the possible values for the field. Press Ctrl-Backspace to delete the invalid Emp no.

6. You are in the Emp no field of record 3 and need to enter the work hours of the Edward Channing who lives on Haight St., and whose employee number you do not know. Press F1 to get help with the fill-in.

7. Once you are in the lookup table, press → twice to move to the Last name field.

8. To find the record, press the Zoom key combination (Ctrl-Z), and when Paradox asks for the value to search for, type **Channing** and press Enter. Since the first Channing is not the one you want, press Zoom next (Alt-Z) to search for the next Channing. This is the record you want. Press F2 to enter Channing's employee number and hourly wage in the Hours table, as shown in Figure 15.8.

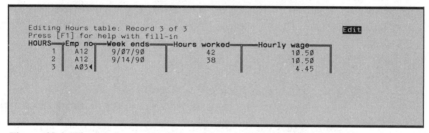

```
Editing Hours table: Record 3 of 3                      Edit
Press [F1] for help with fill-in
HOURS═╤═Emp no╤══Week ends══╤═Hours worked══╤══Hourly wage═══╗
    1 ║ A12 │   9/Ø7/9Ø    │     42        │     1Ø.5Ø      ║
    2 ║ A12 │   9/14/9Ø    │     38        │     1Ø.5Ø      ║
    3 ║ AØ3◀│              │               │      4.45      ║
```

Figure 15.8: The employee number and hourly wage entered automatically

9. Press Enter to move to the Week ends field; type **9/7/90** and press Enter. Type **18.5** in the Hours worked field, press Enter, and then press Enter again to keep the value in the Hourly wage field.

10. Press the Ditto key combination (Ctrl-D) to copy the same employee number, and press Enter. Notice that when you press Enter, the Hourly wage field is automatically filled with the hourly wage from the record in the lookup table that has this employee number.

11. Type **9/14/90** in the Week ends field and press Enter. Then type **21** in the Hours worked field and press Enter. If you wanted to, you could edit the hourly wage using the usual methods, but instead just press Enter to confirm it.

The AllCorrespondingFields FillNoHelp option works in the same way that this AllCorrespondingFields HelpAndFill worked when you typed the employee number: it automatically fills the values in fields that correspond to fields in the lookup table. The difference is that it does not allow the user to see the lookup table and use it for help. Like the PrivateLookup feature, it is meant for programmers who are setting up a system and want to protect the security of the lookup table: you will not need it when you are working on your own database.

In order to have enough data to work with when you are learning about reports and queries in multitable databases, you need more records in the Hours table. Add the records listed in Table 15.1 in the same way that you just added the first four records in the Hours table. You can use the Ditto key (Ctrl-D) to add multiple records for the same employee. Use the help feature occasionally when you are adding the first record for an employee; otherwise, just copy the employee number from the table.

Table 15.1: Additional Records for the Hours Table.

A01	Alice	Channing	9/07/90	38
A01	Alice	Channing	9/14/90	39
A02	Sally	Bean	9/07/90	45
A02	Sally	Bean	9/14/90	47
A03	Edward	Channing	9/07/90	19
A03	Edward	Channing	9/14/90	21
A04	Jean	Abbott	9/07/90	39
A04	Jean	Abbott	9/14/90	42
A05	Jane	Walker	9/07/90	40
A05	Jane	Walker	9/14/90	40
A06	Robert	Lin	9/07/90	30
A06	Robert	Lin	9/14/90	32
A07	Dianne	Lee	9/07/90	43
A07	Dianne	Lee	9/14/90	38
A08	Joan	Garfield	9/07/90	35
A08	Joan	Garfield	9/14/90	36
A09	Andrea	Norton	9/07/90	42
A09	Andrea	Norton	9/14/90	37
A10	George	Silk	9/07/90	41
A10	George	Silk	9/14/90	42

Table 15.1: Additional Records for the Hours Table (continued).

A11	Francine	Bowen	9/07/90	30
A11	Francine	Bowen	9/14/90	32
A12	Albert	Cruz	9/07/90	42
A12	Albert	Cruz	9/14/90	38
A13	Samuel	Smithson	9/07/90	40
A13	Samuel	Smithson	9/14/90	38
A14	Rosalyn	Rogers	9/07/90	20
A14	Rosalyn	Rogers	9/14/90	20
A15	Joseph	Tuckerman	9/07/90	32
A15	Joseph	Tuckerman	9/14/90	33
A16	Joseph	Miller	9/07/90	41
A16	Joseph	Miller	9/14/90	38
A17	William	Channing	9/07/90	26
A17	William	Channing	9/14/90	24
A18	Alice	Walter	9/07/90	32
A18	Alice	Walter	9/14/90	30
A19	Edward	Channing	9/07/90	37
A19	Edward	Channing	9/14/90	38
A20	Josephine	Buckminster	9/07/90	26
A20	Josephine	Buckminster	9/14/90	24
A21	Henry	Ware	9/07/90	31
A21	Henry	Ware	9/14/90	28
A22	Evelyn	Adams	9/07/90	35
A22	Evelyn	Adams	9/14/90	37
A23	Harriet	Noble	9/07/90	32
A23	Harriet	Noble	9/14/90	30

When you have made all these entries, press DO-IT! (F2) to save them.

There is a more advanced method of setting up data entry in a multitable database using the Modify MultiEntry option of the main menu. This lets you enter records in a single table that will then be added to more than one table.

You have to work hard to set up this feature before you can do any actual entry. It is useful primarily for programmers who are setting up a database for a user who knows nothing about database theory. If you are curious about this feature, there is information about it on pages 148 to 152 of the *Paradox User's Guide*.

What you have learned in this chapter is quite sufficient for working with your own database. You have learned to protect the integrity of the data in the tables on the "one" side of the one-to-many relationship and on the "many" side of the relationship, and that is all you need.

REPORTS FOR
MULTITABLE
DATABASES

———

———

LINKING TABLES

———

GROUPING/
SUPPRESSING
REPEATED DATA

———

ADDING
CALCULATED/
SUMMARY
FIELDS

———

Once you understand how one table is linked to another to create a multitable database, it is easy to design reports on multiple tables. You simply have to link one table to another, as you will see, and then you can produce reports for multitable databases in the same way that you did when you were working with single-table databases.

There are a few useful techniques for reports on multitable databases that were not emphasized when you were using single-table databases. For example, a multitable database tends to have many repeated values: in the case of a report on work hours, the employee's name is repeated for each week's hours. In multitable databases, it is useful to use the report feature that suppresses repeated values, and this feature (which was skimmed over quickly in Chapter 10) will be emphasized in this chapter.

Still, you should find this an easy chapter. Given what you have already learned about multitable databases, you should have no trouble linking the tables; and once the tables are linked, you will be using techniques you already know to produce the reports.

*H*ow to Create Reports Using Linked Tables

Before producing a report on a multitable database, you must decide which table of the database will be the *master table* for the report. After choosing to design a new report for the master table, you must link it with the other table whose fields you want included in the report. This linked table is the *detail table*. When you work with more complex databases, you can link the master table with several detail tables.

As you remember, when you select Report Design from the main menu, Paradox asks you to enter the name of the table that the report will be on. The name you enter at this point will be the master table for the report. To use the report later, you also enter the name of the master table when Paradox asks you for the table name: the multitable report will be in the menu that lists all the numbered reports of the master table, right along with the standard report for the master table and any other reports you have created for the master table alone.

Paradox users often talk about the *family* of a table to refer to that table and all the other Paradox objects associated with it—such as reports and forms. In Part III, you will learn about a Paradox tool that lets you copy a table and its entire associated family. If you use this tool, you may need to remember that a report on a multitable database is part of the family of its master table.

*C*hoosing the Master Table

Which table should you choose as the master table of your report? The answer is clear when you remember that, while designing the report for the master table, you have to link it to the detail table. For the linking operation to work properly, the detail table has to be a lookup table that has a key field designated with an asterisk.

In a database with a one-to-many relationship, such as the one you are working with, the table on the "many" side of the relationship must be the master table, and the table on the "one" side, which has a key field designated with an asterisk, must be the detail table.

In some complex databases, with several lookup tables and linking tables, it is necessary to think about which table to make the master table of a report. You need to choose the table that can be linked to the most lookup tables, remembering that the master table determines the number of lines in the report; there will be one line in the report body for each record in the master table.

In a basic one-to-many relational database, of course, you do not have these problems. It is still useful, though, to remember that the master table determines how many lines there will be in the report. As you will see, the records from the lookup table are repeated for each record in the master table: in this case, the employee's name will be repeated for each week's work hours.

In our sample database, then, the Hours table must be the master table. You would not be able to fit in more than one week of work-hours for each employee if it were possible to make the Employee table the master table, since there would be only one line for each employee. Remembering that the master table determines how many lines there will be in the report makes it even more obvious that the table on the "many" side of the one-to-many relationship must be the master table.

Linking Tables

After deciding which table should be the master table, you must select Report Design to create a report on this table. As always, you will be presented with the report specification screen that has the fields of this table laid out on it in the form of the standard report.

Then you must choose Field Lookup Link to link the master table to the lookup table. This menu choice may be difficult for you to find when you first begin creating multitable reports on your own, because it is not listed on the help line when the cursor is on Field in the Report menu. There is not enough room for a help line that describes all the options under Field, so you should make a special effort to remember where Link is in the Report menu.

After you have linked the tables, you will have access to the fields in the Employee table, and will be able to add them to this report by selecting Field Place Regular from the Report menu.

1. Make sure you are in the Paradox main menu. Press R and then D to select Report Design. When Paradox asks you to enter the name of the table for the report, type **Hours** and press Enter.

2. When Paradox prompts you for the report number, press → once to move the cursor to number 1. As you have not yet created any reports for the Hours table, this number will be an unused report. Press Enter to select it.

3. When Paradox asks you for the report description, type **Work Hours: Early September** and press Enter. Then press Enter to select Tabular. Paradox displays the familiar report specification screen, with only the fields from the Hours table included, as in Figure 16.1.

4. Since the table is not yet linked to the Employee table, you cannot use fields from that table. Press the Menu key (F10). Press F, P, and then R to select Field Place Regular, and you will see that only the fields of the Hours table are available. Press Esc four times to back out of the menu system.

5. In order to link this table to the Employee table, press the Menu key (F10). Press F, L, and then L again to select Field

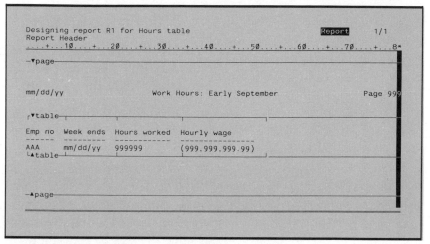

Figure 16.1: The report specification for the master table

Lookup Link. When Paradox asks for the name of the table to link to, type **employee** and press Enter.

6. Paradox asks which field in the Hours table should match the Emp No field in the Employee table, as shown in Figure 16.2. This choice makes it clear that you can only link to the key field of the Employee table, Emp No, which is designated with an asterisk. But you can select any field of the Hours table to link to it.

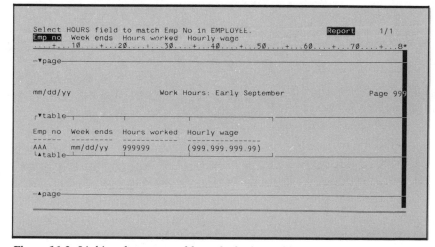

Figure 16.2: Linking the master table to the lookup table

7. Try making an error. Press → to move the cursor to Week ends and press Enter. Paradox displays a message saying the field type does not match and refuses to link the tables. Now press ← to move the cursor back to Emp no and press Enter. Paradox returns to the report screen.

8. To see that the tables are linked, press the Menu key (F10). Press F, P, and then R to select Field Place Regular. Notice that, in addition to the four fields of the Hours table, there is also an [Employee->] choice, which will give you access to the fields of the Employee table.

9. You must make room for these fields before you place them, so rather than choosing to place a field now, just back out of the menu system by pressing Esc four times.

Notice the arrow marker in the added choice, [Employee->], which is made of a hyphen and a greater-than sign. You may remember that, when you learned the rules for naming Paradox tables, one of the more obscure rules was that table names could not include the symbol -> in them. Now you know why: Paradox gives that symbol a special meaning in table names.

Inserting Fields from the Lookup Table

Now that you have linked the two tables, you can insert fields from the lookup table in almost the same way that you insert fields in a single-table report. First you add new columns for the new fields; then you choose Field Place Regular to place the fields. As you saw, now that you have linked the tables, there is also an [Employee->] option on the menu when you make this choice. This option gives you access to the fields of the lookup table.

1. Use ↓ to move the cursor to the table band of the report. It should be in the column where the Emp no is now. Since you do not need the employee number in the final report, you can delete this column. Press the Menu key (F10). Press T and then E to select TableBand Erase. Since the cursor is already in the column you want to delete, press Enter.

2. To insert a new field, press the Menu key (F10). Press T and then I to select TableBand Insert. Since the cursor is already at the left edge of the screen, press Enter to insert the column there. Repeat this step to insert another column.

3. Now you are ready to insert the first name. Press the Menu key (F10). Press F, P, and then R to select Field Place Regular.

4. When Paradox displays the choice of fields, press the End key to move the cursor to [Employee->] and press Enter. When all the fields from the Employee table appear, press → once to move the cursor to First name and press Enter.

5. Since the cursor is already where you want it, at the left edge of the report, press Enter to place the field.

6. Press ← once to make the field mask one character shorter, and press Enter. With this field length, there is a space after the field. Notice that the help line in the upper-right of the screen, which tells you the name of the field that the cursor is in, says [Employee->First name]. It uses the -> symbol to indicate the table that this field belongs to, since it is not one of the fields of the master table.

7. Now you must expand the next column to make enough room for the last name. Press the Menu key (F10). Press T and then R to select TableBand Resize. Press → a couple of times to move to the next column, and press Enter. Press → six times to expand the column until the report hits the right margin, and then press Enter.

8. You are ready to place the Last name field. Press the Menu key (F10). Press F, P, and then R to select Field Place Regular. Press the End key to move the cursor to [Employee->] and press Enter. Press → twice to move the cursor to Last name and press Enter.

9. Use the arrow keys to move the cursor to the left edge of the empty column (just above the line that divides it from the first column) and press Enter. Press Enter again to select that field length.

10. Now you can add titles above the columns. Press ↑ twice to move the cursor to the same level as the titles. Press Ctrl-Home to move to the left edge of the screen. Type **First name**. Press → five times to move to the next column and type **Last name**. Making sure you are not in Insert mode, press Enter to move to the left edge of the next line. Type -------------- (14 hyphens), press → once to move to the next column, and type -------------------- (20 hyphens), to underline both titles.

11. If you want to see the output of this report, press the Menu key (F10). Press O and then S to select Output Screen. Figure 16.3 shows the output. If you do send the output to the screen in this way, you will notice that the output is produced rather slowly, since Paradox must link the two tables while it produces the report. When you are working with larger tables, you probably will not want to use the Output Screen option to preview reports on linked tables, because you have to sit at the computer pressing a key after each screen while Paradox generates the report. With larger tables, it is better to use Output File to preview a report, so that you can leave the computer while Paradox generates the report.

12. To save the report specification, press DO-IT! (F2).

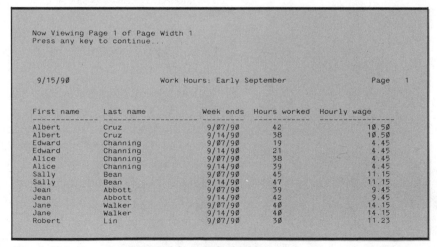

Figure 16.3: A report generated from linked tables

Notice that you just barely managed to squeeze the fields into the width of this report screen. You did not even have room to add the usual two spaces after the First name and Last name fields; there was just enough room for one space. You will often have this space problem when you are creating reports for multitable databases, because you begin with a report form for a master table that is usually narrow and then expand it by adding extra columns.

If you try to add a column when there is not enough room for it on the existing page widths, Paradox displays an error message telling you that there is not enough room. You must add another page width before Paradox lets you add more columns. Though it is not necessary in this report, you should use the menu to add a page width, so that you know how to do it if the need arises.

1. Press the Menu key (F10) to call up the Report menu. Press S and then P to select Setting PageLayout.

2. Press I to select Insert. Paradox automatically adds a second page width to the report. Notice that the help line in the upper-right corner of the screen now says 1/2 to indicate that you are on the first of two page widths.

3. Since you do not need the extra width in this report, you can delete it. Press the Menu key (F10) to call up the Report menu. Press S, P, and then D to select Setting PageLayout Delete.

4. Paradox asks you to confirm whether you want to delete the last page width. Press O to select OK. Notice that the help line in the upper-right corner of the screen says 1/1 again, indicating that you are on the first page width and that there is only one page width. Press DO-IT! to make the change final.

That takes care of the basics of generating a report for a multitable database. Now you can add as many columns as you want by placing fields from the lookup table on the master table report.

*S*pecial Techniques for Multitable Reports

As you can see from Figure 16.3, though, the report looks cluttered. Because there is one line for each record in the master table, data from the detail table is repeated, and there are no separations between records that refer to different employees.

In the rest of this chapter, you will use a variety of techniques that you encountered briefly in Part I of this book in order to make this report less cluttered, easier to read, and more useful.

*H*ow to Group and Suppress Repeated Data

Grouping the records for each employee would, in itself, make the report easier to read. Grouping on Last name might mean that two employees with the same name would be grouped together. Instead, you should group on Employee number, which you know is unique for each employee. Remember that you can group on a field even if it is not included in the report.

1. From the main menu, press R and then C to select Report Change. When Paradox asks for the name of the table for report, type **Hours** and press Enter.

2. Just one report has been created for this table, in addition to the standard report. Press → once to move the cursor to 1: the help line says "Work Hours: Early September," the description you gave to the report you just created. Press Enter to select it.

3. Press Enter again to keep the same report description, and when the report specification screen appears, press the Menu key (F10) to call up the main menu. Press G and then I to select Group Insert.

4. Press Enter to group on a field, and Enter again to select Emp no as the field to group on. Press ↓ a couple of times to move the cursor to the page band and press Enter to insert the group. A band saying "group Emp no" is added to the screen, as shown in Figure 16.4.

5. If you want to generate the report, press the Menu key (F10). Press O and then S to select Output Screen. Figure 16.5 shows the output.

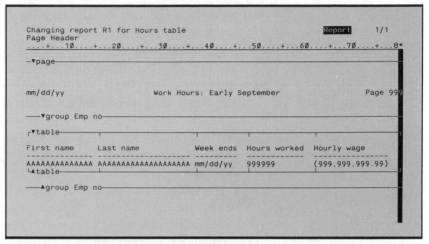

```
Changing report R1 for Hours table                        Report    1/1
Page Header
....+...1Ø....+...2Ø....+...3Ø....+...4Ø....+...5Ø....+...6Ø....+...7Ø....+...8*

 —▼page

 mm/dd/yy                    Work Hours: Early September          Page 999

   ——▼group Emp no
 ┌▼table

 First name      Last name        Week ends  Hours worked  Hourly wage
 ---------------  ---------------  ---------  ------------  ----------------
 AAAAAAAAAAAAAA  AAAAAAAAAAAAAAAAAAAA  mm/dd/yy   999999      (999,999,999.99)
 └▲table
   ——▲group Emp no
```

Figure 16.4: *The report specification with grouping by employee number*

```
Now Viewing Page 1 of Page Width 1
Press any key to continue...


    9/15/9Ø                    Work Hours: Early September          Page   1


    First name      Last name        Week ends  Hours worked  Hourly wage
    ---------------  ---------------  ---------  ------------  ----------------
    Alice           Channing         9/Ø7/9Ø        38             4.45
    Alice           Channing         9/14/9Ø        39             4.45

    Sally           Bean             9/Ø7/9Ø        45            11.15
    Sally           Bean             9/14/9Ø        47            11.15

    Edward          Channing         9/Ø7/9Ø        19             4.45
    Edward          Channing         9/14/9Ø        21             4.45
```

Figure 16.5: *The output with grouping by employee number*

This grouping alone makes the report much more readable. In many cases, though, particularly when there are many records in the master table for each one in the lookup table, you will want to suppress the repeated values in the groups. In this report each name is repeated just twice. You can imagine, though, how it would look if each name were repeated 10 or 15 times.

To suppress repetition, you can choose Setting GroupRepeats from the Report menu. You will be given the choice to Retain or to

Suppress the repetition: Retain can be used to restore repeated values if you decide not to suppress them.

Unfortunately, the GroupRepeats choice only applies to the field that the table is grouped on. Paradox does not have a built-in facility for suppressing other fields. In this case, since you are grouping on the Emp no field, which is not displayed, the output would not look different at all after you chose GroupRepeats Suppress.

There is a way around this limitation, though: create a grouping on the First name field and the Last name field within the existing grouping on Emp no. Since each Emp no represents one person (who has one first name and one last name) there will not be any subgroups created within the Emp no group that you already created. But grouping on these fields will make it possible for Paradox suppress their repeated values.

In the earlier report, two lines were skipped between groups, because the report generator automatically puts blank lines in the group header and footer. In this version, we will delete all the blank lines except one in the headers and footers, to skip just a single line between employees.

1. Press the Menu key (F10). Press S, G, and then S to select Setting GroupRepeats Suppress. Paradox displays a "Settings changed" message. Move the cursor to the table band, and you will see that the help line in the upper-left corner of the screen says "Table Band, suppress," indicating the setting.

2. Press the Menu key (F10). Press G, I, and then F to select Group Insert Field.

3. When Paradox asks for the name of the field to group on, press ← once to move the cursor to [Employee->] and press Enter. Then press → once to move the cursor to the First name field and press Enter. To insert the group, move the cursor to somewhere in the group Emp no band and press Enter.

4. Move the cursor to the group Emp no header band. Press the Ins key to toggle into Insert mode, and press Ctrl-Y to delete the blank line in the header. Now press ↓ once to move to the group [Employee->First name] header band, and Ctrl-Y to delete the blank line in it.

5. Press ↓ six times to move to the group [Employee-First name] footer band. Press Ctrl-Y to delete the blank line in it. The report screen now looks like Figure 16.6. If you were to generate the report now, the repetition of the first name would be suppressed, because you have grouped on it, but the repetition of the last name would not be suppressed.

6. Press the Menu key (F10). Press G, I, and then F to select Group Insert Field. Move the cursor to [Employee->] and press Enter. Move the cursor to Last name and press Enter. Press Enter to insert the Last name group somewhere within the group Emp no band; it does not matter if it is in the First name band or not.

7. Move the cursor to the header of the new group Last name band, and press Ctrl-Y to delete the blank line in it. Do the same to delete the blank line in the footer. The report specification screen should now look like Figure 16.7.

8. If you want to generate the output, press the Menu key (F10). Press O and then S to select Output Screen. Figure 16.8 illustrates the output, with both the first and last name suppressed.

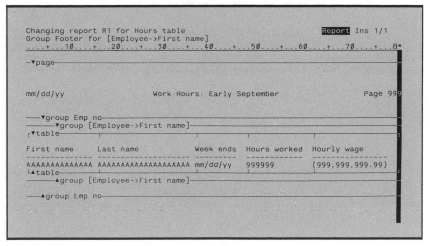

Figure 16.6: The report specification with the first name grouped

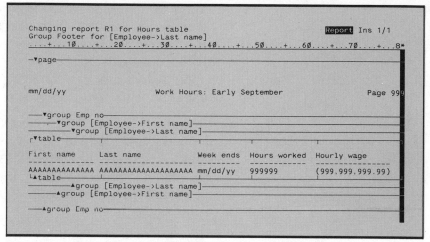

```
Changing report R1 for Hours table                           Report Ins 1/1
Group Footer for [Employee->Last name]
....+...1Ø....+...2Ø....+...3Ø....+...4Ø....+...5Ø....+...6Ø....+...7Ø....+...8*

——▼page————————————————————————————————————————————————————————————————————


mm/dd/yy                      Work Hours: Early September              Page 999

——▼group Emp no————————————————————————————————————————————————————————————
——————▼group [Employee->First name]————————————————————————————————————————
————————————▼group [Employee->Last name]——————————————————————————————————
┌▼table——————————————————————————————————————————————————————————————————

First name      Last name            Week ends   Hours worked   Hourly wage
--------------  --------------------  ---------   ------------   ------------------
AAAAAAAAAAAAAAA AAAAAAAAAAAAAAAAAAAAA mm/dd/yy    999999         (999,999,999.99)
└▲table——————————————————————————————————————————————————————————————————
————————————▲group [Employee->Last name]——————————————————————————————————
——————▲group [Employee->First name]————————————————————————————————————————

——————▲group Emp no————————————————————————————————————————————————————————
```

Figure 16.7: The report specification with first and last name grouped

```
Now Viewing Page 1 of Page Width 1
Press any key to continue...



9/15/9Ø                       Work Hours: Early September              Page    1


First name      Last name            Week ends   Hours worked   Hourly wage
--------------  --------------------  ---------   ------------   ------------------
Alice           Channing              9/Ø7/9Ø         38             4.45
                                      9/14/9Ø         39             4.45

Sally           Bean                  9/Ø7/9Ø         45            11.15
                                      9/14/9Ø         47            11.15

Edward          Channing              9/Ø7/9Ø         19             4.45
                                      9/14/9Ø         21             4.45

Jean            Abbott                9/Ø7/9Ø         39             9.45
                                      9/14/9Ø         42             9.45

Jane            Walker                9/Ø7/9Ø         40            14.15
```

Figure 16.8: The output with both first and last name suppressed

This trick of adding groupings not to create subgroups but purely to suppress repeated fields is often handy when you are working with a multitable database. Whenever you do a report on this sort of one-to-many relationship, you will have a listing of one customer number and customer name with many purchases, of one salesperson's name and location with many sales, of one member's name and address with many years dues, or of something similar.

You can create very neat reports if you eliminate the repetitive data, as you just have. This format looks particularly good if the number of records in each group varies (as it would for salespeople with different numbers of sales) or when you add a summary field in the footer of each group, as you will next.

How to Add Summary and Calculated Fields

Summary and calculated fields are added to reports on multitable databases in the same way that they are to reports on single-table databases.

The only thing you need to remember is that, when you enter an expression for a calculated field, Paradox assumes that field names used by themselves refer to fields in the master table. If you use the name of a field in the lookup table in the expression, Paradox considers it an error or—if there is a field with the same name in the master table—uses that field instead of the field in the lookup table.

To include a field of the lookup table in the expression, you must use the pointer symbol made up of a hyphen and a greater than sign between the table name and the field name.

As you have already seen, for example, Employee->Hourly wage refers to the Hourly wage field in the Employee table. On the other hand, Hourly wage used alone in this report would refer to the Hourly wage field in the Hours table.

To get practice using calculated fields, you can add a line for each employee that calculates the employee's total wage for the two-week period. To get this you add a group summary field that multiplies the person's hourly wage by the number of hours worked. In this case, you must use the Hourly wage field from the Hours table, since you want the actual wage paid to the employee each week. Of course, this must be a summary field, because you want the total paid to the employee for both weeks of the period: an ordinary calculated field gives you a total for each record—in this case, the amount paid for each week.

At the end of the report, you can add two summary fields to analyze the effect of wage increases given during the period. The first will show the total payroll during the period, and will be calculated using the Hourly wage field from the Hours table. The second, which might be used to predict future expenses, will show what the total payroll would have been if employees had worked the same number of hours at their current wage, including raises that have been given during the period: this will use the Hourly wage field from the Employee table.

A third calculated field will be added to show the difference between the two. Of course, there will not be any difference in the table as it stands, since you did not change any of the wages in the Employee table before entering the hours for each week and copying the wage from the Employee table into the Hours table. To test the calculated field, you will lower the wages of one of the workers in the Hours table, imagining that the hours for the earlier week had been entered before that employee got a raise.

1. Use ↓ to move the cursor to the group Emp no footer band: it should be at the left edge of the screen. Type **Total earned for this period:**.

2. To insert the summary field, press the Menu key (F10). Press F, P, S, and then C to select Field Place Summary Calculated. When Paradox asks for the expression, type **[Hours worked] * [Hourly wage]** and press Enter.

3. Press Enter to select Sum, then Enter again to select Per-Group, since you want to total the two records in each group. Press → once to leave a space before the amount and Enter to place the field. Now press ← seven times to shorten the field mask and press Enter, and Enter again to accept the suggested two digit decimal display.

4. Press Ctrl-Home to move the cursor to the left edge of the display. Make sure you are in Insert mode: if not, press the Ins key. Press the spacebar about 35 times to push the summary line toward the right edge of the page.

5. Press Ctrl-End to move to the right end of the line. Press Enter to add a blank line to the footer, so the report still skips a line after each employee. The screen now looks like Figure 16.9.

6. If you want to see the output of this report, press the Menu key (F10). Press O and then S to select Output Screen. The output is illustrated in Figure 16.10.

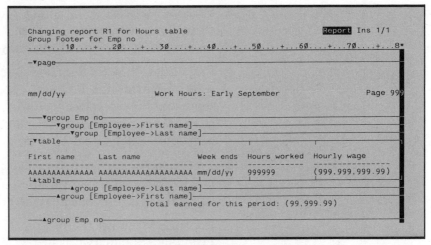

```
Changing report R1 for Hours table                    Report  Ins 1/1
Group Footer for Emp no
....+...10....+...20....+...30....+...40....+...50....+...60....+...70....+...8*
  ─▼page───────────────────────────────────────────────────────────────


  mm/dd/yy                   Work Hours: Early September               Page 999

     ─▼group Emp no──────────────────────────────────────────────────
     ────▼group [Employee->First name]──────────────────────────────
              ────▼group [Employee->Last name]──────────────────────
    ▼table───────────┬──────────────┬────────┬───────────┬──────────

  First name     Last name          Week ends Hours worked Hourly wage
  ─────────────  ──────────────────  ───────── ──────────── ──────────────
  AAAAAAAAAAAAAA AAAAAAAAAAAAAAAAAAAA mm/dd/yy  999999       (999,999,999.99)
   ▲table───────────┴──────────────┴────────┴───────────┴──────────
              ────▲group [Employee->Last name]──────────────────────
     ────▲group [Employee->First name]──────────────────────────────
                          Total earned for this period: (99,999.99)

     ────▲group Emp no──────────────────────────────────────────────
```

Figure 16.9: The report specification with a group summary added

```
  Now Viewing Page 1 of Page Width 1
  Press any key to continue...


    9/15/90                  Work Hours: Early September              Page   1


    First name     Last name          Week ends Hours worked Hourly wage
    ─────────────  ─────────────       ───────── ──────────── ──────────────
    Alice          Channing            9/07/90   38                      4.45
                                       9/14/90   39                      4.45
                             Total earned for this period:      338.20

    Sally          Bean                9/07/90   45                     11.15
                                       9/14/90   47                     11.15
                             Total earned for this period:    1,025.80

    Edward         Channing            9/07/90   19                      4.45
                                       9/14/90   21                      4.45
                             Total earned for this period:      175.77

    Jean           Abbott              9/07/90   39                      9.45
```

Figure 16.10: The output with a group summary added

7. To add the report summary fields, press ↓ to move the cursor
    to the bottom of the report; you can press the key until Para-
    dox beeps to tell you are at end of this report form. You are
    now under the page footer band in the report footer band
    (which is not marked). Type **Total payroll for this period:**.

8. Press the Menu key (F10). Press F, P, S, and then C to select Field Place Summary Calculated. When Paradox asks for the expression, type **[Hours worked]** * **[Hourly wage]** and press Enter.

9. Press Enter to select Sum and O to select Overall, since you want a summary for the entire report. Press → once to leave a space and Enter to place the field. Press Enter twice more to accept the suggested number of digits and the suggested number of decimal places.

10. Press Ctrl-End to move the cursor to the end of the line and, making sure that you are in Insert mode, press Enter to add a new line. Type **Projected payroll at current wages:**.

11. Press the Menu key (F10). Press F, P, S, and then C to select Field Place Summary Calculated. When Paradox asks for the expression, type **[Hours worked]** * **[Employee->Hourly wage]** and press Enter.

12. Press S and then O to select Sum Overall, press → once to leave a space. Press Enter three times to place the field, and Ctrl-End to move to the end of the line. Press Enter twice to add two new lines, and then type **Projected added expense due to wage increases:**.

13. Repeat the first part of step 11 to create another summary field.

14. When Paradox asks for the expression, type **([Hours worked]** * **[Employee->Hourly wage]) - ([Hours worked]** * **[Hourly wage])** and press Enter. Notice that the expression is too long to fit across the screen, but that it automatically scrolls to the left as you type. Notice, also, that you enclosed each half of the expression in parentheses. This is to ensure that the two multiplication operations are performed before the final subtraction is done. As in algebra, operations in parentheses are performed first in Paradox. Whether or not parentheses are needed, it is good to include them in complex expressions for the sake of clarity.

15. Press S and then O to select Sum Overall, press → once to leave a space, and press Enter three times to place the field. The screen now looks like Figure 16.11. Press DO-IT! (F2) to save the report.

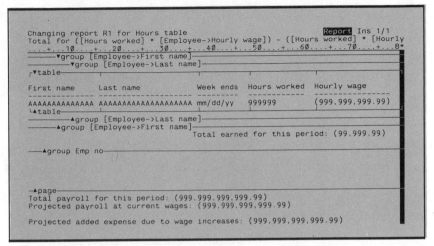

```
Changing report R1 for Hours table                       Report  Ins 1/1
Total for ([Hours worked] * [Employee->Hourly wage]) - ([Hours worked] * [Hourly
...+...10....+...20....+...30....+...40....+...50....+...60....+...70....+...8*
─────────▼group [Employee->First name]─────────────────────────────────
           ─────────▼group [Employee->Last name]───────────────────────
┌─▼table─────────────────────────────────────────────────────────────────┐
│                                                                          │
│ First name     Last name            Week ends   Hours worked   Hourly wage
│ ─────────────  ─────────────────    ─────────   ────────────   ──────────
│                                                                          │
│ AAAAAAAAAAAAAA AAAAAAAAAAAAAAAAAAAA  mm/dd/yy      999999      (999,999,999.99)
└─▲table───────────────────────────────────────────────────────────────────┘
          ─────────▲group [Employee->Last name]────────────────────────
        ─────────▲group [Employee->First name]──────────────────────────
                                      Total earned for this period: (99,999.99)

        ─────────▲group Emp no──────────────────────────────────────────



─▲page──────────────────────────────────────────────────────────────────
Total payroll for this period: (999,999,999,999.99)
Projected payroll at current wages: (999,999,999,999.99)

Projected added expense due to wage increases: (999,999,999,999.99)
```

Figure 16.11: The report specification with overall summary fields

Now that you've saved the report, let's change a wage in the Hours table so you can test it.

1. Press M and then E to select Modify Edit from the main menu. When Paradox asks for the name of the table, type **Hours** and press Enter.

2. Press → four times to move to the Hourly wage field of record 1. Press Backspace five times to erase the current value of 10.50. Type **9.5** and press DO-IT! to save the change.

3. Since this employee worked 42 hours in that week, lowering his hourly wage by one dollar should make the total payroll $42 less than it would be at the current wage. To test the report, press the Menu key (F10). Press R and then O to select Report Output.

4. When Paradox asks for the name of the table, type **Hours** and press Enter. Press → to select report 1, the report with the description, "Work Hours: Early September," and press Enter. Press S to select Screen.

When you get up to Albert Cruz, whose wage you changed, you will see two different hourly wages. Finally, at the end of the report, you will see that the projected payroll has increased by $42 as a result of the wage increase, as shown in Figure 16.12.

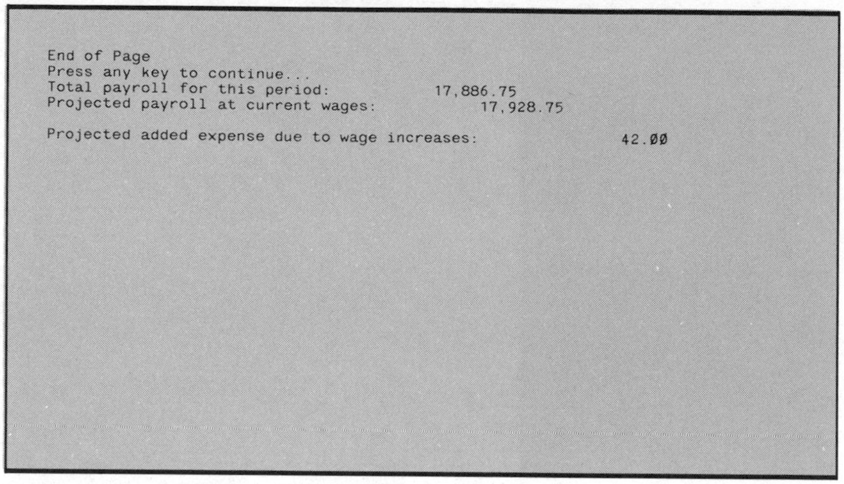

```
End of Page
Press any key to continue...
Total payroll for this period:        17,886.75
Projected payroll at current wages:        17,928.75

Projected added expense due to wage increases:        42.00
```

Figure 16.12: The summary fields showing the difference

You have produced a very sophisticated report, but there is one limitation of the report generator that you cannot get around. Because the report has one line for each record in the master file, with the appropriate fields from the lookup file linked to each, it does not report on people who did not put in any hours for the week.

Remember that, when you were entering data in the Hours table, there was one employee who did not have any values entered: the report generator cannot tell you who that employee is. There are cases when you would want a report on people who have no entries in the master table: for example, to find out which salespeople had no sales in the last month, or which of your mail-order customers hasn't ordered in a year and should be notified that they will stop receiving your catalog if they do not do so soon. In the next chapter, you will learn to do queries on multitable databases that are sophisticated enough to answer these questions.

USING QUERIES WITH MULTITABLE DATABASES

LINKING BY EXAMPLE

ENTERING CRITERIA

LOGICAL AND AND LOGICAL OR

THE INCLUSION OPERATOR

Queries using multitable databases are very similar to queries using single-table databases. As you will see, you merely have to relate the query forms for your two tables by using an example, and then you can treat them almost as if they were a query form for a single-table database. For instance, you can enter criteria using the logical AND on the two query forms just as you would on a single query form.

The one significant difference between multitable and single-table database queries exists because there may be records in one of the tables of a multitable database with no value entered in a corresponding record of the other table.

You saw the same thing in the last chapter. The report on your multitable databases could not tell you which employee had not worked any hours during the period, because it had one line for each record in the master table—and could not possibly incorporate records that were in the Employee table but not in the Hours table.

When you were working with single-table databases, reports and queries would routinely include every record in the table, even if it did not have a value in some fields. In fact, you can make a query using the word "blank" as a criterion in one of the fields in order to find only the records that have no value in that field.

With a multitable database, though, there is no blank field to look for. You never entered any work hours for the employee who did not work for the week, so you did not create any record with a blank field in it for that employee in the Hours table.

Queries in most database management programs work the same way that reports work in Paradox. They leave out records that exist in one table but have no entry in the other table. This is an *exclusive link,* because it links the two tables together but excludes records that do not have any value in one of them.

An exclusive link is what you generally want when you make a query, and it is what Paradox does by default. But Paradox 3 also has a powerful feature that most database management programs lack, which lets you do what is called an *inclusive link*. You can create a query that links the two tables together and includes in the Answer table records that do not have any value in one of them. This feature lets you find out which employees did not work or which salespeople did not make any sales.

This chapter begins by introducing you to the features of ordinary multitable queries before going on to inclusive links.

How to Query Two Related Tables

Before you query a multitable database, you must begin by linking the two tables, as you did with reports, but using a very different method. With reports, you first designed a report on *one* master table and then you linked it to the second table by selecting Field Lookup Link. With queries, you call up query forms for *both* tables and then relate them by using what Paradox calls an *example.*

The word "example" might cause a bit of confusion.

Paradox's general query procedure is called "Query by Example": the criteria you enter are examples of the value you are looking for. For instance, if you want a listing of all the employees from California, you enter CA in the State field of the query form—an example of the state that you want.

When you are working with multitable databases in Paradox, though, the word "example" has another, more specific meaning. It refers, as you will see, to an entry you make using the Paradox Example key (F5) to link the two tables.

Linking Two Tables Using Examples

To query a multitable database, you begin by calling up query forms for both tables, and then enter the same example in the key fields you want linked. You move between the two query forms by using the Up Image key (F3) and the Down Image key (F4), just as you do to move between multiple tables displayed on the screen.

1. From the Paradox Main menu, press A to select Ask. When Paradox asks for the name of the table to ask about, enter **employee** and press Enter.

2. To call up a query form for the second table, press the menu key (F10). Press A to select Ask from the main menu. When Paradox asks for the name of the table to ask about, type **hours** and press Enter. The screen now includes both query forms, as shown in Figure 17.1. Notice that the cursor is in the Hours table, and that table is displayed more brightly to show that it is now active.

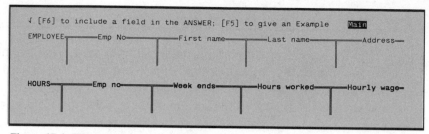

Figure 17.1: Using two query forms simultaneously

3. To enter an example to relate the tables by employee number, press → to move the cursor to the Emp no field of the Hours table. Press the Example key (F5). Type **abcd**. These letters will appear in highlighted form.

4. Press the Up Image key (F3) to move the cursor to the Employee table. Press → to move to the Emp No field. Press the Example key (F5). Type **abcd**. Now that the same example is entered in the two key fields, as shown in Figure 17.2, the two tables are linked.

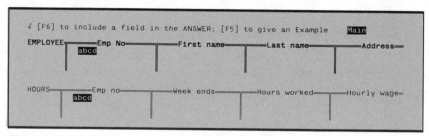

Figure 17.2: Linking the two forms with an example

Notice that you can type any value as the examples, as long as the same value is used in the two fields. The two fields that are being related must have the same field type and the same entries in the two tables so Paradox can relate the records. But the example does not need to be of that field type and does not need to have any of those values: in this case, the employee numbers are three-character alphanumeric fields, and they are linked with an example that is a four-character alphanumeric field. You could also use alphanumeric examples to link key fields that are numbers. The data type and the actual value of the examples does not matter at all.

Now that the query forms are related by examples, the tables are linked for the purpose of this query. The Answer table that appears when you make the queries will include the checked fields from both tables. To get a listing of names and hours worked for all the employees, for example, just put checkmarks in the appropriate fields.

1. Press the Check key (F6) to put a checkmark in the Emp no field. Press → to move the cursor to the First name field and press the Check key (F6). Then use → again to move the cursor to the Last name field and press the Check key (F6).

2. Press the Down Image key (F4) to move to the Hours table.

3. Press → to move the cursor to the Week ends field and press the Check key (F6). Then use → again to move to the Hours worked field and press the Check key (F6). The screen should look like Figure 17.3.

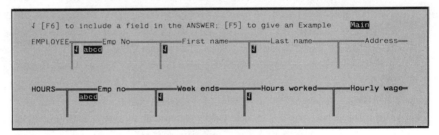

Figure 17.3: *A simple multitable query*

4. Press DO-IT! (F2). The Answer table is too wide to fit in the screen.

5. To view the entire Answer table, press the Menu key (F10). Press I and then C to select Image ColumnSize. Press → three times to move to the Last name column and press Enter. Press ← a few times to narrow the column and press Enter again. The Table now looks like Figure 17.4.

It was necessary to include the Emp No field in this query to distinguish between the two employees named Edward Channing. Remember that answers to queries are normally sorted on the first field, with successive fields used as tie-breakers, so that the records for these two Edward Channings would be mixed up if you did not include the

```
 Viewing Answer table: Record 1 of 46                        Main ▲──

 ANSWER─┬Emp No┬──────First name──────┬─────Last name─────┬───Week ends──┬─Hours work
    1   ║ AØ1  ║ Alice                ║ Channing          ║ 9/Ø7/9Ø      ║    37.5
    2   ║ AØ1  ║ Alice                ║ Channing          ║ 9/14/9Ø      ║    38.5
    3   ║ AØ2  ║ Sally                ║ Bean              ║ 9/Ø7/9Ø      ║    45
    4   ║ AØ2  ║ Sally                ║ Bean              ║ 9/14/9Ø      ║    47
    5   ║ AØ3  ║ Edward               ║ Channing          ║ 9/Ø7/9Ø      ║    18.5
    6   ║ AØ3  ║ Edward               ║ Channing          ║ 9/14/9Ø      ║    21
    7   ║ AØ4  ║ Jean                 ║ Abbott            ║ 9/Ø7/9Ø      ║    39
    8   ║ AØ4  ║ Jean                 ║ Abbott            ║ 9/14/9Ø      ║    42
    9   ║ AØ5  ║ Jane                 ║ Walker            ║ 9/Ø7/9Ø      ║    4Ø
   1Ø   ║ AØ5  ║ Jane                 ║ Walker            ║ 9/14/9Ø      ║    4Ø
   11   ║ AØ6  ║ Robert               ║ Lin               ║ 9/Ø7/9Ø      ║    3Ø
   12   ║ AØ6  ║ Robert               ║ Lin               ║ 9/14/9Ø      ║    32
   13   ║ AØ7  ║ Dianne               ║ Lee               ║ 9/Ø7/9Ø      ║    43
   14   ║ AØ7  ║ Dianne               ║ Lee               ║ 9/14/9Ø      ║    38
   15   ║ AØ8  ║ Joan                 ║ Garfield          ║ 9/Ø7/9Ø      ║    35
   16   ║ AØ8  ║ Joan                 ║ Garfield          ║ 9/14/9Ø      ║    36
   17   ║ AØ9  ║ Andrea               ║ Norton            ║ 9/Ø7/9Ø      ║    42
   18   ║ AØ9  ║ Andrea               ║ Norton            ║ 9/14/9Ø      ║    37
   19   ║ A1Ø  ║ George               ║ Silk              ║ 9/Ø7/9Ø      ║    41
   2Ø   ║ A1Ø  ║ George               ║ Silk              ║ 9/14/9Ø      ║    42
   21   ║ A11  ║ Francine             ║ Bowen             ║ 9/Ø7/9Ø      ║    3Ø
   22   ║ A11  ║ Francine             ║ Bowen             ║ 9/11/9Ø      ║    32
```

Figure 17.4: The Answer table for this query

employee number to distinguish them. This is a common occurrence in multitable databases where the query can produce more than one record for each person, and it is usually a good idea to include the unique key field in queries to avoid confusion.

Notice that the help line on the top says "Viewing Answer table: Record 1 of 46." As you remember, there are 24 employees recorded in your Employee table. But you can see that there are only records in the Answer table for 23 employees, with two weeks of wages for each. The employee who did not work during this period is not included. As you learned at the beginning of this chapter, this result is typical of the exclusive link, which Paradox uses by default if you do not specify an inclusive link. Records are excluded from the Answer table if they do not have entries in both the Employee and the Hours table.

Notice also that the columns in the Answer table appear in the same order as the they did in the query form. Because you called up the query form for the Employee table first, the fields from that table— Emp No, First name, and Last name—appear first in the Answer table. Bear this in mind when you are calling up the query forms: put the fields in the order that you want them in the Answer table. As a general rule, you will want the lookup table with the name, address, and so on to come first, and the table on the "many" side of the relationship to come second.

Using Criteria in a Multitable Database

Now, you can enter a criterion into either of these tables to select records. For example, typing CA in the state field would give you a table very much like the previous Answer table you looked at, except that it would include only employees from California. (Remember that you do not need to put a checkmark in a field to include it in the Answer in order to put a criterion in it.)

It is more interesting to use a criterion in the Hours field, since the table will no longer look like the Answer table you already looked at. Try getting the hours worked for just one week.

1. Press the Clear Image key (F8) to get rid of the image of the Answer table. The cursor moves up to the Hours query form, and there is enough room to display both query forms on the screen.

2. The cursor should be in the Hours worked field. Press ← once to move it to the Week ends field.

3. Type **9/7/90**. The query screen is shown in Figure 17.5.

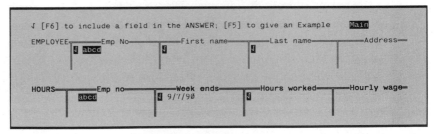

Figure 17.5: A multitable query using a criterion

4. Press DO-IT!

5. To be able to see all the fields, press the Menu key (F10). Press I and then C to select Image ColumnSize. Press → three times to move to the Last name column and press Enter. Press ← a few times to narrow the column and press Enter again. Figure 17.6 shows the Answer table.

As you can see, the Answer table has one record for each of the 23 employees who worked during that week. There is now only one

```
Viewing Answer table: Record 1 of 23                          Main ▲──

ANSWER─┬Emp No┬────First name────┬────Last name────┬───Week ends───┬──Hours worke
     1 │ AØ1  │ Alice            │ Channing        │ 9/Ø7/9Ø       │ 37.5
     2 │ AØ2  │ Sally            │ Bean            │ 9/Ø7/9Ø       │ 45
     3 │ AØ3  │ Edward           │ Channing        │ 9/Ø7/9Ø       │ 18.5
     4 │ AØ4  │ Jean             │ Abbott          │ 9/Ø7/9Ø       │ 39
     5 │ AØ5  │ Jane             │ Walker          │ 9/Ø7/9Ø       │ 4Ø
     6 │ AØ6  │ Robert           │ Lin             │ 9/Ø7/9Ø       │ 3Ø
     7 │ AØ7  │ Dianne           │ Lee             │ 9/Ø7/9Ø       │ 43
     8 │ AØ8  │ Joan             │ Garfield        │ 9/Ø7/9Ø       │ 35
     9 │ AØ9  │ Andrea           │ Norton          │ 9/Ø7/9Ø       │ 42
    1Ø │ A1Ø  │ George           │ Silk            │ 9/Ø7/9Ø       │ 41
    11 │ A11  │ Francine         │ Bowen           │ 9/Ø7/9Ø       │ 3Ø
    12 │ A12  │ Albert           │ Cruz            │ 9/Ø7/9Ø       │ 42
    13 │ A13  │ Samuel           │ Smithson        │ 9/Ø7/9Ø       │ 4Ø
    14 │ A14  │ Rosalyn          │ Rogers          │ 9/Ø7/9Ø       │ 2Ø
    15 │ A15  │ Joseph           │ Tuckerman       │ 9/Ø7/9Ø       │ 32
    16 │ A16  │ Joseph           │ Miller          │ 9/Ø7/9Ø       │ 41
    17 │ A17  │ William          │ Channing        │ 9/Ø7/9Ø       │ 26
    18 │ A18  │ Alice            │ Walter          │ 9/Ø7/9Ø       │ 32
    19 │ A19  │ Edward           │ Channing        │ 9/Ø7/9Ø       │ 37
    2Ø │ A2Ø  │ Josephine        │ Buckminster     │ 9/Ø7/9Ø       │ 26
    21 │ A21  │ Henry            │ Ware            │ 9/Ø7/9Ø       │ 31
    22 │ A22  │ Evelyn           │ Adams           │ 9/Ø7/9Ø       │ 35
```

Figure 17.6: The Answer to the previous query

record per employee, as only one week is selected from the Hours table: the table does not have the repetition that occurred in the Answer table to your first query.

Bear in mind that, if some employees had worked the second week of the period but not during the week entered on the query form, they would not be included in this Answer table at all. In some cases, there could be fewer employees listed in this Answer table than in the answer to your first query. Again, you must use the inclusive link that you will learn about later to get an answer that includes employees who did not work.

Using the Logical AND in Multitable Queries

The logical AND in multitable queries works just as it does in single-table queries. You just have to think of the two linked query forms as if they were a single query form on a single line.

If you enter criteria in fields of the two forms, the Answer will include only the records that meet both of those criteria—just as it would with a single-table database, if you entered the criteria in two fields of a single query form.

Combining the Logical AND with the Logical OR

Combining the logical AND with the logical OR by using the OR operator is the same in a multitable database as it is in a single-table database. But more complex queries, where you must place the query on two lines to represent the logical OR, create one extra wrinkle when you are working with multitable databases: include a separate pair of examples to link the two tables on each line of the query form.

Let's say you want a listing of the hours worked during the week ending 9/7/90 by people in the California office who earn less than $9 an hour and people in the New York office who earn less than $10 an hour.

1. Press the Clear Image key (F8) to get rid of the Answer table and move the cursor to the Hours query form. Then press → until you have moved the cursor to the Hourly wage field.

2. Press the Check key (F6) and then type < **9**. You have added the criterion for California. Now you need to add an entire new line for New York.

3. Press ↓ to move to the next line of the Hourly wage field. Press the Check key (F6) and then type < **10**.

4. Press ← to move to the Hours worked field and press the Check key (F6). Now press ← to move to the Week ends field. Press the Check key (F6) and type **9/7/90**, and press ← again to move to the Emp No field. Then press the Example key (F5) and type **zz**.

5. Press the Up Image key (F3) to move to the Employee query form. Move the cursor to the first line of the State field. Then press the Check key (F6) to add the state to the answer, and type the criterion **CA**.

6. Press ↓ to move the cursor to the next line. Then type **NY or NJ or CT**. (Remember that employees in the New York office can live in any of these states.) Press the Check key (F6) to add the State field to the Answer.

7. Press ← three times to move to the Last name field and Press the Check key (F6). Now press ← to move to the First name field,

and press the Check key (F6). Press ← again to move to the Emp No field and press the Check key (F6). Then press the Example key (F5) and type **zz** to relate the second line of the query in this table to the second line in the other. Press DO-IT!

8. Try rotating a field on the Employee query form, so you can see all the criteria. Press Up Image (F3) twice to move the cursor to the Employee table, then press → three times to move the cursor to the Address field, then Ctrl-R to rotate that field to the far right of the form. The cursor is now in the City field. Press Ctrl-R to rotate the City field to the far right of the form.

9. Press DO-IT! (F2). You can see in Figure 17.7 that there are five records that meet these criteria.

10. Try using the Rotate key on the Answer table. Press → twice to move to the First name column and press Ctrl-R. Press → twice more to move to the Week ends field and press Ctrl-R.

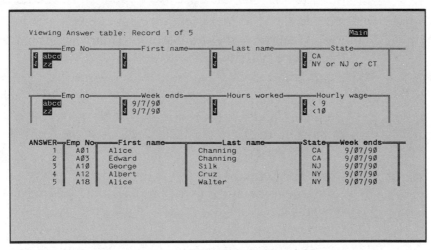

Figure 17.7: Combining the logical AND with the logical OR

You can see clearly that the five records in the Hours table include the wages you indicated for each state.

Of course, this is like what you did with a similar query on a single-table database. The only new point here is that you have related the two query forms twice by entering a set of examples on each line.

When you do this, you are essentially tying the two lines together, so that you can think of them as a single line. As you have seen, two criteria in the fields of either of these two lines will be treated as a logical AND, just like two criteria in the fields of a line of a single query table. Likewise, you need two pairs of examples to tie the lines on the query forms together into the equivalent of two lines in order to use them as a logical OR.

How to Use the Inclusion Operator

All through the examples in this section, you have seen that the record for the employee who did not work any hours during this period has been left out of the answers to your queries—as this record was left out of the reports you created in the last chapter.

To include this record, you just add the inclusion operator, an exclamation mark (!), immediately after the example you enter. You can enter the inclusion operator in either table, and all of the records in that table will be included in the Answer. You can also enter it in both tables, and all the records in both tables will be entered.

With this database, you should never need to use the inclusion operator for the Hours table. Because of the way you enter data, there cannot be a record in the Hours table that does not have a corresponding employee: none of these should be left out of the Answer table. The only reason to use the inclusion operator in the Hours table is to see if there has been a data entry error—an Hours record entered without a corresponding Employee record.

On the other hand, it is possible to have an employee who worked no hours during a period. Sometimes it does make sense to use the inclusion operator in the Employee file. For certain purposes—such as making out paychecks—you do not need to know about the employees who did not work. For other purposes, though—such as reports of absenteeism—you would want to use the inclusion operator to find the employees who did not work.

To do this, you would relate the tables using examples, and place the inclusion operator in the Query form for the Employee table. For instance, you could press the Example key (F5) and type **123** as the example in the Emp no field of the Hours table. Then you could move to the Emp No field of the Employee table and type **123!**. The example itself—the characters 123—would be highlighted, to match the example in the Hours table, but the exclamation mark would not be highlighted.

As you can see, linking queries by example gives you much more power than you have with reports, where you must choose a master table and link it to a detail table. Because reports have one line for each line in the master table, there is no way to include records that are in the detail table without any corresponding entries in the master table. On the other hand, linking queries by using examples lets you use the inclusion operator on either of the query forms.

How to Manipulate the Answer Table

As you learned earlier, the Answer table is a temporary Paradox table. It can be manipulated like any other Paradox table, except that it disappears—along with associated reports, forms, and other members of its family—when you exit from Paradox. An existing Answer table is also written over and destroyed when you create a new Answer table.

You might well want to create reports based on the Answer table that you get from a multitable query. Let's say you need a report on Hours worked and wages—similar to the multitable report you created in the last chapter—but only on employees from New York and including employees who did not work during the period. First, you would do a multitable query using an inclusive join to get the data for just the workers from New York. Then you could select Report Design and design a report on the Answer table produced by that query.

This would be a report on a single table. You would not have to link the Answer table to another table, because you already linked data from the Employee and Hours tables when you performed the query that created the Answer table. This would not actually be a report on a linked, multitable database.

Yet you could use many of the tricks you've learned for reports on multitable databases to produce this report on the Answer table. Like a report on a multitable database, the report on the Answer table would repeat the employee's name for each week of wages. You would want to group by employee number to separate records for the different employees, and to create subgroups on First name and Last name so that you could suppress repeated values in the report on the Answer table, just as you did in the multitable report.

Of course, you would lose this elaborate report form when you exited from Paradox and lost the Answer table. You would be better off changing the name of the Answer table before creating the report, as you will learn to do in the next chapter, so that it and the report on it would be saved permanently.

SHORTCUTS
AND
SPECIAL
TECHNIQUES

TOOLS FOR MANAGING FILES

PARADOX OBJECT MANAGEMENT

USING THE DOS SHELL

CHANGING THE WORKING DIRECTORY

EXPORTING/ IMPORTING DATA

Choosing Tools from the Paradox main menu gives you access to a number of useful utilities for managing Paradox tables, report specifications, and other Paradox objects; for getting information on your database; for exchanging data with other programs; and for performing a number of other jobs incidental to the primary one of maintaining your database.

So many utilities are included that there is no room for all of them in a single menu. The menu has what are sometimes called two *pages*. The first page, illustrated in Figure 18.1, has More as its final choice, on the far right. When you select More, Paradox displays the second page of the menu, illustrated in Figure 18.2. To get back to the first page of the menu from the second, press Esc, just as you would to back out of a submenu. To use the tools on the second page, you have to select Tools from the main menu and then More before you can select the tool you actually want.

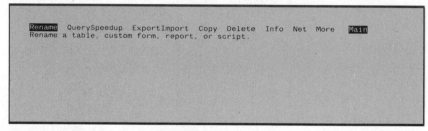

Figure 18.1: The first page of Paradox tools

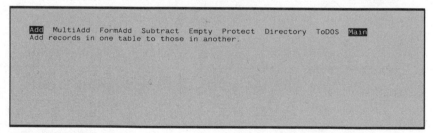

Figure 18.2: The second page of Paradox tools

This chapter begins by looking at tools for managing Paradox objects. These are vital to using the program because they are necessary for manipulating tables. Later in the chapter, some additional tools are discussed briefly.

*M*anaging Paradox Objects

Tables, report specifications, and custom data-entry forms are Paradox objects that you already know about. Other objects you will learn about in the next few chapters include *indexes* and *scripts*.

Technically, an object is anything that Paradox saves as a separate file on your disk. Appendix B describes the names your operating system gives these objects. It is not necessary to know how objects are named, though, to understand what they are. They are the basic building blocks of your Paradox application.

In your work with Paradox, you will need to manage these objects. You may need to delete a table, for example, or to copy a table for a co-worker. Earlier in this book, you saw that there are often occasions when you want to add records from one table to another or to rename a table. For all these reasons, you will find the tools Paradox provides for managing objects indispensable.

*H*ow to Add the Records in One Table to Another Table

In Chapter 6 of this book, when you learned to restructure a table, you did it with trimming. Records that did not fit into the new structure were simply truncated. At the time, you were cautioned that it is best to restructure without trimming. That is, to edit the records that went to the Problems table because they were too long to fit into the new structure, and then return them to the original table.

If you read Part II of this book, on multitable databases, you learned about the Keyviol table, which holds records that have duplicate keys. If you create a key violation in an application, you must edit the records in the Keyviol table so that there are no longer duplicate keys and then return them to the original table.

It is easy to add records from one table to another table. To do so, simply select Tools More Add. Paradox asks you for the source table (where the records are now) and then for the target table (where you want the records to be).

Suppose you decide it is a waste of space to keep a 100-character Comments field in each record of the Employee table, when most comments are much shorter than that. You want to restructure the table so the Comments field is only 30 characters long. After restructuring, you must edit the comments in the Problems table, so that the most important information is retained. Then you can return them to the Employee table.

As you go through the steps of this process, you may be puzzled to see the field for employee numbers in the Employee table. This field was added in Part II of this book, so if you have not yet read that part, your table will look a bit different from the illustrations. This difference will not affect the work you do in this chapter.

1. From the Paradox main menu, press M and then R to select Modify Restructure. When Paradox asks for the name of the table, type **employee** and press Enter.

2. Press End to move to the last field of the table, the Comments field. Press → twice to move to the field type, which is now A100. Press Backspace three times to erase the 100, and type **30**. The field type is now A30.

3. Press DO-IT! (F2). Paradox warns you of a possible data loss and presents the options Trimming, No-Trimming, and Oops!.

4. Press N to select No-Trimming. Paradox takes a moment to update the report specifications associated with this table and tells you it is deleting the modified field from them; but since the comments are not actually included in any report, the reports are not changed. Then the program tells you that it is restructuring the table. Finally, it displays the new Employee table and the Problems table, as in Figure 18.3.

5. The cursor is in the Problems table. Press Ctrl-→ to move it to the Comments field. Press the Edit key (F9) to edit the field. (If you read Part II of this book, you might choose to press the Coedit key (Ctrl-F9) instead to protect your key field.) Backspace eight times to delete the word *program*.

6. Press ↓ to move to the next record, and Backspace to erase the words *Possible advancement*. Press Field View (Alt-F5), and

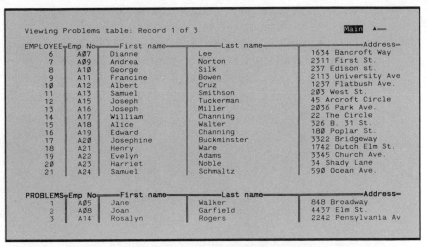

```
Viewing Problems table: Record 1 of 3                                Main ▲══
EMPLOYEE╤Emp No╤═════First name═══════╤═════Last name═══════╤═══════════Address═
      6 │ A07  │ Dianne               │ Lee                 │ 1634 Bancroft Way
      7 │ A09  │ Andrea               │ Norton              │ 2311 First St.
      8 │ A10  │ George               │ Silk                │ 237 Edison st.
      9 │ A11  │ Francine             │ Bowen               │ 2113 University Ave
     10 │ A12  │ Albert               │ Cruz                │ 1237 Flatbush Ave.
     11 │ A13  │ Samuel               │ Smithson            │ 203 West St.
     12 │ A15  │ Joseph               │ Tuckerman           │ 45 Arcroft Circle
     13 │ A16  │ Joseph               │ Miller              │ 2036 Park Ave.
     14 │ A17  │ William              │ Channing            │ 22 The Circle
     15 │ A18  │ Alice                │ Walter              │ 326 B. 31 St.
     16 │ A19  │ Edward               │ Channing            │ 180 Poplar St.
     17 │ A20  │ Josephine            │ Buckminster         │ 3322 Bridgeway
     18 │ A21  │ Henry                │ Ware                │ 1742 Dutch Elm St.
     19 │ A22  │ Evelyn               │ Adams               │ 3345 Church Ave.
     20 │ A23  │ Harriet              │ Noble               │ 34 Shady Lane
     21 │ A24  │ Samuel               │ Schmaltz            │ 590 Ocean Ave.


PROBLEMS╤Emp No╤═════First name═══════╤═════Last name═══════╤═══════════Address═
      1 │ A05  │ Jane                 │ Walker              │ 848 Broadway
      2 │ A08  │ Joan                 │ Garfield            │ 4437 Elm St.
      3 │ A14  │ Rosalyn              │ Rogers              │ 2242 Pensylvania Av
```

Figure 18.3: *The restructured Employee table and the Problems table*

then press ← ten times to move to the beginning of the word *interview.* Press Backspace to erase the words *at personal.* Press Home to move to the beginning of the field. Press Del four times to erase the word *Was,* and Enter to leave Field Editing.

7. Press ↓ to move to the next record. Press Field View (Alt-F5). Press Home to move to the beginning of the field and Del until you have erased the words *Occasional customer.* Press Enter to end Field Editing.

8. Press DO-IT! (F2). You have now edited the comments, as shown in Figure 18.4, and are ready to return the records in the Problems table to the Employee table.

9. Press the Menu key (F10). Press T, M, and then A to select Tools More Add. When Paradox asks for the name of the source table, type **problems** and press Enter; when it asks for the name of the target table, type **employee** and press Enter.

10. If you read Part II of this book and have a key field in the Employee table, Paradox will ask you to choose NewEntries or Update. Press Enter to select NewEntries, which adds the records from the source table into the target table.

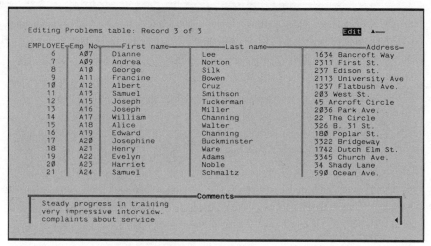

Figure 18.4: The edited Problems table, ready to be added to the Employee table

Paradox adds the records from the Problems table to the Employee table, so that all of the records are now in the table and your restructuring is complete. The source table, Problems, remains unchanged after it is added to the target table, but, of course, the Problems table is temporary and disappears when you exit Paradox.

If you read Part II of this book and have a key field in your Employee table, Paradox gave you the choices of NewEntries or Update before adding the records. The Update option, which can only be used in a table with a key field, uses the records in the source table to change the records in the target table that have the same key fields. This option can cause accidental data loss, though, and should be used with caution.

You may have noticed while you went through this example that fields in the source table and the target table do not have to be identical: the Comments field in the Problems table was still 100 characters long, although it had only 30 characters in the Employee table. Field types must be compatible, but not necessarily identical. Any number field may be added to any other (for example, the data in a $ field in the source table may be added to an N field in the target table), and alphanumeric fields of any length may be added to one another. If the data in an alphanumeric field from the source table is too long to fit in the corresponding field in the target table, it will simply be truncated—so you must make sure to edit your Problems table so its fields fit, or you might lose data.

It is most common and least confusing to use the add option with tables that are similar—for example, when you have a Problems table or a Keyviol table. In any case, the source table remains unchanged.

How to Subtract the Records in One Table from Another Table

Subtracting records in one table from another table is similar to adding them. Select Tools More Subtract, and Paradox asks you for the source table and then for the target table. Any records in the target table that match source table records are removed from the source table.

You might want to use the Subtract option, say, to help you keep track of employees who leave their jobs. It makes sense to keep a table of terminated employees with the same structure as the Employee table. The Human Resources department can maintain the table of terminated employees, and the records in it can be subtracted from the Employee table regularly. Only records that match would be subtracted.

Like Add, Subtract works differently with tables that have key fields. In tables without key fields, only records that match exactly will be subtracted from the target table. In tables with key fields, though, any records with the same key as a record in the target table will be subtracted from the source table, even if the other data is totally different. For this reason, Subtract should be used with great caution—and probably should not be used at all—with tables that have key fields.

How to Rename an Object

Sometimes the need arises to rename a table; for instance to rename a temporary table, such as the Answer table for a query, in order to save it after you exit from Paradox.

As you will see, when you choose Rename, Paradox gives you the option of renaming a form, a report, a script, or a graph as well as a table.

The names of forms and reports really are not important. As you have seen, reports are named R for the standard report and R1, R2, and so on for custom reports; likewise, forms are named F, F1, F2 and so on. You might want to rename one to close a gap in the menu: for example, if you had two reports and deleted R1, then you might want to give R2 the name R1. You can also rename a custom report R; it then becomes the standard report that is produced when you press the Instant Report key combination (Alt-F7).

You may want to rename a table, a script, or a graph just as a convenience, because you prefer to use a new name for an existing object.

It is particularly useful, though, to be able to rename temporary tables, such as an Answer table that you regularly produce reports on, since all the report forms and other objects associated with a table are lost when that table is lost. You can create a report on the renamed table, and it will be available when you perform the same query again.

This is something that you may need to do frequently. Suppose, for example, you needed a report with just the employees' names. Here is how you would proceed:

1. Press the Clear Image key (F8) to clear the screen and call up the main menu. Press A to select Ask. When Paradox asks for the name of the table, type **employee** and press Enter to bring up the query form.

2. Use → to move the cursor to the First name field and press the Check key (F6). Press → to move the cursor to the Last name field, and press the Check key (F6). Press DO-IT! (F2). Paradox takes a moment to process the query and produce the Answer table. You will rename this table Answer1, so it will no longer be a temporary table.

3. Press the Menu key (F10). Then press T and R to select Tools Rename. Paradox presents a menu of objects you can choose to rename, as shown in Figure 18.5. Press Enter to select Table.

4. When Paradox asks for the current name of the table, type **answer** and press Enter; when it asks for the new name for the table, type **answer1** and press Enter. The same table is still displayed, but with the new name Answer1.

5. To create a simple report for this table, press the Menu key (F10). Press R and then D to select Report Design. When Paradox asks for the name of the table for the report, type **answer1** and press Enter. Press → once to move the cursor to

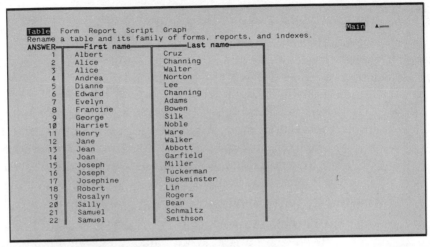

```
 Table  Form  Report  Script  Graph                              Main  ▲━━
Rename a table and its family of forms, reports, and indexes.
ANSWER┬──────First name────────────Last name━━━━
     1 │ Albert          Cruz
     2 │ Alice           Channing
     3 │ Alice           Walter
     4 │ Andrea          Norton
     5 │ Dianne          Lee
     6 │ Edward          Channing
     7 │ Evelyn          Adams
     8 │ Francine        Bowen
     9 │ George          Silk
    10 │ Harriet         Noble
    11 │ Henry           Ware
    12 │ Jane            Walker
    13 │ Jean            Abbott
    14 │ Joan            Garfield
    15 │ Joseph          Miller
    16 │ Joseph          Tuckerman
    17 │ Josephine       Buckminster
    18 │ Robert          Lin
    19 │ Rosalyn         Rogers
    20 │ Sally           Bean
    21 │ Samuel          Schmaltz
    22 │ Samuel          Smithson
```

Figure 18.5: Renaming a table

report 1, the first unused report, and press Enter. When Paradox asks for the report description, type **Employees' Names** and press Enter.

6. Press Enter again to select Tabular. Paradox displays the report specification screen. In reality, you would probably want to create a more elaborate report, perhaps grouping employees or adding a summary field that counts the total number of employees. In this simplified example, you can just save the report in its current form, by pressing DO-IT! (F2).

When you exit Paradox, the Answer1 table and the associated report will be saved permanently.

Later you will want to use this report again after doing another query. Imagine you have made changes in the Employee table and, a month later, need to make your query and produce your report again. Imagine, too, that it is a much more complicated report, so that you do not want to redo all the work of creating the report specification.

After performing the query to get a new Answer table, you cannot simply name the Answer table Answer1 again. If you do that, the reports associated with the old Answer1 table will be discarded when you use the Rename option to destroy the old Answer1 table as you create a new one.

How to Empty a Table

To use the report again, you must empty the Answer1 table of its records. Then you can add the records in the Answer table produced by the new query to the Answer1 table.

1. Press the Menu key (F10). Press T, M, and then E to select Tools More Empty. When Paradox asks you the name of the table to empty, type **answer1**, and press Enter. Paradox asks you to confirm your choice, as shown in Figure 18.6. Press O to select OK to empty the table.

2. Now you can perform the query again and add the Answer table to the empty Answer1 table. Press the Menu key (F10), and then press A to select Ask. When Paradox asks you for the name of the table, type **employee** and press Enter. The Query screen appears above the Answer1 table you were viewing.

3. There should already be a checkmark in the First name and Last name fields. Press DO-IT! to make the query.

4. Press the Menu key (F10). Press T, M, and then A to select Tools More Add. When Paradox asks for the name of the source table, type **answer** and press Enter. When Paradox asks for the name of the target table, type **Answer1** and press Enter. Answer1 is filled again, as you can see in Figure 18.7.

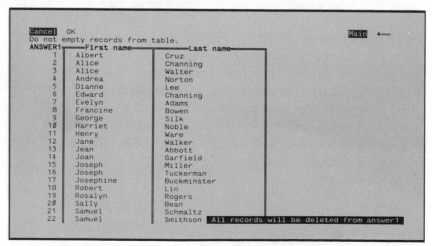

Figure 18.6: Emptying the records from a table

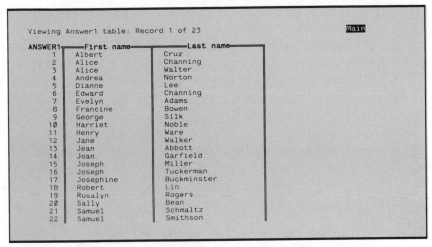

```
Viewing Answer1 table: Record 1 of 23                              Main

ANSWER1     First name              Last name
    1      Albert                  Cruz
    2      Alice                   Channing
    3      Alice                   Walter
    4      Andrea                  Norton
    5      Dianne                  Lee
    6      Edward                  Channing
    7      Evelyn                  Adams
    8      Francine                Bowen
    9      George                  Silk
   10      Harriet                 Noble
   11      Henry                   Ware
   12      Jane                    Walker
   13      Jean                    Abbott
   14      Joan                    Garfield
   15      Joseph                  Miller
   16      Joseph                  Tuckerman
   17      Josephine               Buckminster
   18      Robert                  Lin
   19      Rosalyn                 Rogers
   20      Sally                   Bean
   21      Samuel                  Schmaltz
   22      Samuel                  Smithson
```

Figure 18.7: The Answer1 table refilled

If there had been changes made in the Employee table and the Answer table produced by the last query was different from the previous one, you could produce your regular report on employee's names with the new data. You would simply press the Menu key (F10), and then R and O to select Report Output. When Paradox asked for the name of the table, you would type **answer1** and press Enter. Then, when you pressed → to move the cursor to report 1, you would still get the Employees' Names report that you created earlier.

Needless to say, emptying a table is dangerous, and you should proceed with the greatest caution. You could lose all your data if you entered the name of the wrong table by mistake when Paradox asked which table to empty.

This is why it is good practice to use names such as Answer1 when renaming temporary tables and creating tables you will save but periodically empty and refill with the contents of a newly created temporary table. Using a name similar to that of a temporary table reminds you that the data in this table is temporary. Using only this sort of name in tables you will empty, makes it much less likely that you will empty the wrong table by mistake.

How to Copy a Table

This talk about emptying a table by mistake should have you thinking about the importance of backing up your work. You should back up your data on floppy disks regularly, in case your hard disk fails. Even if you have a backup system to save your data in case of disk failure, you should make a second copy of a table before restructuring it or before any other operation that can cause a loss of data.

You can use the Tools Copy option to copy tables. If you copy a table, Paradox also copies all its associated objects, such as forms and reports. This makes the Copy option particularly useful as a hedge against mistakes; if you delete a table by mistake, all its associated objects are lost too, and if you eliminate a field from a table, that field is also deleted from reports and forms.

First, let's assume you want to back up your data on a floppy disk in drive A of your computer.

1. Place a formatted floppy disk in drive A.

2. Press the Menu key (F10). Press T, C, and then T to select Tools Copy Table.

3. When Paradox asks the name of the table to copy, type **employee** and press Enter.

4. When Paradox asks for the new table name, type **a:employee** and press Enter.

Notice that the red light next to the floppy disk drive goes on while copying is in process. Do not open the drive until the light goes off.

When you do additional backups, copy the Employee table to the same floppy disk. Paradox will tell you that a table with the name already exists and will ask if you want to cancel the command or to replace the existing table. Choose Replace to get rid of the old backup files with obsolete data and replace them with the new data.

You can also use Copy with other Paradox objects: forms, reports, scripts, and graphs. Whenever you copy a Paradox object to a floppy disk, type **a:** plus the old name of the object to copy it to the floppy disk in drive A with the same name it already has. Note that scripts and graphs are not automatically copied along with tables, but must be backed up separately.

One other useful feature of the Copy submenu is the Copy Just-Family option. This copies a table and its associated forms, reports, and indexes just as the Copy Table option does—but it does not copy the data in the table; it only copies its structure. This is handy if you want to create a new application similar to an existing one. For example, if you have a table and a set of reports to run a mailing list, and then you decide to start a second mailing list independent of the first one, you can use Copy JustFamily to create a copy of your whole setup without data, for your new list. If you do this, keep the new application in a different subdirectory on your hard disk. To copy to another subdirectory, enter the entire path name of the new table you want to create, including the subdirectory name—for example, **\newlist\mail**. Appendix A contains a brief discussion of subdirectory names.

How to Delete an Object

Finally, it's important that you know how to delete objects. As an example, delete the Emp-stat table you created in Part I of this book, with the same data as the Employee table.

1. Press the Menu key (F10). Press T and then D to select Tools Delete. Press Enter to select Table.

2. When Paradox asks for the name of the table, type **emp-stat** and press Enter. Press O (OK) to confirm the deletion.

The Emp-stat table and its family are deleted.

Notice that Tools Delete offers two additional important options: KeepSet and ValCheck.

KeepSet lets you return the image of a table to its ordinary appearance by deleting settings you have created with the Image submenu. As you remember, the Image option lets you change the size of columns, the order in which they are displayed, and their format; and if you select KeepSet, the display you create is automatically used whenever you view the table. Tools Delete KeepSet removes these settings. Paradox simply asks you for the name of the table, and after you enter it, displays that table as if you had never changed its image.

ValCheck eliminates validity checks. If you read Part II of this book, you've already set up one validity check. In Chapter 19, you will look at other validity checks you can create. Paradox will not accept data that is invalid according to a validity check you have created. Tools Delete ValCheck lets you get rid of these validity checks.

*O*ther Paradox Tools

The tools that you have looked at so far are absolutely essential for manipulating Paradox objects. Two additional tools for manipulating objects, MultiAdd and FormAdd, are beyond the scope of this book, and are rarely needed, in any case.

Apart from the tools used to manipulate Paradox objects, one of the most important selections on the Tools menu is QuerySpeedup. This option is only used with saved queries, though, and it is discussed in Chapter 20, where you learn how to save queries.

*H*ow to Use a DOS Shell

If you want to use commands from DOS for a short time, you can do so without exiting from Paradox. Just select Tools More ToDOS from the main menu, or press the DOS key combination (Ctrl-O).

Paradox will create a temporary DOS shell, as in Figure 18.8. (The appearance of your screen may differ a bit depending on the version of DOS you have.) This shell lets you use DOS commands just as you normally would. This is useful, for example, to format a floppy disk before making a backup.

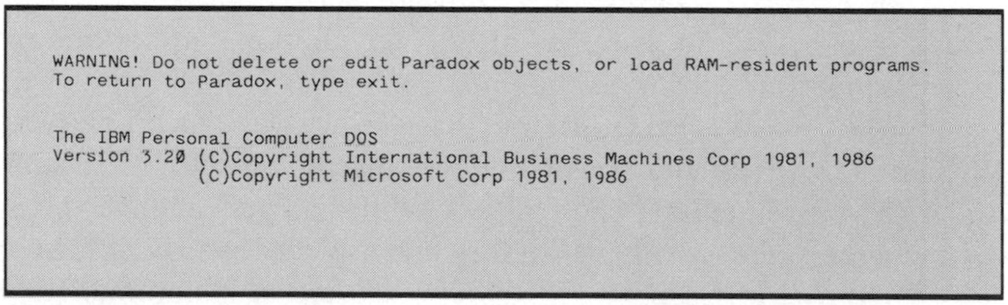

```
WARNING! Do not delete or edit Paradox objects, or load RAM-resident programs.
To return to Paradox, type exit.

The IBM Personal Computer DOS
Version 3.20 (C)Copyright International Business Machines Corp 1981, 1986
              (C)Copyright Microsoft Corp 1981, 1986
```

Figure 18.8: The DOS shell

Notice the warning at the top of the screen: Do not load RAM resident programs or make any changes in Paradox objects from this DOS shell. (Appendix B contains a list of names DOS uses to refer to Paradox objects.) There are a few other pitfalls to avoid:

- If you change directories by using the DOS command **cd**, change back to the original directory before leaving the shell.

- Do not use the DOS **print** or **mode** command.

- If you change floppy disks while in DOS, put the original disk back before leaving the shell.

When you have used the DOS commands you wanted, type **exit** at the DOS prompt and press Enter to return to Paradox.

One disadvantage of the DOS shell, though, is that Paradox still takes up most of your computer's memory (420K, to be exact) and that you must work within the remaining memory, which may not be large enough for your needs. You can minimize this problem with Alt-O, the DOS Big key, to create the shell instead of using the DOS key (Ctrl-O) or the menu. Then Paradox in its suspended state will take only about 100K of memory, leaving you most of your RAM to work with. To do this, Paradox temporarily saves the rest of what is in memory on your disk, so it takes a bit longer to get to the shell and to return to Paradox.

Always return from the shell to Paradox. Do not turn off your computer while you are in the temporary DOS shell or you may lose data. Instead, type **exit** and press Enter to leave the shell, select Exit Yes from the Paradox menu to leave Paradox, and then turn off the computer.

How to Change Your Working Directory

As you have seen, you should not change your working subdirectory by using the DOS shell. Instead, select Tools More Directory from the main menu. When Paradox displays the name of the current directory, delete it, type the full path name of the new directory that you want to use, and press Enter. Note that temporary tables (such as the Answer table) are discarded when you change subdirectories.

This feature is useful if you have several databases in different subdirectories, because you can only use the database that is in the working directory.

How to Export and Import Data

When you begin using Paradox, you might have data in other programs that you want to import into your new Paradox applications. Or you may want to export Paradox data for use in other applications—for example, to do a spreadsheet analysis of your data.

Paradox can interchange data with Quattro, Lotus 1-2-3, VisiCalc, and Lotus Symphony spreadsheets and with dBASE II or III, pfs:FILE, and Reflex databases.

It can also use or create plain ASCII text files. An ASCII text file is a file composed of the characters on your keyboard: letters, numbers, special characters such as the $ sign, and a few control characters, such as the newline character.

To convert a Paradox table into a form that can be used by one of these applications, select Tools ExportImport Export. Paradox asks you to choose from a list of the programs mentioned above, and the help line tells you the file extension of the file it creates for that program.

In some cases, there are minor differences between Paradox data types and those of other programs. See pages 192 to 198 of the *Paradox User's Guide* for descriptions of the small changes Paradox makes in data types when exporting and importing data among various programs.

If you choose to export to an ASCII text file, Paradox asks you to choose Delimited or Text. A delimited file separates fields with commas, puts alphanumeric fields in quotations, and puts each record on a new line. It is most common to export a table to a delimited file. For example, if you wanted to use the names and addresses in your table to do a mail merge with your word processor, you would choose Delimited.

A text file can only be created from a one-field Paradox table. It creates an ASCII text file with each one-field record on a separate line, which makes it of limited use.

How to Get Information about the Database

Choosing Tools Info is a convenient way to get information about your database. If you choose this tool, Paradox presents a submenu with several different types of information you can choose.

Choosing Tools Info Structure lets you display the structure of a table.

Tools Info Inventory gives you a list of all the tables, scripts, and files in any subdirectory.

Tools Info Family lets you look at all the objects associated with a given table. It is probably the most useful of these choices. When you make this selection, Paradox asks you for a table name and then places the names of that table and all its associated objects in a temporary Family table with dates that tell you when each object was last changed. You can use the tools you learned earlier to delete or copy any of these objects.

Tools Info Who and Tools Info Lock are for people using Paradox on a network, as is the Tools/Net option, which provides a whole set of tools for network users. If you are working on a network, see your network administrator for information on these Paradox tools.

VALIDATING

DATA

eaturing

**CREATING
VALIDITY
CHECKS**

**CHECKING FOR A
RANGE OF VALUES**

**SELECTING
DEFAULT
VALUES**

**USING PICTURE
FORMATS**

If you read Part II of this book, on multitable databases, you learned to validate data using TableLookup, which makes sure that values entered in the table you are working on are also present in a lookup table. You needed this feature to make sure that employee numbers entered in the Hours table were also present in the Employee table. TableLookup is most often used in multitable databases. Occasionally, though, it is used in a single-table database, to guard against invalid entries.

This chapter presents some additional ways to validate data, which are useful for both single- and multitable databases. (If you did not read Part II but you are interested in validating data using Table-Lookup, see Chapter 15.)

Creating Validity Checks

As you've seen, Paradox has some built-in validity checks. For example, it will not accept a nonexistent date, such as February 30, in a date field. You can create other validity checks like these built-in ones, which will reduce data-entry errors. You cannot eliminate errors entirely, but you can set up roadblocks that will stop the most obvious ones.

In a sense, validity checks are another set of tools. Like some of those you learned in Chapter 18, they are not indispensable, but they can make your job easier. But validity checks are special tools that only apply when you are modifying data, so they are accessed through the Edit or DataEntry menu rather than the Tools menu.

To set up validity checks, use Edit or DataEntry with the table you want the checks to apply to; then choose ValCheck from the Edit or DataEntry menu. Validity checks are not on the CoEdit menu and cannot be set up in CoEdit mode.

Whatever mode you are in when you set them up, validity checks are saved permanently, and they apply to the table whenever you modify it, regardless of whether you use DataEntry, Edit, or CoEdit. If you are using a multitable database, you might want to set up validity checks for the keyed table while you are in Edit or DataEntry, so you can use them in CoEdit.

How to Check for a Range of Values

After you select ValCheck, Paradox presents the options LowValue, HighValue, Default, TableLookup, Picture, and Required. You may use either LowValue or HighValue by itself, but they are commonly used together to define a range of values for a field.

Imagine, for example, that the lowest possible score in the aptitude test your workers take is 200 and the highest is 800. You can specify these values as the LowValue and HighValue for this field to make sure that all the entries fall within the proper range.

1. From the Paradox main menu, press M and then E to select Modify Edit. When Paradox asks for the name of the table, type **employee** and press Enter.

2. Press the Menu key (F10) to call up the Edit menu. Press V and then D to select ValCheck Define. Paradox prompts you to move the cursor to the field you want a validity check for. Press → to move the cursor to the SEAT score field, and press Enter.

3. Paradox displays the types of validity checks available, as shown in Figure 19.1. Press Enter to select LowValue, and when Paradox asks for the lowest acceptable value for this field, type **200** and press Enter. Paradox displays a message saying that the low value has been recorded.

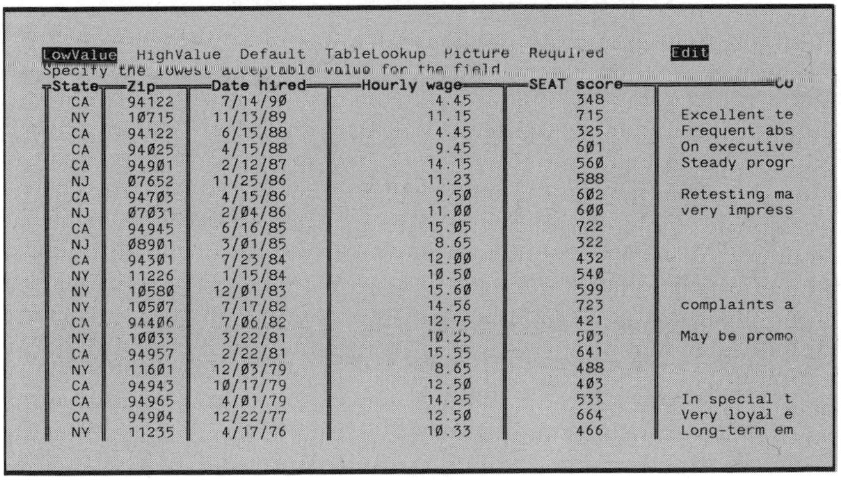

```
LowValue  HighValue  Default  TableLookup  Picture  Required        Edit
Specify the lowest acceptable value for the field
State    Zip     Date hired     Hourly wage      SEAT score              Co
 CA     94122     7/14/90          4.45           348
 NY     10715    11/13/89         11.15           715          Excellent te
 CA     94122     6/15/88          4.45           325          Frequent abs
 CA     94025     4/15/88          9.45           601          On executive
 CA     94901     2/12/87         14.15           560          Steady progr
 NJ     07652    11/25/86         11.23           588
 CA     94703     4/15/86          9.50           602          Retesting ma
 NJ     07031     2/04/86         11.00           600          very impress
 CA     94945     6/16/85         15.05           722
 NJ     08901     3/01/85          8.65           322
 CA     94301     7/23/84         12.00           432
 NY     11226     1/15/84         10.50           540
 NY     10580    12/01/83         15.60           599
 NY     10507     7/17/82         14.56           723          complaints a
 CA     94406     7/06/82         12.75           421
 NY     10033     3/22/81         10.25           503          May be promo
 CA     94957     2/22/81         15.55           641
 NY     11601    12/03/79          8.65           488
 CA     94943    10/17/79         12.50           403
 CA     94965     4/01/79         14.25           533          In special t
 CA     94904    12/22/77         12.50           664          Very loyal e
 NY     11235     4/17/76         10.33           466          Long-term em
```

Figure 19.1: *The types of validity checks available on the menu*

4. Press the Menu key (F10). Press V and then D to select Val-Check Define. Since the cursor is already on the SEAT score field, press Enter to select it, and press H to select HighValue. When Paradox asks for the highest acceptable value, type **800** and press Enter. A message confirms that the high value has been recorded.

5. Now try making some errors. With the cursor on the SEAT score field of the first record, press Ctrl-Backspace to delete the current value. Type **900** and press Enter. Paradox refuses to accept the value and displays a message that tells you what values are valid, as in Figure 19.2.

6. Try another error. Press Backspace once to delete the final 0, so the value is 90, and press Enter. Paradox refuses to accept the value and displays the same error message.

7. Press Ctrl-Backspace to delete the current value. Type **400** and Press Enter. Paradox accepts the value.

```
 Editing Employee table: Record 1 of 24                    Edit
┌State┬─Zip──┬─Date hired──┬──Hourly wage──┬─SEAT score──┬─────────Co
│ CA  │94122 │   7/14/90   │         4.45  │900          ◄│
│ NY  │10715 │  11/13/89   │        11.15  │       715    │ Excellent te
│ CA  │94122 │   6/15/88   │         4.45  │       325    │ Frequent abs
│ CA  │94025 │   4/15/88   │         9.45  │       601    │ On executive
│ CA  │94901 │   2/12/87   │        14.15  │       560    │ Steady progr
│ NJ  │07652 │  11/25/86   │        11.23  │       588    │
│ CA  │94703 │   4/15/86   │         9.50  │       602    │ Retesting ma
│ NJ  │07031 │   2/04/86   │        11.00  │       600    │ very impress
│ CA  │94945 │   6/16/85   │        15.05  │       722    │
│ NJ  │08901 │   3/01/85   │         8.65  │       322    │
│ CA  │94301 │   7/23/84   │        12.00  │       432    │
│ NY  │11226 │   1/15/84   │        10.50  │       540    │
│ NY  │10580 │  12/01/83   │        15.60  │       599    │
│ NY  │10507 │   7/17/82   │        14.56  │       723    │ complaints a
│ CA  │94406 │   7/06/82   │        12.75  │       421    │
│ NY  │10033 │   3/22/81   │        10.25  │       503    │ May be promo
│ CA  │94957 │   2/22/81   │        15.55  │       641    │
│ NY  │11601 │  12/03/79   │         8.65  │       488    │
│ CA  │94943 │  10/17/79   │        12.50  │       403    │
│ CA  │94965 │   4/01/79   │        14.25  │       533    │ In special t
│ CA  │94904 │  12/22/77   │        12.50  │       664    │ Very loyal e
│ NY  │11235 │   4/17/76   │         Value between 200 and 800 is expected
```

Figure 19.2: An error message telling you the entry is not in the defined range

This range of values does not apply to values that are already in the field. If you had set the low value at 500, Paradox would have kept all the values under 500 that are now in the field without objection. It would just prevent you from entering new values or newly edited values under 500.

Though most commonly used with number fields, HighValue and LowValue can be used with alphanumeric and date fields as well. It is unlikely that you would use this feature with an alphanumeric field, but it is conceivable if, for example, you had your employees split into two tables—one for employees with last names beginning with A through L, and the other for last names beginning with M through Z. You could set a high value of Lzz in the Last name field of the first table and a low value of M in the second table, to make sure the names are divided properly.

In date fields, you can use this validity check with the key word TODAY, which is always interpreted as the current system date—that is, the date on your computer's clock or calendar, if you have one, or the date you enter when you start your computer. This is a useful option for many tables.

1. Press ← twice to move the cursor to the Date hired field.

2. Press the Menu key (F10). Press V and then D to select Val-Check Define.

3. Press Enter to select the Date hired field, and H to select HighValue.

4. Type **today** and press Enter.

Now, Paradox will not let you enter a future date in that field by mistake. (This validity check assumes that you enter employees in the table after the date they are hired.)

How to Select a Default Value

There are often cases where one field is repeated during data entry—for example, if you have a large number of people from one city.

You can use the ValCheck feature to enter a default value for a field, so that this value is filled in automatically if you do not type another value in the field. Suppose the New York office just hired 100 people and that half of them live in New York City.

1. Press the Menu Key (F10). Press V and then D to select Val-Check Define. Press ← three times to move the cursor to the City field, and press Enter to select it.

2. Press D to select Default. When Paradox asks for the value to insert if the field is left blank, type **New York** and press Enter.

3. Press End to move to the last record of the table and then press ↓ to add a new record.

4. Press Enter several times. When you get to the City field, New York automatically appears when you press Enter. In an actual application, you would obviously want NY in the State field also.

5. Since this was just an illustration, press Del to delete the extra record.

The default value only appears if you leave the field blank. If an employee lives in another city, type that city's name and the default value is ignored in that record.

This Paradox feature is very handy. Tables often have the same value in a field in most of their records. You cannot always use the Ditto key, because sometimes the common value does not appear twice in a row. If you find yourself working with a database like this, remember the Default option of ValCheck; it can save you hours of work.

How to Require That a Value be Entered

Some fields do not need to have an entry. For example, you might enter the name of an employee who has not yet taken the aptitude test.

Other fields, such as the name field, must have a value entered. If you want to be absolutely sure that a field is not left blank by mistake, you can chose Required as a ValCheck.

1. Press the Menu key (F10). Press V and then D to select ValCheck Define. Press ← to move the cursor to the Last name field, and press Enter. Press R and then Y to select Required Yes.

2. Press ↓ to add a new record and then press Enter several times. When you get to the Last name field, Paradox displays an error message, as shown in Figure 19.3.

3. Do not get help, as suggested in the error message. Just type **Smith** and press Enter. The error message disappears after an instant, and the entry is accepted.

```
Editing Employee table: Record 25 of 25                          Edit
EMPLOYEE┬Emp No┬─────First name─────┬─────Last name─────┬──────Address═
       4  A04    Jean                 Abbott              4445-2312 Technolog
       5  A05    Jane                 Walker              848 Broadway
       6  A06    Robert               Lin                 457 First St.
       7  A07    Dianne               Lee                 1634 Bancroft Way
       8  A08    Joan                 Garfield            4437 Elm St.
       9  A09    Andrea               Norton              2311 First St.
      10  A10    George               Silk                237 Edison st.
      11  A11    Francine             Bowen               2113 University Ave
      12  A12    Albert               Cruz                1237 Flatbush Ave.
      13  A13    Samuel               Smithson            203 West St.
      14  A14    Rosalyn              Rogers              2242 Pensylvania Av
      15  A15    Joseph               Tuckerman           45 Arcroft Circle
      16  A16    Joseph               Miller              2036 Park Ave.
      17  A17    William              Channing            22 The Circle
      18  A18    Alice                Walter              326 B. 31 St.
      19  A19    Edward               Channing            180 Poplar St.
      20  A20    Josephine            Buckminster         3322 Bridgeway
      21  A21    Henry                Ware                1742 Dutch Elm St.
      22  A22    Evelyn               Adams               3345 Church Ave.
      23  A23    Harriet              Noble               34 Shady Lane
      24  A24    Samuel               Schmaltz            590 Ocean Ave.
      25          A value must be provided in this field; press [F1] for help
```

Figure 19.3: An error message appears when a required field is left blank

4. Since this was just an illustration, press Del to delete the added record.

*H*ow to Use Picture Formats

For even more precise control over the values entered, use the Picture option as a validity check.

This option lets you enter a picture format, to which all entries must conform. You can specify how many characters must be entered, and whether each character must be a letter, a number, a given character, and so on.

To define a picture format, you simply create a template in the form of the data you want, using these basic symbols:

Symbol	Meaning
#	Any number
?	Any letter, upper- or lowercase
@	Any character (letter, number, or special character)
&	Any letter, but automatically converts to uppercase
!	Any character, but automatically converts letters to uppercase

Any character, such as a letter, a number, or a hyphen can also be used in a template, and that character itself will automatically be entered in the field.

For example, if you had a field for social security numbers, you could make sure that they were entered in the right format by using the picture format *###-##-####*. The user could enter any number in place of the # symbol.

Characters used literally in picture formats, such as the hyphen in the social security number, are called *constants,* and Paradox types them automatically when you get to them. Once this picture is set up, you can enter social security numbers just by entering the nine digits; the hyphens appear automatically in the right places.

(There is an important exception to this rule: to allow for blank fields, the first letter of a field will not be filled in automatically. If you have a picture format that begins with **AAA**, for example, the field will not be filled in if you press Enter to skip it; but as soon as you enter the first A or press the spacebar, the initial AAA will be filled in.)

The & and ! symbols, which automatically convert letters to uppercase, are useful for state names, which generally appear in uppercase.

1. Press the Menu key (F10). Press V and then D to select Val-Check Define. Press → to move the cursor to the State field, and press Enter.

2. Press P to select Picture. When Paradox asks for a PAL picture format, type **&&** and press Enter.

3. Press Ctrl-Backspace to delete the current state name, (NY), and type **ny** (or whatever the original state name was) in lowercase; the letters appear on the screen in uppercase.

If you use this feature, you can be sure that when you do a query for the records in a given state, you will get all the records for the state; none will be left out because they were mistakenly entered in lowercase.

Apart from these symbols, which match individual letters, a few special characters can be used in picture formats to represent repetition of characters, optional characters, and so on. These are among the most useful:

Symbol	Meaning
*	Repetition
[]	Item is optional
;	Next character should be taken literally

Use the semicolon if you want to include the symbol # or @ or any of the other picture format symbols in a field. If you typed # at the beginning of a picture format, any number could be entered as the first character in the field. If you typed ;#, on the other hand, only # could be the first character. The ; symbol also works on itself; if you type ;; at the beginning of a picture format, then only ; could be the first character.

The optional symbol might be used to let you enter a telephone number with or without an area code, as follows: **[(###)]###-####**.

The repetition symbol (*) is probably the most useful of these special symbols. To make sure that the first letter of a name is capitalized, for example, you could type the picture format **&*@**. The first character of the name would have to be a letter and would automatically be capitalized. It could be followed by any number of characters. (Note that in this case you must use *@ to represent any number of characters, rather than *? to represent any number of letters, because names sometimes have special characters, such as hyphens.)

For information on more advanced features of the picture format, see Chapter 5 of the *PAL User's Guide,* which is one of your Paradox manuals.

*O*ther Features of Validity Checks

As mentioned at the beginning of this chapter, validity checks are automatically saved when you press DO-IT! to complete an Edit or DataEntry session. Whether set from the Edit or DataEntry menu, they are associated with the table, and apply whenever the table is used in Edit, CoEdit, or DataEntry mode. Note that validity checks apply in CoEdit mode, although you can only set them in Edit or DataEntry mode. You'll find this feature especially beneficial if you are using a multitable database.

You can clear validity checks by selecting ValCheck Clear from the Edit or DataEntry menu. Paradox gives you the option of eliminating all the validity checks you have set for a table or of removing them from one field.

For example, try clearing the one that requires an entry in the Last name field.

1. Press V, C, and then F to select ValCheck Clear Field.

2. Use ← to move the cursor to the Last name field; press Enter to select it. Paradox displays a message saying the validity checks have been cleared from that field.

3. Press ↓ to add a blank record to the end of the table. Press Enter a few times, and notice that, without a validity check that requires a value there, you can go right through the Last name field.

4. If you want to take a break, press DO-IT! to save the change you made. Press the Menu key (F10), and then E and Y to select Exit Yes.

Note that you had to choose DO-IT! to save the change that you made in the validity check. If you had chosen Cancel instead, the ValCheck would not have been removed. As you saw in the last chapter, you can also delete the validity checks from a table by choosing Tools Delete ValCheck.

Finally, consider that it is quite possible to create a logically absurd validity check. For example, you might enter 200 as your high value and 800 as your low value by mistake. No matter how many entries you try, you will never convince Paradox that you have entered a number that is less than 200 and greater than 800.

In a case like this, Paradox gives you a slightly bizarre error message, such as the one in Figure 19.4, so you will realize that something is wrong. In other cases, you might not get such an obviously strange error message but Paradox might still refuse to accept any entry as valid, no matter how many times you try. Don't despair; you are not stuck in that record forever. You have already seen how to get out of a record by pressing Del. Try the entry again; and if you have the same problem and can't figure out what's wrong, press Del once more. Then select ValCheck Clear Field to remove all validity checks from the field, and start over, this time being careful to enter all your validity checks correctly.

```
Editing Employee table: Record 25 of 25                    Edit
┌─City──────────┬State┬─Zip───┬─Date hired───┬──Hourly wage──┬──SEAT scor
  Menlo Park       CA   94025    4/15/88               9.45       601
  San Raphael      CA   94901    2/12/87              14.15       560
  Paramus          NJ   07652   11/25/86              11.23       588
  Berkeley         CA   94703    4/15/86               9.50       602
  Hoboken          NJ   07031    2/04/86              11.00       600
  Mill Valley      CA   94945    6/16/85              15.05       722
  New Brusnwick    NJ   08901    3/01/85               8.65       322
  Palo Alto        CA   94301    7/23/84              12.00       432
  Brooklyn         NY   11226    1/15/84              10.50       540
  Rye              NY   10580   12/01/83              15.60       599
  Mt. Vernon       NY   10507    7/17/82              14.56       723
  San Mateo        CA   94406    7/06/82              12.75       421
  New York         NY   10033    3/22/81              10.25       503
  Ross             CA   94957    2/22/81              15.55       641
  Far Rockaway     NY   11601   12/03/79               8.65       488
  Mill Valley      CA   94943   10/17/79              12.50       403
  Sausalito        CA   94965    4/01/79              14.25       533
  San Raphael      CA   94904   12/22/77              12.50       664
  Brooklyn         NY   11235    4/17/76              10.33       466
  Greenwich        CT   06830    7/12/74              14.05       622
  Brooklyn         NY   11226    2/03/69               8.32       321
  New York                               Value between6      is expected
```

Figure 19.4: A bizarre error message for an absurd validity check

20

USING PARADOX
SCRIPTS

In this chapter, you'll learn to create scripts, which save time and effort by allowing you to do repetitive tasks automatically. When you create a script, you tell Paradox to record your keystrokes as you go through some common task. Later, you can simply tell Paradox to play the script, rather than going through the same keystrokes again.

Of course, scripts are most useful for elaborate procedures that take a long time to do by hand. As you learned in Chapter 18, for example, to produce periodic reports on the Answer to a query, you can rename the Answer table Answer1 and design the report for the Answer1 table. To produce each report, you must perform the query; empty the Answer1 table; add records from the Answer table to the Answer1 table; and finally use the Report submenu to output the report you want. Needless to say, making all these menu choices and typing the names of the tables they apply to is time consuming, especially if you have to produce this report every week.

This situation is ideal for a script. You could go through the process once by hand, and have Paradox record your keystrokes in a script called Ansr-rpt. Then, you could just tell Paradox to play the script named Ansr-rpt each week, and it would do all the work for you.

In addition to scripts that record keystrokes, this chapter describes a special feature on the Scripts submenu for saving queries. You will often need to perform the same query repeatedly, to pull the same fields out of a changing database. Filling in the Query form repeatedly is a nuisance—particularly if you are working with a multitable database and need to call up two Query forms and relate them with an example before you even start to enter checkmarks and criteria. If you perform a query often, you can also select Tools QuerySpeedup to reduce the time it takes Paradox to find the information; this chapter explains when QuerySpeedup is useful.

Because the scripts and queries used as illustrations in this chapter are simple, it may not seem worth creating and playing back a script to save so few keystrokes. However, the illustrations are simple just to save you time as you try the examples. The principles they teach will be equally useful when you apply them to more elaborate procedures and queries.

Creating and Using Scripts

Paradox includes two kinds of scripts:

- *Instant* scripts are temporary. You can create them by using the Instant Script Record key combination (Alt-F3) and play them back by using the Instant Script Play key combination (Alt-F4).
- *Ordinary* scripts are permanent. You create and play them back by choosing the Scripts option from the Paradox menu.

Ordinary scripts are more common, but both types can be useful. You will learn to use ordinary scripts first, and then instant scripts.

How to Record a Script

To record an ordinary script, select Scripts BeginRecord from the Paradox main menu. To stop recording, select Scripts EndRecord.

What if you are not able to access the main menu? If you tried to begin or finish recording a script while you are in Edit mode, for example, the Menu key (F10) would call up the Edit menu, which does not have a Scripts option. In this situation, you must press the PAL Menu key combination (Alt-F10). PAL stands for Paradox Application Language, the programming language built into Paradox. Because it is meant for programmers rather than users, the PAL menu key is not included on the function-key template; you must remember that it is Alt-F10.

As a simple example of a script, let's assume that you often add employees to your table using Edit mode. You want to save yourself the trouble of going to the bottom of the table and adding a new blank record each time you add new records, so you create a script named Add-emp that does it for you. (With a multitable database in a real application, you might prefer to use CoEdit in this example.)

1. From the Paradox main menu, press S and then B to select Scripts BeginRecord. When Paradox asks for the name of the new script, type **add-emp** and press Enter. Paradox returns you to the main menu.

2. Press M and then E to select Modify Edit. Notice that an *R* appears in the upper-right corner of the screen to indicate Paradox is recording a script, as shown in Figure 20.1. When Paradox asks for the name of the table to edit, type **employee** and press Enter.

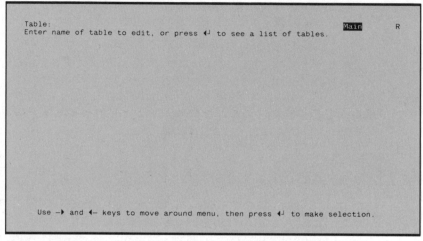

```
Table:                                                          Main      R
Enter name of table to edit, or press ◄┘ to see a list of tables.




















Use ─► and ◄─ keys to move around menu, then press ◄┘ to make selection.
```

Figure 20.1: The R indicates that Paradox is recording a script

3. Press End to move to the last record of the table, and ↓ to add a blank record. You are now ready to make new entries, so this is all you want the script to do. Since you are in Edit mode, you must use the PAL Menu key combination to end recording.

4. Press the PAL Menu key combination (Alt-F10). Paradox presents two options: Cancel, which discards the script; and End-Record, which saves it. Press E to select End-Record.

5. Assume that you have finished your editing for this session, and press DO-IT! (F2) to end editing.

Script names can have a maximum of eight characters. Since scripts are saved as separate files, their names must follow the same rules as the names of tables, listed in Chapter 3. In general, when you are naming scripts, you will probably want to name them using letters, or occasionally numbers if you have several slightly different versions of the same script. If you want to use a name that has more than one word, you can include hyphens or underscores as separators.

If you choose Script BeginRecord and enter the name of an existing script, Paradox warns you that the name is already in use and again presents two options: Replace, which records a new script name and discards the old script; and Cancel, which retains the old script.

How to Play a Script

Now that you have created a script, you can use it instead of repeating the same series of keystrokes.

1. Press the Clear Image key (F8) to clear the screen and call up the main menu.

2. Press S and then P to select Script Play.

3. When Paradox asks for the name of the script to play, type **add-emp** and press Enter. You will automatically be in Edit mode at the start of a blank record at the end of the Employee table.

4. Imagine you have made your additions. Press DO-IT! (F2).

In the previous example, you started to play the script with the screen exactly as it was when you began to record your keystrokes—with the work area blank and the main menu available. When you play this script, you must be in the main mode so the script has the menu available; you cannot begin playing this script in Edit mode, for example. But you do not necessarily need a blank work space, as you do when you start recording the script.

To get a clearer idea of the conditions required to to play a script, try playing Add-emp with the screen the way it is now—in Main mode, but viewing the Employee table. Then try making an error by playing the script in the Edit mode.

1. Press the Menu key (F10). Press S and then P to select Scripts Play. When Paradox asks for the name of the script, type **add-emp** and press Enter. The script leaves you in Edit mode, ready to enter a new record in the table, as before.

2. Now try playing the script from Edit mode. Press the PAL Menu key combination (Alt-F10). The special PAL menu appears, as shown in Figure 20.2 . Press P to select Play.

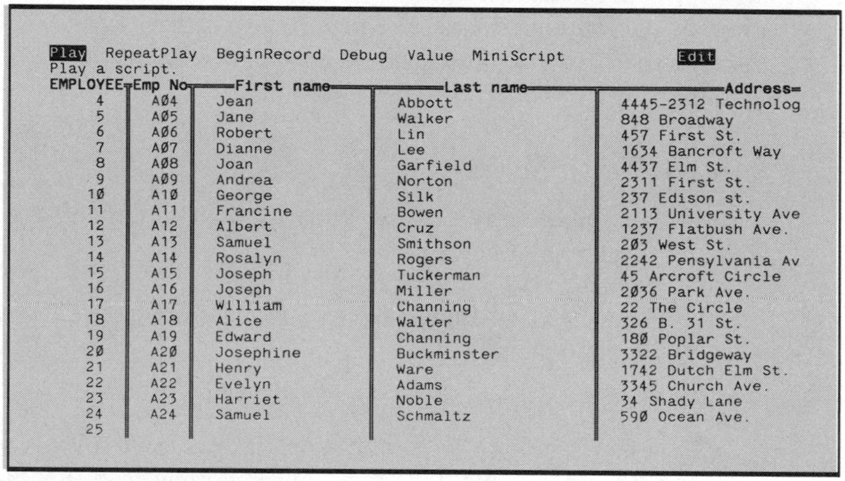

```
 Play  RepeatPlay  BeginRecord  Debug  Value  MiniScript              Edit
Play a script.
EMPLOYEE Emp No      First name          Last name              Address
     4    AØ4   Jean            Abbott            4445-2312 Technolog
     5    AØ5   Jane            Walker            848 Broadway
     6    AØ6   Robert          Lin               457 First St.
     7    AØ7   Dianne          Lee               1634 Bancroft Way
     8    AØ8   Joan            Garfield          4437 Elm St.
     9    AØ9   Andrea          Norton            2311 First St.
    1Ø    A1Ø   George          Silk              237 Edison st.
    11    A11   Francine        Bowen             2113 University Ave
    12    A12   Albert          Cruz              1237 Flatbush Ave.
    13    A13   Samuel          Smithson          2Ø3 West St.
    14    A14   Rosalyn         Rogers            2242 Pensylvania Av
    15    A15   Joseph          Tuckerman         45 Arcroft Circle
    16    A16   Joseph          Miller            2Ø36 Park Ave.
    17    A17   William         Channing          22 The Circle
    18    A18   Alice           Walter            326 B. 31 St.
    19    A19   Edward          Channing          18Ø Poplar St.
    2Ø    A2Ø   Josephine       Buckminster       3322 Bridgeway
    21    A21   Henry           Ware              1742 Dutch Elm St.
    22    A22   Evelyn          Adams             3345 Church Ave.
    23    A23   Harriet         Noble             34 Shady Lane
    24    A24   Samuel          Schmaltz          59Ø Ocean Ave.
    25
```

Figure 20.2: The PAL Menu

3. When Paradox asks for the name of the script to play, type **add-emp** and press Enter. Notice that the Edit menu appears for an instant. When the script tried to use the menu in Edit mode, it called up the Edit menu—not the main menu, as it should have. Paradox cannot execute the script from the Edit menu.

4. Paradox tells you there is a script error and gives you the option to Cancel, which stops the script, or to Debug, which is an advanced option for programmers (see Figure 20.3). Press Enter to select Cancel.

5. Paradox returns you to the Edit menu, which is where the script was when it could no longer continue. Press C and then Y to Cancel editing and leave the menu.

As you see, scripts can do unexpected things if you are not in the right mode when you start playing them, so use them with caution. Paradox must be able to perform the steps you recorded from the place you are when you begin to play the script.

```
Cancel  Debug                                                          Edit
Stop playing script.
EMPLOYEE═Emp No───────First name────────────Last name───────────────Address═
       4    │  A04    Jean              │ Abbott          │ 4445-2312 Technolog
       5    │  A05    Jane              │ Walker          │ 848 Broadway
       6    │  A06    Robert            │ Lin             │ 457 First St.
       7    │  A07    Dianne            │ Lee             │ 1634 Bancroft Way
       8    │  A08    Joan              │ Garfield        │ 4437 Elm St.
       9    │  A09    Andrea            │ Norton          │ 2311 First St.
      10    │  A10    George            │ Silk            │ 237 Edison st.
      11    │  A11    Francine          │ Bowen           │ 2113 University Ave
      12    │  A12    Albert            │ Cruz            │ 1237 Flatbush Ave.
      13    │  A13    Samuel            │ Smithson        │ 203 West St.
      14    │  A14    Rosalyn           │ Rogers          │ 2242 Pensylvania Av
      15    │  A15    Joseph            │ Tuckerman       │ 45 Arcroft Circle
      16    │  A16    Joseph            │ Miller          │ 2036 Park Ave.
      17    │  A17    William           │ Channing        │ 22 The Circle
      18    │  A18    Alice             │ Walter          │ 326 B. 31 St.
      19    │  A19    Edward            │ Channing        │ 180 Poplar St.
      20    │  A20    Josephine         │ Buckminster     │ 3322 Bridgeway
      21    │  A21    Henry             │ Waro            │ 1742 Dutch Elm St.
      22    │  A22    Evelyn            │ Adams           │ 3345 Church Ave.
      23    │  A23    Harriet           │ Noble           │ 34 Shady Lane
      24    │  A24    Samuel            │ Schmaltz        │ 590 Ocean Ave.
      25    │    ◄                      Script error - select Cancel or Debug from menu
```

Figure 20.3: A script error

If you receive a script error message, cancel the script. Try to remember where you were when you began recording the script, and try playing the script again from that position. If there is still a script error, try recording another script to do the same task, noting very carefully where you are when you start recording. If it works when you record it, it should work when you play it back, starting from the same place.

How to Use Instant Scripts

Though instant scripts are not used as often as ordinary scripts, they are sometimes useful. Suppose you've been adding records to a table and discover that you've misread your boss's handwriting, and entered NJ whenever you were supposed to enter NV. You can save time by using an instant script to correct this mistake.

Press the Instant Script Record key combination (Alt-F3) once to record the script, and press it a second time to stop recording.

1. Press the Edit key (F9), and press → to move the cursor to the State field. Press Instant Script Record (Alt-F3). Note the letter *R* in the upper-right corner, and the message that says Paradox is beginning to record the script.

2. Press the Zoom key combination (Ctrl-Z). When Paradox asks for the value to search for, type **NJ** and press Enter. When the cursor moves to the first NJ, press Backspace to delete the *J*, and type **V**.

3. To end recording the instant script, press Instant Script Record (Alt-F3). Note the message that tells you the program is ending recording, and note that the *R* disappears.

4. To change the next NJ to NV, press Instant Script Play (Alt-F4) once, and then a few more times; there are two more NJ's to change to NV's. After the second one, the cursor remains on the same NV, since it cannot find another NJ.

5. Press the Menu key (F10). Press C and then Y to select Cancel Yes and leave the Edit mode without keeping these changes.

Since the script replays exactly the keystrokes you entered, you must be in the State column when you begin playing this script, for Zoom to work.

This script saves so few keystrokes that it would be just as efficient to make the change by hand as to select an ordinary script from the menu. But you can save a significant amount of work by using an instant script.

An instant script is a temporary object named Instant. Unlike a temporary table, it is not discarded when you exit Paradox. You can keep using the same instant script in one session after another. Like a temporary table, though, an instant script is automatically discarded when you create another temporary object of the same type.

Also like a temporary table, Instant can be renamed and made permanent. Just select Tools Rename Script from the main menu and give it another name. It then becomes permanent, so you can use it like any ordinary script. In fact, you can create ordinary scripts by using the Instant Script Record key and then renaming the script you've created, if you find this more convenient than using the menu.

How to Use the Init Script

If you create a script with the name Init, it will execute automatically when you start Paradox.

Rather than creating a new script to see how this feature works, try renaming one you've already created. Imagine you have a temporary data-entry person coming in for the day who knows nothing about Paradox. You want to set things up so Paradox is ready for data entry and editing as soon as the program is started. All you have to do is rename the Add-emp data-entry script Init, and it will be executed automatically.

1. Press the Menu key (F10). Press T, R, and then S to select Tools Rename Script.

2. Press Enter to see a list of scripts. Note that both Add-emp and Instant are available: you can rename an instant script just as easily as an ordinary script. Press Enter again to select Add-emp.

3. When Paradox asks you to provide a new name for the script, type **init** and press Enter. Paradox tells you that it is renaming the script.

4. Press the Menu key (F10). Then press E and Y to exit from Paradox.

5. At the DOS prompt, type **paradox3** and press Enter to restart Paradox. When the program starts, you will be in Edit mode, at the blank new record of the Employee table, ready to add new data. The Init script has executed automatically.

6. Press DO-IT! (F2) to leave Edit mode and press the Menu key (F10). Press T, R, and then S to select Tools Rename Script.

7. Press Enter to see the list of scripts and note that Init and Instant still appear. Press Enter to select Init. When Paradox asks for a new name, type **add-emp** and press Enter.

Of course, you changed the name Init back to Add-emp because you do not always want Paradox to be set up for data entry when you start the program.

*H*ow to Save Queries

The ability to save queries is an invaluable feature of the Scripts submenu. It is common to use the same query repeatedly—to get a new list of California employees every month, for example.

The ability to save queries is particularly useful when you are working with multitable databases; to create queries for them you have to call up two Query forms and relate them with an example, in addition to filling in checkmarks and criteria. Of course, it is always efficient to save complex queries, even for single-table databases.

As you work through this simple example, think how useful the same technique would be with more elaborate queries.

1. Press the Clear Image key to clear the workspace and call up the main menu. Press A to select Ask.

2. When Paradox requests the name of the table to ask about, type **employee** and press Enter. The Query form appears.

3. Use → to move the cursor to the First name field, and press the Check key (F6). Then move the cursor to the Last name field and press the Check key again (F6).

4. Move the cursor to the State field and type **CA**. Now you are ready to save the query.

5. Press the Menu key (F10). Press S and then Q to select Scripts QuerySave. When Paradox asks you to provide a name for the query script, type **calnames**, as shown in Figure 20.4, and then press Enter.

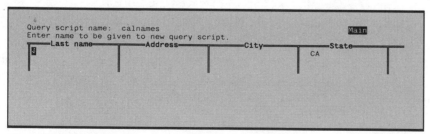

Figure 20.4: Saving a Query

6. You could now make this query by pressing DO-IT!, but for this example, simply clear the workspace and return to the main menu by pressing Clear Image.

Now that the query is saved, you can use it like any script by selecting Scripts Play from the main menu.

1. Press S and then P to select Scripts Play.

2. When Paradox asks for the name of the script to play, press Enter to see a list of scripts. The saved query, Calnames, appears along with the other scripts you've created, Add-emp and Instant.

3. Press C to select Calnames and the Query form you created earlier reappears. Press DO-IT! to make the query, and a listing of employees from California appears.

Notice that playing this script simply calls up the Query form, which you can then change. For example, after playing this script, you could type > = **10** in the Hourly wage field to get a listing of the California employees who earn more than $10 per hour. Then you could play the script again and add < **10** in the Hourly wage field, to get a list of the remaining California employees.

When you save a query, all the forms in the workspace are saved. Make sure that only query forms you want to save are displayed.

How to Speed Up Queries

If you use a query repeatedly, you can take advantage of Tools QuerySpeedup, which reduces the processing time for some queries. You don't have to use Scripts QuerySave and Tools QuerySpeedup together, but it makes sense to do so.

To know when to use QuerySpeedup, you must have some idea how it works. When you select this option, Paradox creates an *index* for every field in the table that contains a selection criterion in the Query form. A database index is like a book index; it is a short, conveniently ordered list that tells you where information is in a longer document or list. Your computer can often process a query more quickly by using an indexed table for the same reason that you can find information faster by using the index of a book.

Indexing also creates extra work for the computer, however. It must update the index to account for new records added to the table.

Indexes created using QuerySpeedup are automatically updated whenever you perform the query. The time Paradox saves by using the index is partly offset by the time it takes to update it.

In fields that have many repeated entries, such as the State field in the Employee table, not much time is saved by using an index. Because half the records in the Employee table contain CA in the State field, it wouldn't take much longer to find these records by reading through the entire table than it would to find them with an index. Thus if you used QuerySpeedup for the query you are working with, where the selection criterion is in the State field, you would not actually save time. The time required to update the index would be roughly equal to the time saved by using the index to locate the records. Reserve QuerySpeedup for queries that have criteria in fields with less repetition.

To use QuerySpeedup, select Tools QuerySpeedup when the query that you want to affect is in the workspace. Paradox automatically creates indexes for all fields that have criteria in the Query form. If none of the fields have criteria entered, Paradox will tell you that a query speedup is impossible; if there are only checkmarks in the Query form, and Paradox has to pull those fields out of every record, there is clearly no advantage to using an index. Key fields designated by an asterisk are always indexed, so a speedup is also impossible if only key fields have criteria entered.

Other Features of the Scripts Submenu

There are a few additional features of the Scripts submenu that you might find interesting, although they are less important than those you've already learned.

It is possible to use one script within another. For example, try using the query you saved above within a script that executes it automatically.

1. Press the Clear Image key to clear the workspace and call up the main menu. Press S and then B to select Scripts BeginRecord.

2. When Paradox asks for the name of the new script, type **calname2** and press Enter.

3. Press S and then P to select Scripts Play and press Enter to see a list of scripts.

4. Use → to move the cursor to Calnames and press Enter. When Paradox calls up the Query form that you saved, press DO-IT! (F2) to make the query.

5. Press the Menu key (F10). Press S and then E to select Scripts End-Record.

You save only one keystroke by using this new script to execute the query automatically, instead of calling up the Query form and then pressing DO-IT!.

Using one script within another becomes useful if you realize you didn't save enough keystrokes when you first created a script. After you've used a script repeatedly, you may notice that you always have to enter the same series of keystrokes before you can execute it. Fortunately, you do not have to record the entire script again to incorporate those few missing steps. In Paradox, you can simply create a new script by typing the few added keystrokes and then playing the old script.

The RepeatPlay feature of the Scripts menu lets you use the same script more than once. When you select Scripts RepeatPlay, Paradox first asks for the name of the script and then for the number of times you want it played. When you have hundreds of entries with the wrong state instead of only three, RepeatPlay can save the day.

The ShowPlay feature is intended primarily to help programmers debug scripts. Normally, you cannot see what a script is doing as it executes; you just see the final result. If a script does not work as you expected it to, though, seeing each step as it is executed can help you figure out where the script is going wrong.

The Add-emp script that you created earlier in this chapter puts you in a position to add records to the Employee table. Let's use ShowPlay to see how it gets you there.

1. Press the Clear Image key (F8) to clear the screen and call up the main menu. Press S and then S to select Scripts ShowPlay.

2. When Paradox asks for the name of the script to play, type **add-emp** and press Enter.

3. Paradox gives you the option of playing the script rapidly or slowly. Press S to select Slow.

As you can see, ShowPlay goes through all the steps that you went through to create the script. The main menu pops up. The cursor moves to Modify. Modify is chosen and the cursor moves to Edit. The prompt asks for the table to edit and the name "employee" appears. Then the table appears, the cursor moves to the last record, and a blank record is added.

If you discover an error this way, it's possible to edit a script, but this is an advanced feature of Paradox that is meant for programmers. If you are having trouble with a script, it is easy to start again. Just select Script Record, enter the same name, and replace the defective script.

You should consider, though, that you have already come close to programming. When you prepared the Init script, you took a step toward setting up a custom Paradox application for someone who doesn't know the program.

What if you wanted the data-entry person to do more than just add records to the table? When Paradox is started, you could have a menu appear that offered a number of choices: one to add records to the Employee table, another to produce a certain report, another to produce mailing labels, and so on. Then, a data-entry person could choose a task from the menu and do whatever needed to be done without knowing the first thing about Paradox.

It is not hard to set up this sort of custom application. You just have to create the tables and reports to hold the data, which you already know how to do. Then you need to do a bit more work to create the initial menu that ties them all together. The Paradox Personal Programmer does most of this work for you. With this tool you can generate applications without doing any programming. For more sophisticated applications, you can use Paradox Application Language (PAL). If you are intrigued by these possibilities, you might want to continue your study of Paradox, and investigate its more advanced capabilities.

Whether or not you want try programming, you have already reached the point where you are no longer a novice who needs a programmer to set up a custom application. You can now do everything you need to manage your own database with Paradox.

INSTALLING PARADOX

This appendix tells you how to install Paradox on your own personal computer. It is not meant to be used by people working on networks. If you are going to use Paradox on a network and it is not yet installed, talk to your network administrator or see the Network Administrators Guide (one of the manuals distributed with Paradox) for installation instructions.

Installing Paradox on a single computer is extremely simple: the Paradox installation program tells you which disk to put in, and does virtually everything else for you.

Before you install Paradox, though, you should understand how to use DOS subdirectories. The first section of this appendix explains subdirectories. If you already know how DOS subdirectories work, go to the second section of the appendix, "How to Create a Working Subdirectory."

*H*ow to Use DOS Subdirectories

To install Paradox 3, you must have a hard disk. Because of the huge number of files hard disks can hold, it is necessary to organize them into subdirectories.

DOS uses a hierarchical directory system, that is easiest to visualize as an inverted tree. The directory at the top of the system is called the *root* directory. You can create subdirectories under the root directory, enter them, and then create new subdirectories under them.

The directory you are in is called the *current* directory, and you only have direct access to files that it contains. When you use the DOS DIR command to list your files, it only lists the files in the current directory. The DOS COPY command can only find those files.

DOS uses three major commands to work with subdirectories:

- *MD* (Make Directory) creates a new subdirectory.

- *CD* (Change or Current Directory) moves from one subdirectory to another.

- *RD* (Remove Directory) eliminates an existing subdirectory. Before you remove a directory, you must delete all the files in it and remove any subdirectories it has.

Each of these commands is followed by the directory name. For example, if you type **MD LEARNPAR** and press Enter at the DOS prompt, DOS creates a new directory named **LEARNPAR** under the current directory.

Apart from these commands, all you need to know to work with subdirectories is the conventions that DOS uses for naming them. A backslash (\) is always used to name the root directory. If you enter the command **CD** \ at the DOS prompt, DOS moves to the root directory, which then becomes the current directory.

The backslash is also used between names of directories when you list the *path name* of a directory. The path name tells you where a subdirectory fits into the directory tree, from the root down. For example, suppose you've created the directory structure shown in Figure A.1. You have a number of subdirectories under the root directory, one of which is named LETTERS and another DATA, and you've also created a number of directories under the LETTERS directory, one of which is named BUSINESS. The full path name of the BUSINESS directory would be \LETTERS\BUSINESS, to show that you are referring to a subdirectory named BUSINESS under the LETTERS directory, which is under the root directory. You could then have another subdirectory named \DATA\BUSINESS. DOS can keep track of multiple directories with the same name, as long as the full path names are different.

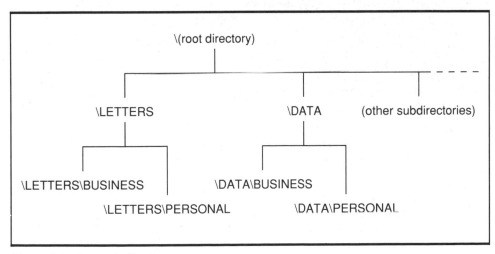

Figure A.1: *A sample directory system*

You also use the backslash to separate the name of a directory from the names of the files in it. For example, if you had a file named MISC.TXT, in each of the BUSINESS directories we just mentioned, the full path name of one would be \LETTERS\BUSINESS\MISC.TXT and the full path name of the other would be \DATA\BUSINESS\MISC.TXT.

A file name used alone refers to the file with that name in the current subdirectory. For example, if you are in the \DATA\BUSINESS subdirectory, and you enter the command **TYPE MISC.TXT**, DOS will display the file \DATA\BUSINESS\MISC.TXT on your screen. If you use the name of a file that is not in the current subdirectory without a path name, DOS will not be able to find the file. But whatever directory you are in, DOS will be able to find a file if you use its full path name, because each file's path name is unique.

A similar naming convention applies to directories. If you use a directory name by itself, DOS will find that subdirectory only if it is immediately under the current directory. On the other hand, if you use the full path name of a directory, DOS will find it wherever you are.

For example, if you were in the \LETTERS subdirectory and you entered the command **CD BUSINESS**, DOS would move you to the directory named BUSINESS immediately under the current directory, that is, the directory whose full path name is \LETTERS\BUSINESS. (Note that you must enter the directory name without the initial backslash. If you entered CD\BUSINESS, DOS would look for a directory named BUSINESS directly below the root directory.)

If you are in the \LETTERS subdirectory and want to get to a subdirectory that is not below it, you must enter the full path name of the subdirectory you want.

For now, you only need to remember two naming conventions in order to use subdirectories:

- If you use a name by itself, DOS will only be able to find it if it refers to a file in the current directory or to a subdirectory under the current directory.

- If you use a full path name, DOS can find any file or directory, regardless of your current location.

Like file names, directory names can have up to eight letters, but they do not have three-letter extensions. The DOS DIR command lists all the files in the current directory and all the subdirectories that are under the current directory. Every subdirectory automatically includes a subdirectory whose name is simply a dot, and another whose name is two dots. Although these directories will appear on the list, you can ignore them; they are tools that DOS creates for its internal use.

How to Create a Working Subdirectory

Paradox automatically creates a subdirectory named Paradox3 to hold the program files you need to run Paradox. It is possible to use this same subdirectory for your Paradox applications, but it is much better to create a separate subdirectory for each application, in order to keep your work organized.

It is easy to create a convenient subdirectory to hold the exercises you will use in this book. Just follow these steps:

1. Make sure you are in the root directory of your hard disk. (You are automatically there if you have just turned the computer on.) If you have any doubts, make sure you are in your hard disk, type the command **CD ** and press Enter.

2. Type **MD LEARNPAR** and press Enter to create the new directory.

3. Type **CD LEARNPAR** and press Enter to get into the directory. Then type **DIR** and press Enter to see a listing of the directory's contents. The listing will include the directory name and will show that there are no files in it, except the DOS files named with one and two dots. Type **CD ** and press Enter to return to the root directory.

Whenever you use this book, start by typing **CD \LEARNPAR** and pressing Enter to get into the LEARNPAR subdirectory. (If you are already in the root directory, just type **CD LEARNPAR**.) Once you are in the LEARNPAR subdirectory, type **PARADOX3** and press Enter to start Paradox. Then all the applications that you create in this book will be conveniently grouped in their own subdirectory.

How to Install Paradox

To install Paradox 3, you should be in the root directory of your hard disk; though this is not necessary, it will make life less confusing. You must have at least two megabytes of free disk space to hold the program. Type **DIR** and press Enter to list the directory. The second line of the listing will tell you what subdirectory you are in. It should say Directory of C:\ (assuming the hard disk you are installing on is disk C.) If you are not in drive C:, just type **C:** at the DOS prompt and press ENTER, then list the directory again to make sure you are in the root directory. If you are in drive C: but in another subdirectory, type **CD ** and press Enter to move to the root directory.

The last line of the directory listing tells you how many bytes are free, and the number must be more than two million. If you do not have this much free space, you must erase some of your existing files before you install Paradox. If you want to install the Paradox Personal Programmer, you need an additional two megabytes of free disk space.

Once you have checked these basics, you are ready to use Paradox's simple installation program.

1. Put the Paradox Installation Disk in drive A. (If you use 3.5-inch disks, use the disk that says Installation/Sample Tables Disk.) Type **A:INSTALL** and press Enter.

2. Follow the instructions on the screen, which tell you to press Enter or to insert a new floppy disk in the drive. (From now on, these instructions only tell you what to do when Paradox offers you a choice. You should press Enter and switch disks in the drive whenever the screen display tells you to.)

3. When Paradox tells you to specify the installation type, press **1** to select Hard Disk Installation, and press Enter.

4. Paradox asks you to enter the source drive. Assuming you are using drive A for installation, just press Enter to confirm the suggested choice. If you are using another drive for the Paradox disks, type the letter of that drive, and press Enter.

5. Paradox asks you to enter the destination drive. Assuming your hard disk is drive C, just press Enter to confirm the suggested choice. Otherwise, enter the letter of the hard disk you are installing Paradox on and press Enter.

6. Paradox asks you to enter the name of the subdirectory in which you want the program installed. Press Enter to select the suggested name, \PARADOX3.

7. Paradox asks which of the five country groups you want to configure the program for. This book assumes that Paradox is installed for the United States. Unless you have a reason to do otherwise, type **1** to select United States and press Enter. Paradox will copy some files and then tell you to switch disks.

8. When Paradox requests them, type your name, your company name, and the Paradox serial number on your installation disk, pressing Enter after each response. (Paradox will not install without a valid serial number.) Type N and press Enter, to tell Paradox you will not be accessing information on a network.

9. Continue switching disks according to the program's instructions. When Paradox is fully installed, it will display a menu listing its optional software. You do not need any of this optional software to use this book. Type **6** and press Enter to complete the installation process.

10. Before you run Paradox for the first time, you must restart your computer. You can turn it off and on, or you can hold down the Ctrl, Alt, and Del keys simultaneously to restart it.

This final step is necessary so your computer can read the system files it needs to configure itself so Paradox can run.

PARADOX
OBJECTS
AND
TEMPORARY
FILES

This appendix lists some technical details about the names of Paradox objects and temporary files. It is not necessary to know the names DOS gives Paradox objects, which are listed in the first section of the appendix; but it is important to know the names of the temporary files, listed in the second section of this appendix, so you can avoid using these names for objects you create.

*P*aradox Objects as DOS Files

When you use Paradox, you can create, delete, or copy Paradox objects by using the menu system, without giving any thought to how your computer's operating system handles these objects. There is no need for you to know how DOS names these objects: Paradox was designed so that you could do everything using its menus, without worrying about the operating system. This section lists them just in case you are curious about all the file names that appear when you look at the DOS directory.

DOS file names have two parts: the first part can be up to eight characters long, and the second part can be up to three characters long. The first part is the file name and the second part is the extension.

The DOS files of all Paradox objects that are in the family of a table have the same eight-letter name as the file that holds the table; only the three-letter extensions that follow the name differ. For example, the Employee table is kept in a file named EMPLOYEE.DB. The .DB extension indicates that this is a table (that is, a database). The standard report for the Employee table is kept in a file named EMPLOYEE.R, and report R1 for the Employee table is kept in a file named EMPLOYEE.R1.

The extensions of all the objects in the family of a table follow (## stands for any one or two digit number):

.DB	Table
.F	Standard form
.F##	Custom form
.R	Standard report

.R##	Custom report
.SET	Image settings
.VAL	Validity checks
.PX	Primary index (index on key field)
.X##	Secondary index (created by QuerySpeedup)
.Y##	Secondary index (created by QuerySpeedup)
.G	Graph specification

Scripts and Graph settings are not part of a table's family. This is why you must give them a name up to eight letters long. Scripts are stored in files with the name that you give them followed by the extension .SC, and graph settings go in files that have the name you give them followed by the extension .GRF. Because they have their own names, and do not share the family name of a table, scripts and graphs can be used with any table that they will work with. Also, note that these objects are not copied when you use the Tools Copy Table or Tools Copy JustFamily commands.

Since Tools Copy Table copies not just a table and its data but also its entire family of objects, you might prefer to use DOS to copy a table by itself. To do so, use the table name followed by the extension .DB.

*P*aradox Temporary Tables

As you have seen, Paradox creates a number of temporary tables, such as the Struct, Answer and Problems table, which are automatically discarded when you exit from the program or when another table of the same type is created. Temporary files are also lost when you choose Tools More Directory in order to change your working directory.

You should be familiar with the names of all the Paradox temporary tables so you do not mistakenly use one of them for a table that you create. Any table that has one of these names will be lost just as a temporary table would be, regardless of how the table was created.

- *Answer* holds the results of a query.

- *Changed* holds unchanged copies of records that were changed using Tools More Add, Tools More Multi-add, or an advanced query.

- *Crosstab* holds the results of a cross-tabulation used to prepare data for a graph.

- *Deleted* holds records that were deleted using an advanced query operation.

- *Entry* holds records that were added to a table using Modify DataEntry.

- *Family* holds a list of reports and forms for a table that was created using Tool Info Family.

- *Inserted* holds records that were inserted using an advanced query operation.

- *Keyviol* holds records that have duplicate key fields.

- *List* holds lists created by Tools Info. They can be lists of Paradox objects, of users on a network, or of locks applied to a table and its family on a network.

- *Password* holds auxiliary passwords on networks.

- *Problems* holds records that do not fit into a table after it has been restructured or after records have been imported from another table.

- *Struct* holds the structure of a Paradox table.

You do not need to worry if you don't understand what some of these temporary tables do; many of them are used by advanced Paradox features that are not covered in this book. You should just be aware of their names so you can avoid using them for your own tables.

Index

A

Answer table, 170–178, 184, 255–258, 262–263, 298, 322
arithmetic operators for calculated fields, 138
ASCII file creation, 282

B

backup of tables, 277–278
beep signal, 20
BLANKLINE, 144–149

C

Check key (F6), 169–170
columns
  changing size, 96–99, 119–122
  modifying in reports, 117–118
  moving, 95–96
command functions
  AllCorresponding Fields, 225
  HelpAndFill, 222–223
  JustCurrentField, 225
  Move columns, 96–99
  PageLayout for print reports, 150
  PrivateLookup, 222
computer, basic operation of, 8–14
constants, 292

D

data
  asterisks as short field indicator, 100
  changing data type in table, 79
  date entry shortcuts, 66
  editing, 52–67
  entering, 40–49
  exporting/importing, 281–282
  in Form View, 48–49
  interchanging with other programs, 282
  in multitable databases
    adding and editing, 216–222
    adding to, 214–229
    editing problems, 217–218
    protecting with DataEntry, 218–219
    protecting with Coedit, 220–221
  number entry shortcuts, 66
  one-to-many relationship, 193, 222–229
  protecting, 218–221
  truncation of, 99–102
  validating, 286–295
    automaticity of, 293–294
    default value, selection of, 289–290
    Edit menu, use of, 286

TO JOIN THE SYBEX MAILING LIST OR ORDER BOOKS
PLEASE COMPLETE THIS FORM

NAME _____ COMPANY _____

STREET _____ CITY _____

STATE _____ ZIP _____

☐ PLEASE MAIL ME MORE INFORMATION ABOUT **SYBEX** TITLES

ORDER FORM (There is no obligation to order)

PLEASE SEND ME THE FOLLOWING:

TITLE	QTY	PRICE
_____	____	____
_____	____	____
_____	____	____
_____	____	____

TOTAL BOOK ORDER _____ $_____

CUSTOMER SIGNATURE _____

SHIPPING AND HANDLING PLEASE ADD $2.00 PER BOOK VIA UPS _____

FOR OVERSEAS SURFACE ADD $5.25 PER BOOK PLUS $4.40 REGISTRATION FEE _____

FOR OVERSEAS AIRMAIL ADD $18.25 PER BOOK PLUS $4.40 REGISTRATION FEE _____

CALIFORNIA RESIDENTS PLEASE ADD APPLICABLE SALES TAX _____

TOTAL AMOUNT PAYABLE _____

☐ CHECK ENCLOSED   ☐ VISA
☐ MASTERCARD   ☐ AMERICAN EXPRESS

ACCOUNT NUMBER _____

EXPIR. DATE _____ DAYTIME PHONE _____

CHECK AREA OF COMPUTER INTEREST:

☐ BUSINESS SOFTWARE

☐ TECHNICAL PROGRAMMING

☐ OTHER: _____

THE FACTOR THAT WAS MOST IMPORTANT IN YOUR SELECTION:

☐ THE SYBEX NAME

☐ QUALITY

☐ PRICE

☐ EXTRA FEATURES

☐ COMPREHENSIVENESS

☐ CLEAR WRITING

☐ OTHER _____

OTHER COMPUTER TITLES YOU WOULD LIKE TO SEE IN PRINT:

_____

_____

OCCUPATION

☐ PROGRAMMER   ☐ TEACHER

☐ SENIOR EXECUTIVE   ☐ HOMEMAKEF

☐ COMPUTER CONSULTANT   ☐ RETIRED

☐ SUPERVISOR   ☐ STUDENT

☐ MIDDLE MANAGEMENT   ☐ OTHER:

☐ ENGINEER/TECHNICAL   _____

☐ CLERICAL/SERVICE

☐ BUSINESS OWNER/SELF EMPLOYED

CHECK YOUR LEVEL OF COMPUTER USE

☐ NEW TO COMPUTERS

☐ INFREQUENT COMPUTER USER

☐ FREQUENT USER OF ONE SOFTWARE
   PACKAGE:
   NAME _____

☐ FREQUENT USER OF MANY SOFTWARE
   PACKAGES

☐ PROFESSIONAL PROGRAMMER

OTHER COMMENTS:

_____

_____

_____

_____

_____

_____

_____

PLEASE FOLD, SEAL, AND MAIL TO SYBEX

SYBEX, INC.
2021 CHALLENGER DR. #100
ALAMEDA, CALIFORNIA USA
94501

SEAL

SYBEX Computer Books
are different.

Here is why . . .

At SYBEX, each book is designed with you in mind. Every manuscript is carefully selected and supervised by our editors, who are themselves computer experts. We publish the best authors, whose technical expertise is matched by an ability to write clearly and to communicate effectively. Programs are thoroughly tested for accuracy by our technical staff. Our computerized production department goes to great lengths to make sure that each book is well-designed.

In the pursuit of timeliness, SYBEX has achieved many publishing firsts. SYBEX was among the first to integrate personal computers used by authors and staff into the publishing process. SYBEX was the first to publish books on the CP/M operating system, microprocessor interfacing techniques, word processing, and many more topics.

Expertise in computers and dedication to the highest quality product have made SYBEX a world leader in computer book publishing. Translated into fourteen languages, SYBEX books have helped millions of people around the world to get the most from their computers. We hope we have helped you, too.

For a complete catalog of our publications:

SYBEX, Inc. 2021 Challenger Drive, #100, Alameda, CA 94501
Tel: (415) 523-8233/(800) 227-2346 Telex: 336311
Fax: (415) 523-2373

Designing a Report

CHAPTERS NINE, TEN, AND ELEVEN

Paradox lets you design tabular reports, which have the fields listed in columns, or free-form reports. The program begins with the standard report format, shown here. You can use the Report menu to move fields, add new columns, group records by their contents, and add calculated and summary fields.

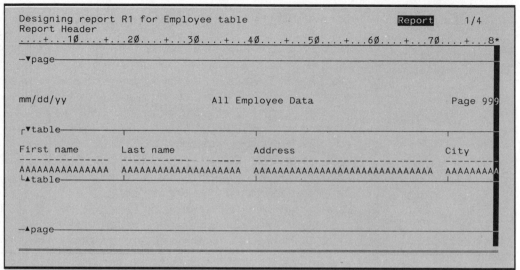

The tabular report specification screen

You can also use the report specification screen as a full-screen editor, moving the cursor and typing in the report title, headers, and footers, just as you would with a simple full-screen word processor. You can even create form letters using Paradox.

Use of the keys in the report editor:

Key	Action
Home	Moves cursor to the first line
End	Moves cursor to the last line
Ctrl-Home	Moves cursor to the far left
Ctrl-End	Moves cursor to the last character of the line
Del	Deletes a character
Ins	Toggles from insert mode to type-over mode
Left and Right arrow	Move cursor left or right one character
Up and Down arrow	Move cursor up or down one line
Ctrl-Left arrow and Ctrl-Right arrow	Move cursor a half-screen left or right
PgUp and PgDn	Move up or down one screen
Backspace	Deletes the letter left of the cursor
Ctrl-Y	Deletes from the cursor to the end of the line
Ctrl-V	Displays or hides the vertical ruler